The Creole Incident

The Beginning of the End of Slavery

John Hyde Barnard

The Creole Incident
The beginning of the end of slavery.

Coldwell & Hyde Publishing, LLC
San Francisco, California

U.S. Copyright Office Registration Number: TXu-868-79
Writer's Guild of America West Registrant Number: 2114736
Submission Date: 04/22/2021

ISBN: 979-8-9895918-0-0
Library of Congress Control Number: 2023922190

Table of Contents

The Creole Incident is an American story for all Americans

In Appreciation

A debt of gratitude and appreciation to William Barnard, my older brother who first enlightened me to the wonders and marvels of History; brother Paul, sister Beth and brother Tom; the History Department at California State University at San Marcos, U. C. Riverside and Saddleback College. The editors: Dan Marcus, Ronny Schiff, Morgan Ames, the invaluable insights from Suzi Morris, Wendy Conrad, Marilyn Hassett, Bernard Espinet, Joel Gotler, Cindy and Neville Johnson and Cool Titles, Lisa Wyscoky, the folks at the San Francisco Institute For Historical Studies; The San Francisco Writers Conference and Lissa Provost; the Sausalito Writers Group: Cindy, Steve, Edmond, Evelyn and Marc; and Jeff Battis and Cheryl Popp at Books By the Bay.

A big thanks to Katie and Kent Philpott, especially the patience, guidance and wisdom of Katie who willed the book over the finish line.

Finally — A very special and loving thanks to Merrily, whose belief and love sustained and supported me — without qualification, without question.

And Madison Washington. We did it!

Prologue
Mutiny and Murder

In October of 1841, a hurricane came ashore at the Carolinas, disrupting the shipping lanes of the Mid-Atlantic. As it clawed its way up the eastern seaboard, the storm wreaked havoc on New England, depositing eighteen feet of snow in some areas of Connecticut, destroying the Georges Banks fishing fleet, and so devastating the Cape Cod area that it caused a local financial collapse. For the remainder of the month the weather would continue to be stormy.

Along the Chesapeake ports, from Baltimore to Richmond, shipping slowed. Ships at sea that couldn't outrun the weather, were forced into numerous ports along the eastern seaboard. Two of these vessels were the American flagged bark *Louisa* and the brig *Congress*. Each had encountered the brunt of the hurricane, been dismasted, and sought safe harbor in the port of Nassau, Bahamas, as they awaited supplies and repairs.

However, by late October, commerce once again began to venture out on the high seas. On Sunday, October 31, 1841, the brig *Creole*, out of Richmond, Virginia, bound for New Orleans, heavily laden with supplies and cargo, left the Chesapeake Bay and proceeded to sea. The ship's cargo consisted of manufactured tobacco in boxes, cases of wine shipped by Senator Henry Clay of Kentucky[1] and one hundred and thirty-five individuals, who were slaves.[2]

The *Creole* was one of several ships employed in the intercoastal slave trade, an established commercial venture in human cargo that plied its commerce between the Chesapeake ports and those ports of the deep South: Charleston, Mobile, and New Orleans. The master of the *Creole* was Robert T. Ensor of Richmond, Virginia, age thirty-seven, who was accompanied by his wife Eliza Ann Sewell, his daughter Margaret, and a niece. The remainder of the crew was made up of the first mate Zephaniah C. Gifford, age twenty-six, of Richmond, Virginia (and a close neighbor of Captain Ensor); ...second mate, Lucius Stevens of New Haven, Connecticut; William Devereux, the cook, steward, and a free Black man; Jacques Lacomb, the helmsman from France who spoke little English, and sailors; Anthony John Silvy, a native of Portugal; Henry Speck, a Dutch sailor; Blinn Curtis, age thirty, from Owls Head, Maine; and an eighteen-year-old named Francis Foxwell.

Also on board were four passengers: Jacob Lietener (sometimes referred to as Jacob Miller), who assisted as a steward to augment his passage; John Hewell, a slavedriver who was the overseer of the slaves owned by Thomas McCargo; William H. Merritt, the overseer of the remainder of the slaves on board the *Creole* and Theophilus J.D. McCargo, age twenty-one, the nephew of Thomas McCargo. Theophilus was accompanied by his slave, referred to as "old man Lewis."[3]

Although it was economically feasible to arrive with as many slaves as possible in prime condition, so as to achieve the highest possible price, the passage by ship from the Upper-South to the Lower-South markets was not an easy trip. The manner in which the slaves were shipped was a controlled and calculated business, arranged down to the last detail. The slaves were allocated exact areas, packed into the hold of the *Creole* in much the same manner as practiced during the "middle passage," when slave ships sailed from West African ports to the New World. It was also a routine practice on these vessels to keep a separation between male and female slaves, so as to ensure a controlled environment on board the cramped ships. Male slaves were stowed in the forward hold, away from the crew's quarters, and female slaves in the aft hold. The remainder of the cargo was stored between the men and women's sections of the brig.

The boarding of the slaves began on October 20, 1841 at Shockoe Bottom, the notorious riverfront district of Richmond, Virginia. When the *Creole* left Richmond at midnight on Monday the 25th, in tow of the steamboat *Ben Shepard*, there were 121 slaves on board.[4] The ship's log indicates that on Tuesday morning she cast off from the *Ben Sheppard*, proceeded down the James River under sail, and came to anchor that evening off Hog Island. The following day she moved to Day's Point, where three more slaves were brought aboard. At this point, Captain Ensor left the *Creole* and embarked on another ship to pick up more slaves in Norfolk. At Newport News, Ensor returned to the *Creole* sometime after five p. m. with thirty-three more slaves.

The ship's log states the following:

Thursday, 28th Oct. 1841—All this day fresh breezes from S. E. At noon got under way. At five p. m. came to anchor at Newport News. Capt. Ensor came on board with thirty-three negroes. So ends this day.[5]

Although the log showed 154 slaves as steerage cargo, there were in fact 135 slaves on board.[6] This discrepancy may be attributable to insurance claims regarding the issue of indemnity for loss of property. The insurers of the cargo of slaves being shipped onboard the brig *Creole* declined to reimburse the policy holders for their losses; claiming that the policies excepted insurrection, suicide, desertion or natural death as causes of recovery. The owners brought suit against the insurance companies in Commercial Court in New Orleans where it was established that there were discrepancies in the actual number of slaves onboard the *Creole* when it entered Nassau, as compared to what the owners of the slaves claimed.

As groups of slaves were brought aboard during the trip down the James

River, it would have been difficult, if not impossible, for those already in the holds to know if, by chance, a wife, mother, daughter, sister, father, son or brother were now also on the ship.

The next day, October 29, the *Creole* made its way to Sewell's Point, and on Saturday to Lynnhaven Bay, where she anchored for the night while awaiting favorable tides and weather.[7] While anchored at Lynnhaven Bay, the *Creole* was in the company of two other intercoastal slave ships that also awaited favorable conditions—the brigs *Orleans* and *Long Island*.

The next morning the *Creole*'s log stated: "Nothing of importance. Got under way and proceeded to sea. Winds S. E. etc."[8]

The *Creole* sailed east-southeast as the weather deteriorated and the seas grew heavy. On the fourth of November, the vessel began shipping water to the point where a man was ordered on the pumps.

[f]resh breeze, took in lite [sic] sales [sic] heavy seas vessel labouring [sic] heavy making considerable water kept one man at the pump So ends this day.[9]

The inclement weather would have required the attention and time of the crew to maintain the ship's seaworthiness. A series of air ports on either side of the ship allowed fresh air to circulate below decks, but when the seas were rough, it became necessary to cover these openings to avoid shipping water. With the hatches battened down, portholes sealed, and gratings covered, the areas below deck were secured from the weather, while at the same time, sealing in the slaves below decks. The slaves, usually allowed on deck for feeding, were fed in the hold where the air became thick and noxious to breathe. Suffice to say, they were not as closely watched under these conditions.

For several days the *Creole* labored heavily as waves broke over the bow, but by late Saturday the weather began to clear. On Sunday, November seventh, the log reported that Captain Ensor ordered all sails set as the *Creole* sailed south by southwest at six knots. As evening approached, the exhausted crew began to relax as the ship neared Hole-in-the-Wall, the southern end of Great Abaco Island in the Bahamas. It was here that the *Creole* intended to resupply its fresh water.

It was a moonless night when Captain Ensor ordered the ship "hove to" at eight p. m., believing he was near Abaco Island. He then retired below decks, leaving the first mate, Mr. Gifford, in charge. According to the deposition of Mr. Gifford, at or around nine o'clock that night, "[a] black man came and told me (1st mate, Mr. Gifford) there was a man in the whole [sic] with the woman . . ."[10]

Gifford sent for Mr. Merritt, as he was in charge of the slaves on board the *Creole*. Merritt came on deck, and after securing a match and lamp, descended into the aft hold and discovered a male slave named Madison Washington among the females. When Merritt tried to detain Madison, he refused and forced his way on deck.

Upon reaching the deck Madison Washington ordered all the slaves up on deck.

"Come on boys," he shouted, "we have commenced. We must go through with it!"[11]

With this reported command, Madison Washington, with as many as twenty-two known accomplices, began the largest successful slave revolt in American history.

In the darkness, several slaves rushed aft to the crew and passenger cabins. In the struggle that ensued, the crew was overwhelmed. The captain, a crewmember, and two slaves suffered severe wounds, and the slave driver, John Hewell, and one of the slaves, George Grundy, were killed.

Once the mutineers secured the *Creole*, orders were issued by Madison Washington to set a course for the nearest British port, Nassau, Bahamas. The 135 slaves on board the *Creole* were now free—and masters of the brig.

All day Monday, a tense quiet permeated the ship as it sailed toward New Providence, Bahamas. The crew was closely watched and were prohibited any conversation among themselves or with the passengers, with only the writing of compass headings tolerated by the newly freed slaves. Captain Ensor, badly wounded from several stab wounds received in the initial fray, was seen to by the ex-slaves, and his wounds dressed. It is noteworthy that, prior to reaching Nassau, Madison Washington, "[g]ot the pistol from the nineteen, and said he did not want them to have any arms when they reached Nassau." [12]

On Tuesday morning, the *Creole* was spotted from the harbor tower at Nassau and a pilot boat was sent out to meet the vessel. Mr. Gifford was allowed to go ashore on board the quarantine boat, and went directly to the American Consul, John Bacon, to report the incident. Bacon and Gifford immediately made their way to the offices of the Royal Governor of the Bahamas, Sir Francis Cockburn. After several days of back and forth between the American Consul and the Colonial authorities, the passengers, as the British referred to the people on board the *Creole*, were given their liberty.

At the same time, after a brief investigation by the colonial attorney general, those who led the insurrection were detained on charges of mutiny and murder.

This revolt came to be known as The Creole Incident.

What has been documented about the incident focuses mainly on the obvious facts: slaves being transported to New Orleans on a common intercoastal slave vessel rose up and mutinied the ship.

Yet, this is only a small part of the story.

The struggle for freedom and emancipation onboard the *Creole* by nineteen individuals unequivocally and dramatically altered the course and nature of American history. Without a doubt, the actions taken by Madison Washington and his compatriots on that fateful night set in motion a series of events that significantly transformed the dynamics between the free states of the North and those Southern states that practiced and defended the institution of slavery.

What role did an obscure slave revolt have on the conflict that raged between the Southern planters' stubborn defense of their peculiar institution and those who petitioned vehemently for freedom and Union? It can be argued that the fate of the Union was decided twenty years prior to the Civil War, with the actual disposition of that conflict predisposed, *all because of this one incident.*

The act of mutiny and murder onboard the brig *Creole* was more than a simple conspiracy of nineteen individuals who sought their freedom. Their story reveals an undeniable link that ties the revolt on board the *Creole* with a calculated, premeditated course of action that involved a handful of radical abolitionists and some of the highest officials in the United States government. It clearly defines the beginning of the end of slavery.

The reason this American saga has remained unknown and little reported can be attributed to this simple fact: *The circumstances surrounding the revolt on board the brig* Creole *were never intended for public perusal.* The layers of history that surround this event conceal a careful, step-by-step process of subterfuge, cunning, and boldness taken by a select group of individuals who acted in concert to save the Union from the domination of slavocracy.

In the years leading up to the revolt on board the *Creole*, the cancer of slavery had become so ubiquitous and ineradicable, that it threatened the very existence of constitutional law and Union. What stood between freedom and the total domination of the government by Southern slave interests were two remarkable men who came from widely divergent backgrounds; one was an aging champion of Constitutional ideals and the other was a slave.

This is their story and the story of America.

The Creole Incident

THE BEGINNING OF THE END OF SLAVERY

BOOK I: DIVISIONS

1
Washington, DC: 1835–1836

A power for one part of the people to make slaves of the other can never be derived from the consent, and is, therefore, not a just power. —Diary of J Q Adams, March 3, 1820.

In October of 1835, Halley's Comet, as it has every seventy-six years, appeared on an orbit through our solar system. It was widely reported to be visible in the night skies over the eastern seaboard of the United States and was thought by certain people then, and is still considered by some today, to be a foreshadowing of certain events. To those who attend to such divination, the comet's appearance can either be a harbinger of good fortune or ill will.

Halley's Comet was first recorded by the Chinese in 240 BCE, and was interpreted as a "broom star," believed to sweep the heavens of evil, while in other parts of the world it was considered to be an omen of calamitous events. It seems the comet's fortune is reliant on which side of a historical moment one observes the phenomena. For example, its appearance in 1066 bode well for William the Conqueror, but not as favorably for King Harold.

As to whether Halley's Comet foreshadowed events on this particular passage is a matter of interpretation and conjecture. The actual real-world events that did occur, occurred in their usual plodding manner in that they were relevant and new at the time, but have since become history.

During the celestial visit of 1835 certain events took place that would have an influence on the character and course of history in varying degrees: Hans Christian Anderson published the first four of his 168 tales for children; Charles Darwin, on board the HMS *Beagle*, visited the Galapagos Archipelago; and in London, several short stories by Charles Dickens appeared in a British weekly sporting paper called *Bell's Life in London, and Sporting Chronicle*. Also in London, the British Colonial Office completed a detailed report concerning the disposition of newly emancipated slaves in the British West Indies, with particular attention to the resettling of former slaves in the Bahamas, so as to provide "subsistence & receiving the benefit of British Law & Manners."[13]

Her Majesty's government had recently passed the Slavery Abolition Act of 1833. Prior to the act, Great Britain had abolished slavery in England in 1787 and instituted the Slave Trade Act in 1807 that outlawed the African slave trade. The Royal Navy established the West Africa Squadron (or Preventative Squadron) in 1808, the same year the United States made the importation of slaves illegal. The Preventative Squadron patrolled the West African coastline in search of illicit shipping of slaves. Although the Royal Navy was active in suppressing the slave trade, the United States lagged in its enforcement. British boarding of American ships suspected of participating in the slave trade was one factor that led to the War of 1812. It would not be until 1862, during the Civil War, that the United States actually tried and hanged a slave captain for the crime of illegal slave importation—one Captain Nathaniel Gordon of Portland, Maine.

In 1835, the Royal Navy expanded its enforcement of the Preventative Squadron. It instituted the practice of seizure of ships that may not have slaves on board but were clearly equipped to store and ship slaves. It was hoped that the newly expanded enforcement would end the practice of throwing slaves overboard while being pursued by the Preventative Squadron.

In February of that year the United States ship, *Enterprise*, carried a cargo of seventy-eight slaves between Alexandria, Virginia and Charleston, South Carolina, and was forced by bad weather into the British port of Hamilton, Bermuda. Upon interviewing the slaves, the colonial government freed seventy-two who desired to remain in Bermuda as free people. Suffice it to say, there existed bad feelings between the United States and Her Majesty's government over this and similar incidents.

Other matters of history during the comet's passing also involved the institution of slavery. In North America, Texas revolted against Mexico. One of the main points of contention for Texas was the fact that the Mexican government did not recognize the institution of slavery. American settlers, who had immigrated into the Texas territory at the invitation of the Mexican government, carried with them their worldly possessions—including their slaves. This affront to Mexican law contributed to the inevitable separation of Texas from Mexico and the establishment of the Republic of Texas.

In New York City, Phineas Taylor Barnum began his career as a showman with the exhibition of Joice Heth, a black woman and a slave, alleged to be George Washington's childhood nurse and advertised to be over 160 years old.

Another American icon made his appearance during this time period. On November 20 in Florida, Missouri, Jane Lampton Clemens gave birth to a boy she named Samuel. Ironically, the next time Haley's Comet appeared, Mr. Clemens would pass from the earth after leaving a rich legacy of literature.

Near Fort King (Ocala), Florida, the Second Seminole War began. Major General Thomas Sidney Jesup, the commander in Florida during this period of the Seminole War, declared emphatically, "This is a negro, not an Indian war."

Throughout the Southern slave states, abolitionists were being expelled and the mailing of anti-slavery propaganda became forbidden, based in large part on a paranoia brought about by the recent Nat Turner slave uprising.[14] John Quincy Adams, then a member of the United States House of Representatives, noted in his diary that in Mississippi "[m]obs are hanging up blacks suspected of insurgency, and whites suspected of abetting them."[15]

In the White House, President Andrew Jackson, who had fought in the first Seminole War, was nearing the end of his second term. Earlier, in January of 1835, an attempt on President Jackson's life took place, the first in American history. But for the moist air that fouled the fine gunpowder in the assailant's pistol, causing the ignition to fail and thus rendering the gun useless, Jackson could have been the first assassinated President. Although frail and not well, Jackson attacked the would-be assassin with his cane and avoided killing the man when the crowd separated Jackson and subdued the perpetrator, Richard Lawrence.

By the time Halley's Comet began to fade into the night sky at the end of December, the Blue Ridge Mountains were blanketed with a mantle of snow and one of the harshest winters in memory had firmly established itself throughout the eastern seaboard.

In Congress, a political chill had also set in.

The 24th Congress of the United States convened on December 7, 1835. The accepted practice of convening Congress in December was mandated in the Constitution of the United States, Article I, Section 4. "The Congress shall assemble at least once every year, and such meetings shall be on the first Monday in December, unless they shall by law appoint a different day."

A "different day" was eventually appointed with the passage of the Twentieth Amendment, ratified in 1933, which changed the date of convening Congress to January third. However, in 1836 the character and principal industry of the United States was agriculture, and the timeline was directly connected to the convening being after the harvest with further allowance for the conditions of the roads and newly formed rail transportation. Some traveled great distances from the Western frontier, while others, from the Southern plantation system, made the journey complemented by their personal slaves. Others, who represented northern climes and the attitudes of a buttoned-up New England society, made their way to the nation's capital by the well-established rail, ferry, and road systems of the northeast.

They convened to carry on the business of government, each representing their own provincial opinion as to how the nation was to be governed. Issues that dealt with the federal banking system, internal improvements, and many other legislative matters confronted Congress in December of 1835. However, the one issue that became an irritant to the body politic involved petitions that prayed for the abolition of slavery in the District of Columbia.

When a petition was presented to Congress, it followed a routine practice. If accepted, it was read into the record and then assigned to the proper committee. If rejected, it was said to be "tabled," and no further action was taken.

The petitions that prayed for the abolition of slavery in the District of Columbia were the result of a growing agitation by those who were active in the newly established anti-slavery societies that began to make their presence known in the late 1820s. The following is an example of such a petition:

To the Congress of the United States

Your Petitioners, Ladies of the town of West Springfield, in the county of Hampden, and state of Massachusetts, beg leave to represent to your honorable body, that the people of the United States have vested in Congress, by the first Article of the Federal Constitution, "exclusive legislation, in all cases whatsoever," over the District of Columbia.

Your Petitioners do not ask your honorable body to legislate for the abolition of slavery in the several states where it exists, but they do respectfully represent that duty to their country, to mankind, and to God, forbids Congress to exercise their power of "exclusive legislation," to Perpetuate Slavery And The Slave Trade in the Capital of the American Republic. The acts of Congress hitherto passed for the government of said District in fact do this.

If these laws are *ever* to be repealed, and slavery and the slave trade in that District are thereby *ever* to cease, it must be by the action of Congress. Your Petitioners believe that no time can be more favorable for such action than the present. They therefore most respectfully but earnestly entreat your honorable body to pass without delay such laws, as to your wisdom may seem right and proper for the entire abolition of slavery and the slave trade in the District of Colombia.

And your Petitioners, &c.[16]

It wasn't just the subject matter of the petitions, but the sheer volume of the petitions being presented that raised the ire of Southern members:

In the 1837-38 Congressional session, they dumped over 130,000 petitions calling for abolition in the district, following them up with 32,000 against the Gag rule, 22,000 against the admission of new slave states. And 23,000 in favor of abolishing the domestic slave trade.[17]

Anti-slavery materials were not only directed at Congress but were being sent via the United States mail into the deep South. Many believed the inflammatory nature of the petitions and anti-slavery materials acted as a catalyst for slave insurrections. Often cited as a case in point: the Nat Turner slave revolt that occurred in August of 1831.[18] The incendiary material became such a concern that both President Jackson and Senator John C. Calhoun supported legislation censoring the mail of publications deemed abolitionist. In his annual report to Congress, December 1, 1835, President Jackson wrote the following: "The General Government to which the great trust is confided of preserving inviolate the relations created among the States by the Constitution, is especially bound to avoid in its own action anything that may disturb them [sic] I would, therefore, call the special attention of Congress to the subject, and respectfully suggest the propriety of passing such a law as will prohibit, under severe penalties, the circulation in the Southern States, through the mail, of incendiary publications intended to instigate the slaves to insurrection."[19]

On Dec. 21, 1835, Senator Calhoun asked that the portion of Jackson's statement, regarding antislavery material being sent through the public mail be referred to a select committee for immediate action. The pushback from Calhoun's fellow senators put an end to his designs and killed the request regarding consideration in a select committee, or any further consideration.

Although their attempts failed, the Southern postmasters denied delivery of abolitionist materials as each individual Southern state found a means to thwart these materials from reaching their respective communities. However, this had no effect on the flood of anti-slavery petitions directed at Congress. Due to the volume and subject of petitions, the Southern leadership declared the time had come to seek a resolution. The debate centered on the existence of slavery in the District of Columbia, a territory that came under the jurisdiction of the federal government and Constitutional restrictions and protections. The issue quickly became a bone of contention between the Southern members of Congress and a small group of representatives who protested against the existence of slavery in the nation's capital.

Southern planters claimed the legality of their peculiar institution fell under the jurisdiction of state and municipal codes, rather than federal law. They based their argument on the Fifth Amendment (property rights) and Tenth Amendment (powers reserved to the states) of the Constitution. At the same time, Southern politicians claimed the status of slavery had a somewhat ambiguous legal recognition in the Constitution, based on passages that referred to "[p]erson held to service or labor."[20]

The Southern representatives believed these slave clauses, purposely vague in their wording, supported an implied legal imposition of the institution on the nation as a whole. Furthermore, the Southern representatives claimed that the District of Columbia was a creation wrought from parts of Virginia and Maryland, both slave states. It was an obvious conclusion on the part of the Southern representatives that the newly formed District of Columbia should be a slave district, regardless of its status as a federal territory.

On the other side of the debate were those members who decried the South's blatant attempt to legitimize slavery on a federal level. Many members who opposed slavery were considered a fringe element, with radical ideas regarding the institution. They emphatically stated that slavery was not a condition found in the Constitution, since the word "slave" did not appear anywhere in the body of the document. They also argued that the jurisdiction of slavery in the South was not recognized under federal law but was, instead, regulated under state and municipal codes. Thus, a federal territory that was under the jurisdiction of federal law would not recognize the institution of slavery.

The flood of petitions that prayed for the abolition of slavery in the nation's capital focused their complaint on the discrepancy of federal versus state sovereignty with regard to the District of Columbia. The American Anti-Slavery Society, established in Philadelphia on December 4, 1833, explicitly stated that slavery in the District of Columbia was an affront to federal jurisdiction and constitutional law. This one issue was so important that it was written into the society's constitution.[21]

The issue boiled to the top of legislative matters during the opening days of the 24th Congress when several resolutions presented by John Fairfield of Maine prayed for the abolition of slavery in the District of Columbia. Although not unusual, petitions praying for the abolition of slavery in the nation's capital had reached a level that could no longer be ignored or tolerated by the Southern membership of Congress. The reaction to the insistent petitions set in motion a series of debates on how Congress should, or should not, address the matter. Representative William Slade of Vermont argued that the petitions deserved further consideration of the Congress and should not be arbitrarily tabled (when a petition is tabled, no further action is taken).

The Bill of Rights established the use of petitions as a Constitutional guarantee of public expression on issues facing Congress:

> Congress shall make no law respecting an establishment of religion, or prohibiting the free exercise thereof; or abridging the freedom of speech, or of the press; or the right of the people peaceably to assemble, and to petition the Government for a redress of grievances.

In the first session of the 24th Congress, a select committee under the leadership of Henry Laurens Pinckney of South Carolina, whose father was a signatory of the Constitution, was established to review the abolitionist's petitions and report on what action should be taken. The expectation was that Pinckney would reaffirm the South's stance that Congress had no jurisdiction over the issue of slavery in any individual state. As for the District of Columbia, the planter's attitude was to avoid a showdown on the issue, while at the same time vigorously defending the continuation of slavery in the District.

On February 8, 1836, Pinckney presented a resolution to establish the select committee that would deal with this contentious issue. It read in part:

> *Resolved,* That all memorials which have been offered or may hereafter be presented to this House, praying for the abolition of slavery in the district of Columbia, and also the resolutions offered . . . be referred to a select committee, with instructions to report that Congress possesses no constitutional authority to interfere in any way with the institution of slavery in any State of the Confederacy; and that, in the opinion of this House, Congress ought not to interfere in any way with slavery in the District of Columbia . . . assigning such reasons for these conclusions as in the judgment of the committee may be best calculated to enlighten the public mind, to preserve the just rights of the slaveholding States and of the people of the District, and to reestablish harmony and tranquility among the various sections of the Union.[22]

There were others who called for stronger measures. Southern representatives, led by South Carolina's James Henry Hammond, moved that the House emphatically reject abolitionist petitions. What was concerning about Hammond's pronouncement was that there was no precedent that allowed for a petition *not* to be received. This flew in the face of the First Amendment, wherein the people of the United States are guaranteed the right to "petition the government for a redress of grievances."

The idea of abolishing slavery in the District of Columbia sent economic shudders through the financial body of the nation and was perceived by Southern planters as a direct threat to the very existence of their peculiar institution. In 1836, the abolition of slavery was unheard of and unthinkable. The fact was, the institution of slavery was frozen into the economic body of civil America at the sum of two billion dollars. By 1860, the capital investment in slaves was worth more than three billion dollars and surpassed the combined capital investments in railroads and factories. The idea that such accumulated wealth would suddenly cease to exist seemed unimaginable to most Americans. In the words of Representative Hammond, "Slavery can never be abolished."

Although debate over the petitions subsided while Congress awaited the Pinckney committee's recommendations, the bitter antagonism between the planters and those who championed abolition was never far from the surface. The winter dragged on as each side remained frozen and intractable over its position on the petitions. As Congress awaited the committee's findings, it was obvious that each side was unwilling to compromise. This in turn preordained the outcome of Pinckney's findings as unsatisfactory to either side.

In May of 1836, the inevitable spring thaw began in earnest, if only with regard to the weather. But in Congress, a similar thaw had failed to occur. It was expected that on May 18 the Pinckney committee would finally present their recommendations. The committee hoped a series of resolutions, to be considered by the House, would settle the issue, once and for all. In fact, the consequence of the Pinckney resolutions would act to further turn up the heat on the question of slavery.

2
Divisions: Washington, DC
House of Representatives.

*He offered the resolution before the House with the most temper-
ate reflection, and with firm conviction that it was the best course
to be pursued...he had three objects in view in offering that resolution: the first was...to arrest discussion of the question of slavery
on that floor...the second to bring the whole matter to a practical
result...the third and great object was, to put down fanaticism and
produce harmony and tranquility...*

—Representative Henry Laurens Pinckney, South Carolina's 1st district.

From the gaps in the Blue Ridge Mountains, rushing streams swelled the rivers of the Appalachian Plateau as they flowed toward the Piedmont Upland, searching for a path to the coastal plain. At Harpers Ferry, the confluence of the Shenandoah and Potomac Rivers flowed east to form a boundary between Maryland and Virginia. The Potomac then passed through Mather Gorge and Great Falls as it made its final descent to the coastal plain. From that point on, the river became lazy and wide as it made its way to the Chesapeake, and on to the open sea.

Along the banks of the Potomac dogwood trees were in bloom and in the low marshy areas adjacent to the river, Paulownia and white-flowered black locusts were in evidence. As the river flowed past the nation's capital at spring crest, the scent of honeysuckle permeated the air. Residents of the District, after the long harsh winter, hiked trails along its banks, had picnics, and enjoyed the beauty and serenity of the river.

On the eighteenth of May, a lone elderly gentleman could be seen walking along the banks of the Potomac, recalling how just a few years earlier he had swum in its waters. He had noted in his diary that it seemed the weather had changed abruptly and the sudden appearance of spring had occurred overnight: "Tuesday, May 17, 1836. The change from winter to summer has taken place in 24 hours."[23]

For the man walking along the Potomac, it was another spring in a long life of service. His history in government and his years in Washington established him as an aging champion of Union who bridged the generation of the Founding Fathers with the present. He had been in service to the Republic, in one form or another, for most of his life and presently served in the House of Representatives. His name was John Quincy Adams.

His propensity to serve never seemed to get old, unlike himself. He would have smiled as he reconciled himself to the fact that he had become old, the years falling away like the leaves of an autumn tree. With age, some said he had become harsher in his judgment of those with whom he did not agree. He did admit to himself that at times he was a bit self-righteous, but he was as harsh a judge of himself as he was toward those who opposed him. Yet, here was another spring with its hope eternal. Although he pursued many varied interests, he desired no other avocation than the life of service he had dedicated to the Republic. His love affair with the city, and the nation it presided over, was his sustenance. He had spent his entire life in the protection and defense of the ideals and principles of governance found in the nation's Constitution.

As he turned to walk back toward the city, the view of the squat Bulfinch dome of the Capitol building atop Jenkin's Hill (the highest point in the community) was clearly visible.[24] The other prominent structure of the District in the spring of 1836 was the White House, where the leaves of the many English elms began to offer shade along the walkways of Pennsylvania Avenue. The remainder of the capital was made up of a scattering of homes and government buildings, interspersed with pastures and roads that frequently led nowhere. In places, the streets were muddy from a mix of late snows and spring showers, but for the first time in months dust was in evidence from passing carriages. Although a chill in the night air persisted, by mid-afternoon the insufferable humid oppression of summer began to make its presence known. Winter had finally relinquished its hold on Washington.

The capital of the United States sought to define its identity as a center of government, but in 1836 Washington had yet to achieve the eminence of a European capital. On a visit to Washington a year earlier, Harriet Martineau, an English political author, wrote her impression of the new capital. "The city itself is unlike any other that ever was seen, straggling out hither and thither, with a small house or two a quarter of a mile from any other; so that in making calls 'in the city' we had to cross ditches and stiles, and walk alternately on grass and pavements, and strike across a field to reach a street."[25]

Imposed upon a marshy stretch of land, the District of Columbia may have conveyed a suggestion of harmony with nature on that spring day, but in reality, this image belied the conflict wrenching at the very foundation of the young republic it presided over. A clash of governance, based on varied interpretations of constitutional protections handed down by the previous generation, embroiled the nation, its capital, and its lawmakers. The catalyst for this contention was as pervasive as the scent of honeysuckle. From the very steps of the Capitol, where inside, members of both Houses debated and championed the inalienable rights of man, one could discern the crack of a whip, the clanking of chains, the misery, stench, and brutality of slavery.

The English abolitionist, E. S. Abdy, on a visit to Washington in 1833, related his impression of a slave pen near the Capitol:

One day I went to see the "slaves' pen"—a wretched hovel, 'right against' the Capitol, from which it is distanced about half a mile, with no house intervening. The outside alone is accessible to the eye of a visitor; what passes within being reserved for the exclusive observation of its owner, (a man of the name of Robey,) and his unfortunate victims. It is surrounded by a wooden paling fourteen or fifteen feet in height, with the posts outside to prevent escape and separated from the building by a space too narrow to admit of a free circulation of air. At a small window above, which was unglazed and exposed alike to the heat of summer and the cold of winter, so trying to the constitution, two or three sable faces appeared, looking out wistfully to while away the time and catch a refreshing breeze; the weather being extremely hot. In this wretched hovel, all colors, except white—the only guilty one—both sexes, and all ages, are confined, exposed indiscriminately to all the contamination which may be expected in such society and under such seclusion. The inmates of the gaol, of this class I mean, are even worse treated; some of them, if my informants are to be believed, having been actually frozen to death, during the inclement winters which often prevail in the country. While I was in the city, Robey had got possession of a woman, whose term of slavery was limited to six years. It was expected that she would be sold before the expiration of that period, and sent away to a distance, where the assertion of her claim would subject her to ill-usage. Cases of this kind are very common.[26]

Slavery was a cancer on the soul of the Republic. It revealed stark, discernible differences between the political philosophies of the Northern free labor states and the Southern agrarian slave states. Each side sought to define the role of government—rhetorically, emotionally, and civically—based on their respective regional interpretations of the Constitution. Despite a series of tenuous compromises, these differences had become increasingly protracted by the late 1830s. With the expansion of the nation beyond the original thirteen colonies, newly elected representatives proclaimed their allegiance either for free labor, or slavery, and added fuel to the fire of discontent. Passionate, heated voices debated, prayed, petitioned, and proclaimed for each side. Some sought compromise, while others vehemently adhered to a narrow reading of the Constitution based on the principle of state sovereignty.

Southern members of Congress believed the role of the federal government was subservient to that of individual states, and argued against any perceived attempt by Washington to impose its governance. This contentiousness can be traced back to the very inception of the Constitution. The framers debated the issue of state versus federal authority, and to ensure ratification of the Constitution by states that were leery of losing sovereignty to a central government, compromises were inserted into the Constitution. Particular regard was given to slavery, yet it did not give any direct reference to that institution.

The importance of these compromises was that they allowed privileges to those who supported slavery, while at the same time they avoided the insertion of the word "slave" anywhere in the Constitution. The jurisdiction of slavery as a legal institution was delegated to individual states, based on the Tenth Amendment: "The powers not delegated to the United States by the Constitution, nor prohibited by it to the states, are reserved to the states respectively, or to the people."[27]

Slavery, based on state law or municipal codes, negated any jurisdiction by the federal government. This enabled the Southern planter establishment to lawfully defend against any and all perceived encroachment by federal authority. This, in turn, created a competition between those who believed in a strong federal government and those who proclaimed for the sovereignty and independence of individual states.

As early as Jefferson's presidency (1801-1809), the lines had been clearly established between the supporters of national supremacy, the Federalists, and those who advocated for states' rights, the Republicans. Thirty years later, the divide had become pronounced. By the 1830s, the South was so adamant about protecting states' rights that they came to perceive the government in Washington as an overarching threat to state sovereignty, with particular regard to slavery. One example of imposed federal authority cited by Southern representation was the American system, wherein the federal government set tariffs, funded the building of roads, canals, and other internal improvements, and claimed jurisdiction over interstate commerce.

The South's attitude toward these perceived encroachments is best exemplified by its response to what many Southerners firmly believed were unfair tariffs. In the South, the tariffs were disdainfully referred to as abominations, perceived by the Southern planters as a threat to both their commerce and their institutions. Enough so that Southern politicians took dramatic steps toward defying the tariffs, and in so doing, put their interests in a position of defiance against the federal government.

On November 24th, 1832, by a vote of 136 to 26, the South Carolina legislature adopted an Ordinance of Nullification. Covertly written by the vice president of the United States, John C. Calhoun, the ordinance asserted that each state had the right to nullify, or refuse to obey, any act of Congress it believed to be unconstitutional, based in part on Jefferson's Kentucky and Virginia Resolutions of 1799. [28] The Virginia and Kentucky Resolutions, authored by James Madison and Thomas Jefferson in 1798, were in response to Federalist legislation named the Alien and Sedition Acts. Jefferson believed the union of states was a compact between the states and that individual states retained the autonomous authority to declare legislation passed by the Federal government, that violated state sovereignty, to be null and void. This ran counter to the Constitution's Supremacy Clause that established federal law superseded state law.

When Jefferson became President, he realized that, in order to govern diverse states, the Supremacy Clause in the Constitution need take precedent and abandoned his concept of state sovereignty in the Virginia and Kentucky Resolutions.

Calhoun centered his argument on the principle of interposition, wherein a state could place itself between its citizens and the national government to prevent enforcement of what was deemed to be unfair national laws. The people of each state, he argued, were sovereign when the Constitution was ratified, and in the process of ratification each state retained its position within the Union as a sovereign and separate entity. The Union was "[a] union of states as communities, and not a union of individuals"

The following excerpt from the Ordinance clearly reveals the direction and type of government Calhoun envisioned:

> Those governments only, which provide checks, which limit and restraint within proper bounds the power of the majority, have had a prolonged existence, and been distinguished for virtue, power and happiness. Constitutional government, and the government of the majority, are utterly incompatible, it being the sole purpose of a constitution to impose limitations and checks upon the majority. An unchecked majority, is a despotism . . .[29]

The language found in the Ordinance of Nullification alarmed many in the North, as well as others who supported a free, democratic union. It was viewed not only as a serious threat to the nation, but also a reckless attempt by a small minority to control federal policy. In fact, the ordinance was in direct violation of the Supremacy Clause of the Constitution (Article VI, section 2), wherein it states the Constitution shall be the supreme law of the land.[30]

This did not deter Calhoun. He, and those who supported his call for nullification, let it be known that if the Southern planters did not get their way, the talk of Southern slave states leaving the Union and establishing their own nation was a serious consideration—if not a blatant threat. Calhoun argued that the institutions of the South could only survive by one of two means: taking control of the federal government with the expressed intention of reforming the Constitution to legally incorporate slavery, or a dissolution of the present union and the establishment of a separate nation based on Southern institutions:

> . . . [t]hat each state of the union has the right whenever it may deem such a course necessary for the preservation of its liberties or vital interests, to secede peaceably from the Union, and that there is no constitutional power in the general government, much less in the executive department, of the government, to retain by force such State in the Union.[31]

In the end, the possibility of a war of secession was avoided through a series of actions taken by President Jackson and Congress. Jackson stated without equivocation that he would use the powers vested in him by the Constitution to suppress any attempt at secession and take military steps necessary, in the form of a Force Bill, to back up his words.[32]

At the same time, Senator Henry Clay of Kentucky offered a compromise bill that would provide for the gradual reduction of tariff duties until 1843, at which point they would be maintained at an across-the-board level of twenty percent.

The nullification crisis passed, but the underlying issue persisted. Suffice to say, it was not tariffs. Calhoun reflected this view when he succinctly laid out his concerns and ambitions in a letter to Virgil Maxcy, a friend and ardent supporter:

> I consider the Tariff but as the occasion rather than the real cause of the present unhappy state of things ... The truth can no longer be disguised that the peculiar domestic institution of the Southern States, and the consequent direction, which that and her soil and climate have given to her industry, has placed them in regard to taxation and appropriations in opposite relation to the majority of the Union; against the danger of which, if there be no protective power in the reserved rights of the states, they must in the end be forced to rebel, or submit to have their permanent interests sacrificed.[33]
> —Calhoun to Virgil Maxcy, Fort Hill, September 11, 1830.

Calhoun accepted the inevitable, hedging his bets, and waiting for a future opportunity to gain control of the government. He resigned his position as vice president[34] on December 28, 1832, and was then appointed to the Senate from South Carolina.

As the debate over slavery and states' rights grew ever more contentious over the ensuing years, the realization that constitutional democracy could never be compatible with slavery further divided the country. In the Senate, Daniel Webster and Henry Clay worked to contain Southern agrarian interests, but it was in the House where the strongest and steadiest voice against the actions of Calhoun and the Southern planter establishment was to be found:

> It is among the evils of Slavery that it taints the very sources of moral principle—It establishes false estimates of virtue and vice; for what can be more false and heartless than this doctrine which makes the first and holiest rights of humanity to depend upon the colour of the skin—It perverts human reason, and reduces men endowed with logical powers to maintain that Slavery is sanctioned by the Christian religion.[35]—John Quincy Adams

John Quincy Adams stood as a bulwark against the onrushing tide of Southern ascendancy. His commitment to a strong Union was rooted in the Puritanical ethics of New England, and a family tradition of public service. His father had been the country's second president and he, its sixth. He had served the nation with a long illustrious career: appointed by President Washington to be Minister of the United States to the Netherlands in 1794, elected to the United States Senate as a Federalist, serving from 1803 to 1807, appointed by President Madison in 1809 to the post of United States Minister to Russia, all before he was fifty.

While serving in Russia, Adams reported the rout of Napoleon's army and was also present in Paris when Napoleon returned from Elba. As Minister to England from 1815 to 1817, he was in London when Waterloo occurred. He served as Secretary of State in the Monroe administration from 1817–1825 and achieved the highest office in the land when he was elected president of the

United States in 1824 for one term.

He could have easily retired to a life of idle refinements, but instead accepted the challenge of continued public service. His greatest accomplishment was still in front of him when he entered the House of Representatives in 1831 at the age of sixty-four. He now stood as the singular impediment to a complete Southern domination of the government.

Although many still addressed him as Mr. President, he was often referred to as "Old Man Eloquent," in large part due to his ability to hold the floor for extended periods during debates. His debating prowess was legendary, and many a fellow representative came to regret the day they opposed him on a point of procedure. As to the South's peculiar institution, Adams not only recognized the threat slavery imposed on the nation, but was revolted by its practice. He railed against any perceived threat to the Union and had little patience with the states' rights contingent in Congress.

> Slavery . . . is the great and foul stain upon the North American Union, and it is a contemplation worthy of the most exalted soul whether its total abolition is or is not practicable: if practicable, by what means it may be effected, and if a choice of means be within the scope of the object, what means would accomplish it at the smallest cost of human sufferance. A dissolution, at least temporary, of the Union, as now constituted, would be certainly necessary, and the dissolution must be upon the point involving the question of slavery, and no other. The Union might then be reorganized on the fundamental principle of emancipation. This object is vast in its compass, awful in its prospects, sublime and beautiful in its issue. A life devoted to it would be nobly spent or sacrificed.[36]

Diametrically opposed to Calhoun and his governing philosophy, Adams spoke against the threat presented by the South Carolina Exposition. In attacking nullification Adams exposed the underlying cancer that was eroding the very foundation of the republic:

> Nullification was generated in the hot-bed of slavery. It drew its first breath in the land where the meaning of the word democracy is that a majority of the people are the goods and chattels of the minority; that more than half of the people are not men, women, and children, but things, to be treated by their owners, not exactly like dogs and horses, but like tables, chairs, and joint stools; that they are not even fixtures to the soil, as in countries where servitude is divested of its most hideous features, not even beings in the mitigated degradation from humanity to beasts, or birds, or creeping things, but destitute of the sensibilities of our own race of men, but of the sensations of all animated nature.[37]

The nullification crisis not only revealed how slavery threatened democracy, but in turn it showed how the American system threatened slavery. Adams relates this point in the following excerpt from a speech he made at Braintree, Massachusetts, in the fall of 1842.

The root of the doctrine of nullification is that if the internal improvement of the country should be left to the legislative management of the national government, and the proceeds of the sales of the public lands should be applied as a perpetual and self-accumulating fund for that purpose, the blessings unceasingly showered upon the people by this process would so grapple the affections of the people to the national authority, that it would, in process of time, overshadow that of the state governments, and settle the preponderancy of power in the free states; and then the undying worm of conscience twinges with terror for the fate of the peculiar institution. Slavery stands aghast at the prospect promotion of the general welfare, and flies to nullification for defense against the energies of freedom, and the inalienable rights of man.[38]

Adams and Calhoun would duel each other over the direction and control of the government—Calhoun in the Senate, Adams in the House—with the competition being both personal and professional. However, by 1836 the advantage in both houses clearly favored the South.

One major factor that buttressed the South's advantage was its focused energy on the preservation and expansion of slavery as the engine for its industry. The North's representation in Congress stood in stark contrast to the solidarity of the South, rarely united on a single issue. Adams related his frustration with the voting record of his Northern cohorts when he proclaimed: "Do you not see that the one hundred representatives of persons, property, and slavery, marching in solid phalanx upon every question of interest to their constituents, will always outnumber the one hundred and forty representatives only of persons and freedom, scattered as their votes will always be by conflicting interests, prejudices, and passions?"[39]

With Calhoun as the anointed high priest of Southern ideals, the Southern contingent in Congress stood as one formidable bastion whenever slavery was threatened. As early as 1820, Calhoun wrote to a friend, Michael Sterling, that "[n]othing can be more congenial to our excellent political institutions, than the habits produced by agricultural pursuits."

Calhoun perceived slavery to simply be the practical application of labor to agriculture production. And how did he reconcile this with a constitution that guaranteed freedom for all? In his *A Disquisition on Government*, he dismissed completely the natural rights theory as expressed in the Declaration of Independence. For Calhoun, the statement "all men are created equal" was without merit.

These great and dangerous errors have their origin in the prevalent opinion that all men are born free and equal; than which nothing can be more unfounded and false. It rests upon the assumption of a fact, which is contrary to universal observation, in whatever light it may be regarded. It is, indeed, difficult to explain how an opinion so destitute of all sound reason, ever could have been so extensively entertained unless we regard it as being confounded with another, which has some semblance of truth; but which, when properly understood, is not less false and dangerous. I refer to the assertion, that all men are equal in the state of nature; meaning, by a state of nature, a state of individuality, supposed to have existed prior to the social and political state; and in which men lived apart and independent of each other. If such a state ever did exist, all men would have been, indeed, free and equal in it; that is, free to do as they pleased, and exempt from the authority or control of others—as, by supposition, it existed anterior to society and government. But such a state is purely hypothetical. It never did, nor can exist; as it is inconsistent with the preservation and perpetuation of the race. It is, therefore, a great misnomer to call it *the state of nature*. Instead of being the natural state of man, it is, of all conceivable states, the most opposed to his nature—most repugnant to his feelings, and most incompatible with his wants. His natural state is, the social and political—the one for which his Creator made him, and the only one in which he can preserve and perfect his race.[40]

By the spring of 1836, the regional competition for control of the government was quickly reaching critical mass. Congress had been in session since early December, dealing with a variety of issues confronting the nation: the federal banking system, a recession, the on-going Seminole wars, territorial disputes with England, a host of local matters and the approaching Texas question. Although each of these issues presented Congress with divergent views based on civic, social and economic sectionalism, each was entwined in the tentacles of slavery.

This was not only evident in the legislative arena, but in the executive and judicial branches of government as well. No branch of government was immune from slavery's influence, since all three branches of government experienced changes in 1836 that would directly affect this bitter debate.

For the executive branch, 1836 was a presidential election year. A new political party, the Whigs, became active in presidential politics for the first time. Part National Republican Party and Anti-Mason Party, the Whigs would eventually evolve into the Republican Party of Abraham Lincoln some twenty years later. A major part of their platform was for western expansion, based on the American system of canal and road building, supported by a strong central government.

The leading voice for the Whigs was Senator Henry Clay of Kentucky. Politically empathetic to both Northern interests and Southern institutions, Clay supported a broad interpretation of the Constitution. Although he was a slaveholder, he legislated for protective tariffs and liberal aid for internal improvements, while at the same time acting to maintain a balance between North and South by appearing to have a hands-off approach to slavery. The issue of slavery and the internal struggle in the Whig party would eventually divide the party along sectional lines, and contribute to its demise by 1858.

In the judicial branch of government, the courts faced a new era of jurisprudence. Property rights and the role of new forms of non-tangible property, such as corporate franchises, were just some of the legal questions that faced the courts with the advent of the industrialization. There was also a new chief justice.

The Supreme Court's fifth chief justice, Roger B. Taney, appointed by President Jackson, took his place on the bench that year. Unlike the previous chief justice, John Marshall, Taney was dedicated to the security of slavery and displayed a penchant for the protection of state sovereignty. Ironically, while the Taney court championed slavery by upholding state law and municipal codes, it inadvertently laid the legal groundwork for slavery's demise. In establishing the legal interpretations of property under the auspices of corporations, the court made it possible for the federal government to strengthen its jurisdiction over matters of interstate commerce. These decisions, as we shall see, would become a critical tool in the hands of Northern abolitionists in Congress.

But on May 18, 1836, the focus was on the legislative branch of government. The divergent views in the 24th Congress concerning slavery and sectionalism had manifested into a contentious debate on the issue of petitions. The task to resolve the petition question seemed destined to only create a larger paradox. A long shadow fell over the future of the nation and its Constitution, but in that same instant an individual's resistance to the event was an adumbration of the end of a peculiar institution.

3

The Gag Rule: Washington, D.C.
Wednesday, May 18, 1836

Immediately after the reading of the journal, H. L. Pinckney presented the report of the select committee to whom all abolition petitions were referred, and said that the report had the unanimous assent of the committee.—J Q Adams[41]

Washington was consumed with the business of government on that spring day when the dogwood trees were in full bloom. John Quincy Adams, along with other members of the 24th Congress, arrived at the Capitol on foot, horseback, and carriage. At the age of sixty-eight, he ascended the steps with the vigor of a much younger man, his thoughts focused on the issues facing Congress. It had been rumored that the Pinckney committee would report today. The other topic of interest being discussed was Texas.

News of the Alamo and the death of a fellow representative, Davy Crockett, had first been reported in the New York newspapers in early April, and the defeat and capture of Santa Ana at San Jacinto had been reported in the *New Orleans Picayune* on May 9.

Three years earlier, Adams had written in his diary of an encounter with Crockett:

[I] had a morning visit from Dr. Sewall, and before dinner walked to the Capitol. There I met Chilton Allen of Kentucky, Mr. Foster of Georgia, and Mr. Potts of Pennsylvania. On coming out, I met in the Avenue, Herman Allen of Vermont and afterwards Colonel David Crockett of Tennessee. I did not recognize him till he came up and accosted me and named himself. I congratulated him upon his return here, and he said, yes, it had cost him two years to convince the people of his district that he was the fittest man to represent them; that he had just been to Mr. Gales and requested him to announce his arrival and inform the public that he had taken for lodgings two rooms on the first floor of a boarding-house, where he expected to pass the winter and to have a fellow-lodger Major Jack Downing, the only person in whom he had any confidence for information of what the Government was doing . . .[42]

Although the death of Crockett would have been a topic of conversation, the real focus of attention was centered on the newly formed Republic of Texas. There was already talk of Texas entering the Union as several states. The Southern leadership in Congress recognized the benefits and advantages of an annexation of the Republic of Texas.

One of their distinguished politicians (referring to the Virginia legislation) published a series of essays on the policy of annexing Texas to the United States; a territory, which he contended, was large enough to be divided into *nine* slave States, which would counterbalance the increasing number of free States at the North.[43]

Of particular concern was the recognition of the institution of slavery by the Republic of Texas in its Constitution. If Texas came into the Union as several slave states, the added representation in Congress would tilt the precarious balance of power in favor of the ranks of "slavocracy." The debate was not "if," but how and when Texas would be admitted to the Union. It was important that there be discussion about allowing a free state to enter the Union along with Texas, so as to maintain the balance of power in Congress.

A few days earlier in the Senate, William Preston of South Carolina broached the subject. He argued in favor of the annexation of the Republic of Texas on the proposition that papist hordes were a threat to the constitutional practice of separation of church and state. Preston deemed abhorrent the contemplation of a "Spanish" race competing with the American-based Anglo-Saxon for the hearts and minds of Texas.

[b]y a superstition Catholicism, goaded on by a miserable priesthood, against the invincible Anglo-Saxon race. It was once a war of religion and liberty. Texas might or might not belong to us, or us to it; but talking, as the people there did, the same language with us, and having the same feelings with us, they were too homogeneous not to belong to us.[44]

Adams's apprehension over the admittance of Texas was based on the possible creation of several slave states from the Republic. This in turn would give the Southern representation in Congress a majority vote, based in part on the three-fifths clause in the Constitution, and with that, total control over the course of governance.

To understand the significance of the three-fifths clause a brief explanation of what the clause was and its role in government. Although the three-fifths clause is no longer a part of the Constitution, in 1836 it played a significant role in the allocation of funds to states, the ability to elect members to the House as well as the Presidency of the United States.

Article I, Section 2 read in part:

"Apportionment of Representatives. 3. Representatives and direct taxes shall be apportioned among the several states which may include within the union, according to their respective numbers, which shall be determined by adding to the whole number of free persons; including those bound to service for a term of years, and excluding Indians not taxed, three-fifths of all other persons."

The number of persons that are elected to The House of Representatives is based on the Congressional District's population found in each state. States like New York will have a larger number of representatives than a state like Delaware, based on each respective population. This added representation would vote according to the mandate and wishes of its constituents. The "three-fifths of all other person" was how the population of slaves was to be counted - but not represented. The slave was property; thus it had no voice regarding its desires and demands for representation; only the owners of the property had the prerogative as to how these added person were to be represented. Thus, the added representation based on slave population voiced its demands on the protection and continuation of the institution of slavery.

In 1840 the slave population in the United States was 2,873,648 persons, when calculated would add 1,492,413 person to the population. A significant number.

Further, the electoral college that elects the President of the United States is also based on population, in that the number of electors in each state is based on the population of each state. Again, a state like New York will have a much greater number of electors than a smaller state with a smaller population, such as Delaware.

The matter of concern in 1836 rested on the number of free states versus the number of slave states and the added representation that would vote on legislation favorable to each vision of governance; from funding to a reformation of the Constitution.

The stated goal of the Southern planter was to establish slavery as a federally protected institution. They believed that once slavery was constitutionally recognized, it would end debate about slavery's legal right to exist.

Further, if the call for abolition persisted, the South would have enough votes to legislate a legal separation from the Union. Representative Hammond, as well as many other Southern representatives, made it abundantly clear they would not hesitate to dissolve the Union if there was a perceived threat to the institution of slavery. Hammond proclaimed:

> But Congress has no right to legislate on the subject of slavery; and if ever the Government dared to take up and act on it, there would be civil war. If ever the proposition should come into the House, while he was there, he would not even remain to record his vote on it, but would go home and preach and practice disunion.[45]

Adams protested against such designs in a speech delivered in the House on May 31.

> The war now verging in Texas is a Mexican civil war, and a war for the re-establishment of slavery where it was abolished. It is not a servile war, but a war between slavery and emancipation, and every possible effort had been made to drive us into the war, on the side of slavery . . . Your war, sir, is to be a war of races—the Anglo-Saxon American pitted against the Mor-

rish-Spanish-Mexican American; a war between the northern and southern halves of North America . . . And again I ask what will be your cause in such a war! Aggression, conquest and re-establishment of slavery where it has been abolished. In that war, sir, the banners of *freedom* will be the banners of Mexico; and your banners, I blush to speak the word, will be banners of slavery.[46]

The lines were clearly being drawn. Those who wished to preserve the status quo of free versus slave states required that a free state be admitted for every new slave state. As long as the votes in the House and Senate were kept in this precarious balance, neither side could dominate. The key to maintaining this balance was to insure continued debate on the issue of slavery. Little did anyone realize how quickly that was all about to change.

As Adams joined the crush of representatives entering the House chamber, the greetings and conversations between the members grew to a cacophonous rumble. The old House chamber, known today as Statuary Hall, was laid out in a semi-circle with a high dome that was supported by a series of columns. The desks of the representatives faced the Speaker's dais and formed concentric half circles. Curtains of scarlet moreen (a strong, ribbed cotton or wool fabric) hung between the marbled columns that followed the curve of the room and the heavy material, along with the carpeted floor, acted to muffle the echoes of the speakers. Over the center of the chamber hung a large chandelier that was lowered and lit in the evenings.[47]

On the Senate side of the Capitol building, the columns in the old Senate chamber were adorned with tobacco leaf, a reminder of the importance of Southern agrarian institutions and their influence on the nation. The production of tobacco and all its connotations as a pillar of American society is further represented in a collection of essays that are considered, even today, the foremost commentary on the United States Constitution: *The Federalist Papers.*

Authored by Alexander Hamilton, John Jay, and James Madison, the cover page of the 1788 publication simply read "A Tobacco Plantation," with an engraving of plantation life, complete with slaves. Besides conveying the success of tobacco as an early agricultural industry, the illustration indicates how accepted and important slavery was in American society.

Back in the House chamber, the arriving representatives made their way to their desks amid greetings and glad-handing, and the visitor's balcony began to fill with spectators. In a clear voice, rising above the din, the Speaker hammered his mallet as he called the House to order. The chamber quieted and the House began the business of the day.

The following record of that fateful day reveals the sway Southern legislators held over Congress. Each of the petitions presented by Northern members was tabled, yet those presented by Southern members were read into the record and referred to committee.

From the *Congressional Globe,* dated Wednesday, May 18, 1836, the clerk recognized Mr. Whittlesey of Ohio:

[w]ho reported, without amendment, a bill from the Senate for the relief of the owners, officers, and crews, of the private-armed schooners Neptune and Fox[48]; and the same was committed.

Mr. Mercer, from the Committee on Roads and Canals, reported a bill to grant to the New Orleans and Nashville Railroad Company the right of way through public lands; which was read twice and committed.

Mr. M., from the same committee, laid before the House sundry documents in relation to the Louisville and Portland canal; which were laid on the table.

Mr. Thomas, from the Committee on the Judiciary, reported a bill to compensate the marshals and attorneys of the United States for the districts of South Carolina and Georgia for extra services; which were read twice and committed.

Mr. Pinckney [of South Carolina], on leave,[49] presented a petition; which was referred.

Abolition of Slavery

Mr. Pinckney, on leave, presented a report from the select committee on the subject of the abolition of slavery. In making this report, Mr. P. remarked, that it had received the unanimous assent of the committee, and he trusted it would meet the unanimous approbation of the House. By the instruction of the committee, he moved that it be read and printed.

Mr. Mercer moved that the report be laid on the table without reading, and printed.

Mr. Claiborne, of Mississippi, asked for the reading of the report; which was accordingly done. The reading occupied about an hour and a half. The report concluded with the following resolutions:

Resolved, That Congress possesses no constitutional authority to interfere in any way with the institution of slavery in any of the States of this Confederacy.

Resolved, That Congress ought not to interfere in any way with slavery in the District of Columbia.

And whereas it is extremely important and desirable that the agitation of this subject should be finally arrested for the purpose of restoring tranquility to the public mind, your committee respectfully recommends the adoption of the following resolution, viz:

Resolved, That all petitions, memorials, resolutions, propositions, or paper, relating in any way, or to any extent whatsoever, to the subject of slavery, or the abolition of slavery, shall, without being either printed or referred, be laid upon the table, and that no further action whatever shall be had thereon.

From his diary, dated May 18, 1836, Adams notes the events of the House session. "Immediately after the reading of the journal, H. L. Pinckney presented the report of the select committee to whom all abolition petitions were referred, and said that the report had the unanimous assent of the committee. He moved that five thousand copies of the report should be printed for the House. It was immediately attacked with extreme violence, and a fiery debate arose, which continued until one o'clock, and then, by a suspension of the rules, for another half-hour. Motion was made to print ten thousand and twenty copies, and Waddy Thompson, the representative of South Carolina's 6th congressional district, said he would commit it to flames or to the hangman. The Gag Rule, as it came to be known, was accepted in the House by a vote of 117 to 68."

In the Senate, John C. Calhoun of South Carolina failed in his attempt to establish a gag rule.

> The Senate, in deciding that this petition [on the abolition of slavery in the District of Columbia] should be received, established the principle that they were bound to receive petitions on the subject, no matter what language might be, on all occasions. This was a principle to which he could not give his consent. It gave a fatal stab at our liberties, and neutralized the effect of all the balm that had been attempted to be poured on the wounded feelings of the South.[50]

However, partially in response to Calhoun's protestations, coupled with an apprehension that a gag rule would further inflame abolitionists and their petitioning for an end of slavery in the District of Columbia, the Senate opted for a series of convoluted, complex procedures that would call for a vote, not on whether to receive such a petition, but rather on whether to accept the question to receive a petition.

In response to a petition presented by Senator Daniel Webster calling for the abolition of slavery in the District of Columbia, Senator Hubbard from New Hampshire applied such tactics.

> He hoped that the Senate would at one proceed to vote upon the question of reception, and prevent any further discussion at this time; and should the Senate, as he had no doubt they would, vote to receive the petition, he presumed that some one Senator would move to lay the motion of the Senator from Massachusetts and the petition on the table. The proceedings of the Senate on Friday last satisfied his mind that it is not the intention of this body, at this session, further to agitate the question of slavery within the District of Columbia.[51]

This parliamentary device avoided the appearance of any infringement of the right to petition guaranteed in the First Amendment of the Constitution. Calhoun later explained his justification for censoring debate on the subject of slavery: "What political grievances existed that required petitions? . . . The truth is the right of the petition could scarcely be said to be the right of a freeman. It belongs to despotic Governments more properly and might be said to be the last right of slaves."[52]

For all intents and purposes, the subject of slavery would no longer be debated in either the House or Senate. All petitions or resolutions pertaining to slavery would be laid upon the table, with no further consideration or action taken on behalf of the petitioner. A basic right—protected by the First Amendment—ceased to exist.

Not only did the Gag Rule give an advantage to the South concerning slavery in the District of Columbia—it also acted to censor debate on the admission of future territories into the Union as either free or slave states. The newly instituted rule, coupled with the South's solid voting bloc in the Congress, the states' rights sympathies of the Supreme Court, the majority of Cabinet members in the executive branch being slave owners, and the scattered interests of the North, all but guaranteed slavery's unabated continuance in both the District and in future states.

Yet, there were divisions in the Southern camp over the wording of the Gag Rule as it related to the District. The initial gag rule stated that Congress "ought not interfere" with slavery in the District, but many of the Southern members felt the statement was not emphatic enough. Pinckney acted to placate any doubts on May 19; when he stated: "What would be the thought of any Southern man who should move the resolutions declaring that Congress does possess the power to abolish slavery in the District of Columbia? Now, he had no doubt, that if the House were pressed to vote upon a resolution denying such power, it would be rejected, and most probably by a large majority. He did not know the fact of course, as no man can know anything that has not actually taken place; but it was his decided conviction, that such would be the result."[53]

Southern representatives basked in their victory over the abolitionists and their instigation by petition. With the Gag Rule in place, the South acquired an immense amount of power over the direction and course of governance. Pinckney stated the obvious when he addressed the House at the conclusion of the debate on the Gag Rule; "As matters now stand, everything is operating favorably to the South. The Senate, by a large majority, has rejected the prayer of the abolition memorials. This House has adopted resolutions pledging the national faith not to interfere with slavery in the District of Columbia. The tone of public sentiment is sound and patriotic in all the non-slaveholding States. The South, so far, is victorious, and everything goes well for her advantage and security."[54]

The initial Gag Rule would be followed by yearly gag resolutions. By 1841, the refusal to accept anti-slavery petitions became a permanent standing rule of the House. Of particular importance was the fact that the Gag Rule would now extend its censorship to cover slavery in both states and territories.

> *Resolved*, That no petition, memorial, resolution, or other paper praying the abolition of slavery in the District of Columbia, *or any State or Territory* (emphasis added), or the slave trade between the States or Territories of the United States in which it now exists, shall be received by this House, or entertained in any way whatever.[55]

Adams came to the sobering realization that, if left in place, the Gag Rule would forever alter the landscape and direction of the United States. He vowed to establish a means to break the Gag Rule. If successful, the nation would stand united, but if he failed, the Union faced the very real possibility of legal secession. Thus would end America's noble experiment in constitutional government. Adams was under no illusion as to what lay ahead—the Gag Rule must not stand. A masterstroke of legal maneuvering must be found that would present a compendium of facts circumventing state sovereignty.

What would eventually be determined was that the means to break the Gag Rule existed within the system of slavery itself.

4

The Evolution of a Peculiar Institution

Be it enacted and declared by this Grand Assembly if any slave resists his master (or other by his master's order correcting him) and by the extremity of the correction should chance to die, that his death shall not be accounted a felony, but the master (or that other person appointed by the master to punish him) be acquitted from molestation, since it cannot be presumed that premeditated malice (which alone makes murder a felony) should induce any man to destroy his own estate. —Virginia Slave Codes, October 1669

A cursory account of slavery's evolution and the divergent paths of two English colonies, Jamestown and Plymouth, foretold the divisiveness that plagued the nation by 1836. As a legal institution, slavery existed on the North American continent for more than 240 years. The origin of this institution can be traced back to the very first English settlement in the new world: Jamestown.

In 1606, a royal charter was granted to a trading company that obtained funding by stock subscriptions. With these funds, the Virginia Company of London formed an expedition for the purpose of establishing a colony based on the simplest of all business designs: profit.

On the twentieth of December of that year, 120 colonists sailed from London aboard the *Susan, Godspeed,* and the *Discovery*. They reached the Chesapeake Capes on the twenty-sixth of April, 1607, where they founded a trading post named after King James. Although their intentions were to establish a commercial venture, and then a permanent settlement, neither goal initially met with much success. Contrary to popular descriptions that promoted Virginia as an Eden, its reputation as a death trap soon became evident. In the first six months, fifty-one of the original colonists died from disease and starvation. As the harsh realities of colonization became public knowledge in England, further interest in securing passage to Virginia waned.

There were other aspects of the colony that dissuaded migration: harsh working conditions, the fact that colonists held no property and worked for stockholders back in England, the absence of women and families, and most important to investors, the failure of the first materials of pitch tar and turpentine for naval application to generate a profit.

Jamestown bravely struggled along, but after four years, the colony was almost abandoned. It was reinvigorated by the arrival of Thomas De La Warr, who brought needed supplies and relief to the starving colony.[56] The expedition managed to keep the venture afloat until a profitable product could be found.

John Rolfe, a member of De La Warr's expedition, is noted in history for his courtship and marriage to Pocahontas. Although the marriage brought a period of peace between the settlers and native tribes, Rolfe's impact on the colony's survival was due to something other than marital bliss. In 1613, Rolfe introduced a product that all but guaranteed the colony's commercial success: tobacco. What made this tobacco a success was the fact that it was not *Nicotiana Rustica,* the harsh tobacco grown by the local indigenous peoples. Rolfe had obtained seeds of the coveted *Nicotiana Tabacum* strain that was then being grown in Trinidad and South America. Spain attempted to protect its monopoly on *Nicotiana Tabacum* by declaring that "anyone caught selling *Nicotiana Tabacum* seeds to a non-Spaniard faced the penalty of death." Regardless, tobacco soon became a profitable enterprise for the English colony at Jamestown. More important, it established the plantation system for the purpose of commercial cultivation.

The success of tobacco, coupled with the eventual granting of private property to laborers, the allowing of families and women to migrate to the colony, and the establishment of English common law as the basis for governing, created a stability that assured the colony's continuation. With this success a new problem arose that played a significant role in the evolution of the colony—the role of labor.

The use of indentured servitude during the early years was a two-edged sword. It allowed a cheap labor pool that was paramount to the success of the plantation system, while at the same time it frustrated the planter's attempts to maintain a steady labor force due to manumission. The status of indentured servitude required that the indentured individual, after a seven-year period (if one lived that long), would be freed. Once free, he could marry or send for family back in England. He was also granted property, something that rarely happened in England. More important, the newly freed indentured servant could begin his own agricultural pursuits, which placed an increasing demand on an already taxed labor pool.

Attempts were made to use local native labor, but this proved to be as unstable as the reliance on imported English labor. The natives often ran off into the wilderness, a wilderness they knew much better than the colonists. Once escaped, the native easily found shelter and aid from fellow tribespeople, who resisted attempts by the colonists to capture and return the runaway to labor.

Another factor concerning native labor was the vulnerability to disease from contact with Europeans, which decimated many of the local tribes. Disease also contributed to the ill health of European laborers. The arduous routine of tobacco farming was demanding, and allowed for little to no leisure time. This, coupled with the inadequate living conditions in early Jamestown and the lack of provisions for the laborers, resulted in a high mortality rate. The dilemma facing planters was that many servants died before they fulfilled their contracted period of indenture.

Then there was the lengthy and risky matter of replenishing and maintaining a labor source. It required time, money, and dependence on a largely non-volunteer labor source that was shipped from England upon hazardous seas. Furthermore, the supply was frequently disrupted by events at home such as political manipulations and foreign wars.

Yet another factor that made indentured labor precarious for planters was the class of Englishman recruited for the colonies. Many who were sent to the colonies as indentured servants were sent by force, either through sentencing for infractions in England, or for payment of debt. These people were, at times, difficult to control. To guarantee a semblance of control over the unruly (though valuable) labor force, planters began to institute harsh measures. At the time, the servant, in particular an indentured servant, under English law was classified as *personal chattel*. This gave the servant the same legal distinction as farm implements, livestock or furniture, and made the laborer a commodity, with all the legal interpretations of property.

For example, indentured servants were used as security in financial dealings, formed parts of marriage settlements, and were considered inheritances in wills. Those who were indentured to the Virginia colony entered a society controlled by planters. They quickly came to the stark realization that the majority of laborers were, to a large degree, unfree.

The first step toward institutionalizing servitude in Virginia came in 1619 when the first General Assembly of Virginia, made up of wealthy plantation owners, established a "company system." The planters recorded the status of indentured servants for the purpose of enforcing labor contracts, preventing double-dealing, and stopping unlawful marriages of servants. Under the company system it seemed everyone bore some obligation of service to the colony. Yet these measures failed to correct the problem that continually plagued the planters: replenishing the workforce.

In the years following 1619, a means by which planters achieved a stable, cheap, long-term work force was methodically rectified. The solution was a new system of servitude, for in 1619, the arrival of the first Africans in Jamestown was documented. It was the beginning of what became commonly referred to as "a peculiar institution," otherwise known as slavery.

That year, Dutch pirates, who had been raiding Spanish shipping vessels, sailed into Jamestown in need of provisions. On board were twenty slaves of African descent who were bartered and traded for supplies. The exact fate of these people is not clear, but by 1621 the importation of Africans for labor had become common.

It is an undeniable fact that both African and European people equally participated in the growth and development of American society. Within the first generation of settlements in North America, not only the white Englishman, but also the Black African, became an active participant in the venture, although under drastically different circumstances. From the very beginning of the early settlements of Virginia, a precedent for relations between Europeans and Africans began to establish itself. By the time of the American Revolution, Africans represented 20 percent of the population, yet the degree of participation and ability to achieve status as an equal partner in the American experience varied greatly between black and white.

There is no doubt that the economics of dealing with slavery were supported by racism. The one feature that clearly fostered this was skin color. The dichotomy of white and black greatly facilitated an ethnocentric view of race by the Virginia colonists. To Europeans, Africans were different. They were not Christian, were not within the social norms of English society, were perceived to be lustful, and were deemed by popular belief to be on a different social and evolutionary scale than whites. These perceptions greatly facilitated the inevitable change from servant to slave, and with it, dictated the place in Southern society into which Africans would be forcibly regulated.

A stranger amongst strangers in a strange land, the newly arrived from Africa would not have the benefit of language, culture, law, or the community of his native land. He or she was now at the mercy and whim of European settlers, who were also outside the comforts and security of their own society. The one difference was that Europeans were in control of colonial society, while Africans were to be controlled.

The colonists who founded, created, and governed the first settlements in Virginia were of the gentry class of English society. Accomplished at adventure, they were little prepared for the rigors of colonization. It would be these wealthy planters of early Virginia who played a significant role in decisions that concerned the legal interpretation of servitude, which greatly precipitated the progression toward the institutionalization of slavery.

The governing planters created a series of legal statutes based on old-world precedents of indentured servitude that established slavery as a unique American institution. The preconceived notions of a class system, attitudes of gentry, racism that was an accepted norm of English society; and the demand for a cheap, reliable source of labor acted as catalysts for the evolution of indentured servitude into slavery. This process of turning indentured servitude into slavery had no basis in English common law. Instead, a new form of law concerning labor was established in the American colonies. Based on colonial records, the steps taken to secure slavery as an institutional fact in the agriculture industry of the South were clear.

At first, Africans were treated like previous workers, in that they were brought, held, and eventually freed under indentured servitude stipulations. In colonial records from 1621, an individual named Anthony Johnson arrived from Africa as a laborer. He survived Indian attacks, fulfilled his servitude, and eventually married an African woman named Mary. By 1641 he was a freeman with four children, land, and cattle. Court records reveal Johnson sued a white colonist over a servant, and won, but the attitudes and legal status toward

Africans were already beginning to change.

Beginning in 1621, laws were enacted to change servitude into slavery as it pertained to those of African descent. That year, Virginia and Maryland instituted into law the status of African servitude as "Durante Vita" (for life). In 1622, Virginia mandated that slavery must follow through the mother, and in 1667 Virginia law declared that baptism would not free a slave:

December 1662

Whereas some doubts have arisen whether children got by any Englishman upon a Negro woman should be slave or free, be it therefore enacted and declared by this present Grand Assembly, that all children born in this country shall be held bond or free only according to the condition of the mother; and that if any Christian shall commit fornication with a Negro man or woman, he or she so offending shall pay double the fines imposed by the former act.

September 1667

Whereas some doubts have risen whether children that are slaves by birth, and by the charity and piety of their owners made partakers of the blessed sacrament of baptism, should by virtue of their baptism be made free, it is enacted and declared by this Grand Assembly, and the authority thereof, that the conferring of baptism does not alter the condition of the person as to his bondage or freedom; that diverse masters, freed from this doubt may more carefully endeavor the propagation of Christianity by permitting children, though slaves, or chose of greater growth if capable, to be admitted to that sacrament.[57]

The progression toward slavery accelerated in 1689 when Africa was opened to free trade,[58] and Virginia, Maryland, and South Carolina quickly became inundated with newly arrived slaves. This called for strict measures to control the burgeoning slave population. Over the next ten years Virginia established slave codes that restricted the travel of African American slaves, declared interracial marriage unlawful, and prohibited the ownership of property by slaves—based on the premise of slaves *being* property—further establishing slavery as an institution based on property rights.

Slaves were not allowed to vote or assemble, and were put under a sunset-to-sunrise curfew. With the growth of the Negro slave population in the Southern colonies, restrictions on slaves were rigorously, and often times, brutally enforced. To enhance the authority and dominance of white owner-planters, laws were enacted that required owners of slaves to punish runaways. These measures became fixed in municipal codes, and further institutionalized slavery into the political and social framework of colonial society. By the 1700s, as agriculture became the South's principal industry, the engine that drove the industry became the accepted basis for wealth. The plantation system of labor with its separate quarters for slaves, the hierarchy of overseers and the frequent absentee owner, contributed to an ever-widening gulf between whites and blacks, free and slave. A status quo was created and clearly defined.

To the north, a very different society was being established.

At one time the area of North America now called New England was referred to as Northern Virginia. This distinction was officially granted to the domain by James the First in 1606 when he issued a royal charter to the Northern Virginia Company for the purpose of settling and establishing a trading post on the Kennebec River in present-day Maine. The first expedition lasted one winter, and the following spring all embarked for return passage to England. For several years the area of New England held little interest to early entrepreneurs.

But, John Smith wrote a glowing report on his exploration of the coast in 1616 titled "Description of New England," which contained, among other praises, the high quality of the fishing. The territory was frequented by French and English fishermen, but not much else until November 9, 1620 when the ship *Mayflower*, tossed on rough seas for sixty-four days and blown off a course originally set for the mouth of the Hudson River, made the tip of Cape Cod. The sea-weary travelers then came ashore at a place that, much later, became known as Plymouth Rock.

The rugged men and women who originally established Plymouth were part of a group of Separatists, or Puritans, who had suffered persecution in England for their religious beliefs. James the First did not hide his disdain for the Puritans, or nonconformists as they were called, and vowed to reform them or harass them from the country. In anticipation of severe actions behind these threats, the Pilgrims exiled themselves from England and sought refuge in the Netherlands. Although the Dutch treated these religious zealots fairly, the living was hard and the Puritans longed for a community of their own.

Their leader, William Brewster, sought and obtained a grant from a Sir Edwin Sandys for a particular plantation in what was then called Southern Virginia, but what we know today as the Hudson River Estuary. With regard to the present borders of the state of Virginia, in the 1600s the territory of Virginia covered a much larger area.

Upon realizing that the area they came to after their rough passage was not clearly defined as part of the territory of Virginia, those on board the *Mayflower* decided to establish their own governing compact. The Mayflower Compact, signed by forty-one adult males, is only a paragraph long but this simple statement creates a self-governing covenant that, ". . . Combine ourselves together into a Civil Body Politic . . . to enact, constitute and frame such just and equal Laws, Ordinances, Acts, Constitutions and offices . . . for the general good of the colony . . ."

The establishment of a rule of law in those early colonies reflects the determination of Englishmen at the time toward self-government. This self-determination is striking with regard to other European colonies, wherein strict governance by a supreme authority, appointed by the home country's monarch, was imposed. The fact that England tolerated autonomous governance by their respective colonies contributed to the evolution of a body of law peculiar to each colony.

Although English-speaking people settled both Plymouth and Jamestown, the class of people and the philosophy each brought to bear on their respective settlements varied greatly. The Puritans based their creed on the teachings of John Calvin, whose ideals became a revolutionary force in seventeenth century England. These teachings sought to restructure and reform the Church of England, and eliminated practices associated with Catholicism. Puritans perceived the Catholic Church, and the edicts issued from Rome, as a corrupting influence on English society that compromised England's autonomy. They demanded a reversion back to the early Christian church by purging the Church of England of any influences thought to be associated with Rome. Issues that concerned the retention of bishops, and vestments and rituals associated with the Roman Catholic Church, caused the Puritans to break from the Church of England, and in so doing, the Crown.

In New England, the Puritan ideal not only professed to reform the Church of England but to also create a society they believed would best exemplify the New Testament. The Puritans came to recognize the colonies they established as a new promised land for the true Christian, and believed New England was set apart for them, not by the king or the state, but by the Almighty himself as an experiment in Christian living. They had set out to establish, in the words of John Winthrop, a "city on the hill," that would be a beacon for those who had given up their life to the ways of Puritanism.

The Puritans based their ideals of community on the civility and virtuosity found in their religious teachings. They believed firmly that they were not only to excel at establishing a model Christian community, but were to create a successful business enterprise, based on Puritanical teachings that encouraged industriousness, good works and piety. In this manner, the people of New England committed themselves to creating a community, rather than a mere colony, and balanced religious zeal with practical applications of survival.

Another factor that further established independent governance in the colonies, in particular the New England colonies, dealt with matters occurring back in England. The growing dissatisfaction between the Crown and Puritans led to civil war, the regicide of Charles the First, and the replacement of the monarchy with Oliver Cromwell, who proclaimed himself Lord Protectorate in 1649.

The establishment of a commonwealth in England nurtured the independence of the colonies in North America, due to the fact that Cromwell had little interest in governing the colonies. The English settlements were pretty much left to themselves. In both Virginia and Massachusetts, the concept of self-government took root and blossomed during the commonwealth period of Puritan rule in England. Not until the restoration of the Crown did the colonies again have royal interference in their own matters of governance. By that time each colony had achieved a degree of autonomy and, equally important, had become successful, self-sufficient business ventures.

The Puritans had established on their stern and rock-bound coast a new order with a preoccupation for structure. From its inception, Plymouth established itself as an enterprise that fostered longevity. This was greatly facilitated in 1628 when the Puritans were granted land patents and from these grants obtained a royal charter that legally created the Massachusetts Bay Company. This status, coupled with the inhospitable political climate in England, persuaded ten thousand Puritans to emigrate and settle in New England by 1634. However, with the onset of the English Civil War, this migration dramatically slowed and the first American depression occurred, described by a local poet as "the fall of the cow." This reversal of fortune forced the colony to look elsewhere for its livelihood.

A new prosperity soon came to New England based on a form of mercantilism. Built on manufacturing, shipping, and slavery, this triangular trade, often referred to as the "golden triangle," lasted until the American Revolution. In the Caribbean, sugar plantations created a demand for New England goods and New England shipping to deliver those goods. New England ships sailed to Africa's Gold Coast to load their ships with slaves, then sailed to the sugar plantations of the Caribbean to offload their cargo of slaves for sale and profit. They then reloaded the ships with sugar and molasses, and sailed to New England for the purpose of distillation of spirits that would be sold at home, shipped to England, or traded for slaves on Africa's Gold Coast.

The stain of slavery was not regulated to only those colonies below the Mason-Dixon line. Although slavery was not institutionalized in the New England colonies to the degree that existed in the Southern colonies, its influences were prevalent. For example, during the establishment of New Amsterdam (later to be renamed New York), early Dutch settlers created a slave market near the present-day site of Wall Street. A mile from this location is the site of the largest slave burial ground north of the Mason-Dixon line. By the 1700s, forty percent of white homes in New York City had slaves. Further, there is no denial that many of the fortunes of New England shippers were derived from the African slave trade.

The main difference, however, is that the institution of slavery had a larger and longer impact on the Southern colonies--far beyond the English colonies to the north. The different philosophical, economic and political approaches to colonization and the type of labor employed in each respective colony contributed to these differences. So much so, that by the end of the eighteenth century, these differences went to the heart of the divisiveness that plagued the United States by the first half of the nineteenth century. It can be argued that these deep rooted differences persist to the present day.

From early on, the New England colonies developed a land system of townships governed by the authorities of the colony. This system guaranteed that virtually all families owned land, which created a sense of equality and an independent identity. Although religion was a fundamental characteristic of early New England communities, the Enlightenment played a large part in the intellectual life of Massachusetts. Puritans believed scientific knowledge increased one's awareness of God's works. This broad approach toward scientific teachings facilitated the availability of education to all, regardless of class or wealth.

Starting around 1640, it was required that everyone receive a free education. In the communities of New England, where the majority of the population was centrally located, it was feasible to create and accomplish such goals. In fact, the literacy levels of these Puritan settlements were the highest in the English-speaking world. In turn, mandatory education helped erase any class distinction, and gave all an equal opportunity to establish wealth and secure a home. An egalitarian society evolved in New England that differed from the strict social structure found in Virginia.

In Virginia, the leading citizens were of the gentlemen class, or the wealthy landowners. Next were the yeomen, who might own a small parcel of land. This was followed by landless folk and indentured servants, and at the bottom of the social ladder were the slaves, who constituted about half the population. To maintain a safe civil society for the free population of the Southern colonies, severe measures were instituted to control the un-free population. From these imposed controls, a rigid hierarchy of class distinction evolved. In comparison, New England's class order was basically of two categories, one being a gentleman, and the rest referred to as "the people." The aloof status and patriarchal sway of the gentleman class of Virginia planters, lording over their many dependents and slaves, was absent in New England society.

Another variance between the two colonies dealt with leisure and the pursuit of pleasure. The leisurely elegance and class found in the South were in stark contrast with the accepted manner of life based on Puritan ethic. Due partly to the more rugged environment, but in greater part to religious philosophy, idle refinements were not accepted or tolerated in Puritanical society. The Puritans adopted the teachings of St. Augustine's image of man as a beast of burden, while the Southerner looked upon a certain segment of humankind as beasts of burden.

The Virginian maintained an air of gentlemanly leisure to simulate his ideal of a wealthy planter. Personified as the elite class of English gentry, although in the fashion of the *nouveau riche* based on *gaucherie*, the Southern gentleman came into being. To others, the planters were depicted as climate-struck, reflecting a lifestyle that had a thorough aversion to labor. A reference found in Hugh Jones's 1724 book, *The Present State of Virginia*, suggests the mild climate of the Southern colonies tended toward laziness. The depictions of everyday life in Virginia are of contemplation, but little actual accomplishment. As to the validity of these and other observations of the South in early colonial times, the historian Richard Beale Davis concluded: "Hedonism was a quality of character common to all Southern classes . . ."

This persona of the leisurely landowner played a pivotal role in the governance of Virginia, for the main duty of the planter was to govern. In the Massachusetts colonies the majority of males, both gentlemen and the people, participated equally in the political process. Unlike the Virginia General Assembly, which had a bicameral body consisting of a lower house (the House of Burgess with one hundred members), and an upper house, (called the Senate of Virginia), there was no upper house or equivalent to the English House of Lords in Massachusetts; class distinction was not present in the political governance of New England.

The basic principle of government practiced by the early settlers of New England laid the foundation for community service that would evolve into what would be called "the federal system of government." In the South, with large plantations and few centers of community, an agricultural society would evolve into the Jeffersonian form of government that fostered an agricultural society. Each would view their respective role differently, based on their own evolving social and commercial way of life.

As the colonies grew and became more independent from England, the growing dissatisfaction with the Crown and Parliament led to revolution and independence. It is of little wonder that the first instigation, if not the first shot that brought about the revolution against England, occurred in New England, and that the epicenter was Boston. With the war for independence and the establishment of a new nation on the North American continent a reality, the differing sectional views on the course of the new nation came to light.

In Philadelphia, during the Constitutional Convention in 1789, the existence of slavery as an institution became a matter of some disagreement. Here was the first test of union and we, as a nation, almost didn't pass it. To placate Southern reservations over the ratification of the Constitution, and their suspicions of a strong central federal government, certain clauses were written ambiguously into the Constitution to appease Southern slave states and gain their ratification. These are known as the "slave clauses." These clauses not only guaranteed property rights to the owner of an escaped slave, but more important, based on the three-fifths clause, granted additional representation in Congress to slave owners.

Population is the basis for the number of congressional representatives assigned to Congress, and with the three-fifths clause, any added seats in the House of Representatives was answerable to only the slave owners, not the slave.[59]

Slave Clauses United States Constitution: Article I Section 2.

Representatives and direct taxes shall be apportioned among the several states which may be included within this union, according to their respective numbers, which shall be determined by adding to the whole number of free persons, including those bound to service for a term of years, and excluding Indians not taxed, three fifths of all other Persons...

However, the words "slavery" or "slave" were not part of the Constitution. Rather, the word "person" is used so as to avoid the term *slave* being a sanctioned part of the Constitution. This distinction between person and slave avoided any appearance that the Constitution sanctioned the institution of slavery, while at the same time it provided enough ambivalence to suggest a recognition of slavery. Suffice to say, both sides argued their respective view on the validity of slavery, based on these vague clauses.

As the United States grew beyond the original thirteen colonies, the issue of slavery persisted in plaguing the nation, and created an ever-widening gulf between North and South. In 1820, John Quincy Adams eerily foretold the consequences of the continued existence of the institution.

> If slavery be the destined sword in the hand of the destroying angel which is to sever the ties of the union, the same sword will cut in sunder the bonds of slavery itself. A dissolution of the Union for the cause of slavery would be followed by a servile war in the slave-holding States, combined with a war between the two severed portions of the Union. It seems to me that its results must be the extirpation of slavery from this whole continent; and, calamitous and desolating as this cause of events in progress must be, so glorious would be its final issue, as God shall judge me, I dare not say that it is not to be desired.[60]

By 1836, the institution of slavery threatened the very existence of constitutional law.

The Creole Incident

THE BEGINNING OF THE END OF SLAVERY

BOOK II: RUNAWAY

5

The Close of 1839, Northern Pennsylvania

Hurry on my soul
My weary soul,
And I yearde [sic] from heaven today,
hurry on my weary soul,
and I yearde from heaven today,
My sin is forgiven
and my soul set free

—I Hear From Heaven Today. Virginia slave song.[61]

In late November of 1839, the days dawned gray and cold, and remained so, with the dull light of the sun penetrating just enough to let one realize it was day. Bare trees stood as silent silhouettes against the cold, stark, snow-covered ground, the solitude interrupted by occasional gusts of wind that raked the woods with a numbing cold.[62]

This particular day became a passage of time, stuck between other days where events occurred, where a man could act upon his future or reflect upon his past. However, this day was meant to exist only as a connector to other days. It would be lost in history, with no event to shape the course of time, no special meaning recalling memories of passion, of longing, or of a fear of eternal salvation. The day existed only to allow another day to follow.

On such a day, a man could relate to the beasts of burden, plodding along at their toil with no reflections of the past, no hope for the future, only the task at hand, the immediateness of "now." The mind would focus on thoughts that would sustain survival, keeping the soul occupied, and avoiding any doubts concerning the validity of the task, so as not to despair and cease. For with the stopping of progress, without the relentless push to continue, defeat would soon overcome the soul and death would follow.

He would not allow that to happen. He had come too far to stop now. He told himself, "This will not last forever."

His mind strayed to thoughts of when he would be warm again, sitting close to a fire, with this day seeming like a dream—distant and fading. It was then his leg sank deep into snow that had drifted even with the land, concealing the depth it covered. Shaken from his reverie, he stumbled forward and felt the cold snow slap him in the face. He lay there, exhausted, while his breath spewed from his lungs in great clouds of steam. The wind blew the snow, stinging his cheeks and watering his eyes. He turned his face away from the wind, pushed himself up and continued to walk north, trying to close out the cold and weariness that dogged him. Each step was a struggle as his feet sank deep into the snow, causing him to lift each foot higher. As long as he kept moving, there would be a destination where he could find rest.

He lived with an ever-present fear of discovery and capture where he would be returned to a life guaranteed to be harsher than what he had left. The strain of the long flight was telling. For several weeks he had been in hiding, moving from location to location. There had been days without meals, and often, when he did eat, it was hurried and cold. The hardships of being a fugitive contributed to a physical change in him, with a loss in weight emphasized by a haggard and dirty appearance. The mental anguish of the flight wore at his determination, and at times tempted his resolve.

Yet, he endured. He had come too far to let doubt impede him, to stop him, to let them win. The goal that sustained him, that kept him moving was simple: freedom.

He came upon a clearing bordered on one side by a road. As he approached, he observed that in places the wind had sculpted the snow into drifts that resembled frozen waves, while in other places the road lay exposed, swept clean by the same wind. In all probability the road had not been used for the entire day, considering the severity of the weather. To his left, the road dipped and reappeared as it crossed a frozen creek and then cut its way through the woods. To his right, it was exposed as it worked its way up an incline. At the crest of the hill the wind-swept snow blurred the road's detail.

On the far side of the road was a Virginia fence, the type made of rough-hewn poles laced into an interlocking pattern, commonly referred to as a "split rail." It bordered an open field of old stubbles of corn stalk, yellowed and withered that poked up through the snow in thin lines that stretched white and stark until it reached the woods several hundred yards beyond. A small shed sat across the field toward the line of woods, apart from the main buildings of a farm by some two hundred yards, a safe distance. It was the only building he had seen that looked abandoned enough in which to seek shelter. Feeling the exhaustion and the cold beginning to strip away his endurance, he decided to make for the shed. He looked again, up and down the road, and then made his way across and over the fence.

As he trudged across the open field his tracks became obliterated by the wind that cut into him like a knife. Upon reaching the shed he made his way around to a door, it being located on the far side, away from the wind. The latch was not locked, but secured with a string of leather. His numb fingers poked from worn mittens, and worked at the knot with great difficulty. His mind seemed to have little communication with his hand, for the cold had rendered them slow and clumsy. He bent down to the knot and bit at it, his spit freezing within a few seconds. Finally, in desperation, he jerked at the latch, and to his relief, it gave way and fell to the ground.

Snow had piled up against the door, giving an impression that the shed had not been used since the fall harvest. With some difficulty he slowly pulled the door open enough to enter. He squeezed past the small space, shut the door behind him, and secured it with a piece of rope he found attached to the inside handle. He stood in the middle of the darkened shed, waiting for the cold to loosen its grip. The fury continued to rage outside, but now the wind was not the only sound. With his focus no longer on the exertion of moving through the snow, and the sudden absence of the constant drone of the wind, his hearing became sensitive to the slightest sound. He could now hear his own breathing and the creak of the walls as the wind buffeted the shack. From where he stood in the middle of the shed, he inspected the interior, his breath a visible fog. What dim light invaded the space showed he was its only inhabitant.

A variety of farm implements were stacked along one wall, and feed hay was piled at the far end. Ropes and a few traps hung on the other wall. The floor was of rough-cut boards. He could stand erect in the middle of the shack, but because the roof slanted to either side he had to bend to inspect either wall.

He moved to the opposite end of the shed, where the hay was piled, and let himself fall back into a sitting position onto the hay. The cold still robbed him of fluid motion, but the shelter of the shed was beginning to ease the numbness. He clapped his hands several times, and wiggled his fingers until they became a bit nimbler. Then he unbuttoned the middle of his coat, reached inside, and drew out a chunk of salted pork and some hardtack. The bread was cold, but not totally frozen, it being kept somewhat warm from his body. He slid a knife from the inside of his left boot and sliced a sliver of the pork. He stuck the knife into the floor and slowly ate as he surveyed the room. He then unbuttoned the remainder of his coat and settled back into the hay. As the cold began to wear off, a restful sleepiness came over him. He spoke out loud to himself as he glanced around the inside of the shed, as if to reinforce his observation that he was alone and safe. "Damn cold as hell. Too cold for this runaway to go no further."

The unanswered empty room shook with a rush of wind, and then fell silent. He reassured himself that this would suffice for the time being and mumbled a weary approval. "As good a place as any to spend the night."

His voice was firm but thoughtful, his stature dignified and calm. His name was Madison Ruffin Washington. Born in Virginia, he was twenty-one years of age, stood five-foot-nine-and-a-half-inches-tall, and had spent his entire life in slavery.

William Wells Brown, another fugitive from slavery who had sought refuge in the North, wrote this description of Madison Washington:

> Among the great number of fugitive slaves who arrived in Canada towards the close of the year 1839, was one whose tall figure, firm step, and piercing eye attracted at once the attention of all who beheld him. Nature had treated him as a favorite. His expressive countenance painted and reflected every

emotion of his soul. There was a fascination in the gaze of his finely-cut eyes that no one could withstand. Born of African parentage, with no mixture in his blood, he was one of the handsomest of his race. His dignified, calm, and unaffected features announced at a glance that he was one endowed with genius, and created to guide his fellow-men. He called himself Madison Washington, and said that his birthplace was in the 'Old Dominion.'[63]

Madison Washington was playing out a scene in one of the greatest migrations in American history, when countless slaves broke their shackles and made their way north. Faced with imminent sale, the threat of physical harm, or to bear witness to the brutal application of the institution of slavery on family members, friends, and spouses, the one unifying aspect of a runaway was his or her desire to be free.

Although Madison Washington's early life is not documented, an accurate portrayal of a slave's life, circa 1830s Virginia, is accessible through a variety of primary sources. The community of slaves found in the plantation system of the 1830s was a system with few variations.

From the narrative of ex-slave Charles Ball, an insight is achieved into this peculiar institution.

> The general features of slavery are the same everywhere; but the utmost rigor of the system, was only to be met with, on the cotton plantations of Carolina and Georgia, or in the rice fields which skirt the deep swamps and morasses of the Southern rivers. In the tobacco fields of Maryland and Virginia, great cruelties are practiced—not so frequently by the owners, as by the overseers of the slaves.[64]

It has been written that Madison Washington was held in bondage on the Johnston plantation located one county east of Richmond, Virginia. The Johnston name, the proprietor of the area where Madison Washington was reportedly from, dates back to the 1700s and was considered one of the established families of the area. Several sources suggest Judge Johnston's father fought in the war for independence and later served in both houses of Congress.[65] Based on existing records, there were Johnston families living in the Richmond area in 1839. An index of the 1840 Census of Virginia shows two households in Henrico County and two in James City County.[66]

The majority of the planters in Northern Virginia at this time typified the wealthy landowner, deriving a portion of their wealth from tobacco cultivation. The labor required in the cultivation and production of tobacco was demanding, but not as strenuous as cotton cultivation, and certainly it does not compare to the hardships endured by the slaves on the sugar plantations of Louisiana. Although less labor intensive, tobacco cultivation required careful maintenance for most of the year. Slave narratives bring to light the routine of servitude faced by Madison and others on a tobacco plantation in 1830s Virginia.

> From the period when the tobacco plants are set in the field, there was no resting time until it was housed; but it was planted out about the first of May,

and must be cut and taken out of the field before the frost comes. After it was hung and dried, the labor of stripping and preparing it for the hogshead in leaf, or of manufacturing it into twist, was comparatively a work of leisure and ease. Besides, on almost every plantation the hands are able to complete the work of preparing the tobacco by January, and sometimes earlier; so that the winter months, form some sort of respite from the toils of the year. The people are obliged, it was true, to occupy themselves in cutting wood for the house, making rails and repairing fences, and in clearing new land, to raise the tobacco plants for the next year; but as there was usually time enough, and to spare, for the completion of all this work, before the season arrives for setting the plants in the field; the men are seldom flogged much, unless they are very lazy or negligent, and the women are allowed to remain in the house, in the very cold, snowy, or rainy weather.[67]
—ex slave Charles Bell

Tobacco accounted for almost 80 percent of the revenue produced by the planters in the Upper South and was valued at $17.90 million between 1830-40, far outpacing the combined incomes derived from rice (2.18), Sea Island cotton (2.08) and short-fiber cotton (9.66). However, by 1849 the production value of tobacco from the same region fell to 6.92 (million).[68] This drastic decline in revenue was due to the depletion of nutrients in the soil.

By the late 1830s, tobacco cultivation had denuded much of the arable soil of valuable minerals in coastal Virginia, and soil could only be maintained with expensive fertilizers. As tobacco stripped the soil, it also began to erode the profits of the planters of Virginia and the other tobacco states of the Upper South. The planters, looking to offset their losses and reduce expenses, became economically dependent upon selling a substantial number of their laborers to the new expanding cotton regions of the Lower South. Some accounts suggest the sale of slaves in the Upper South was equal to 20 percent of the staple crop production in the region.

An ever-increasing demand for slaves in the expanding cotton states and the sugar-growing regions of southern Louisiana acted as the catalyst for a complex and sophisticated trade between the major Chesapeake ports and New Orleans, commonly referred to as the "intercoastal slave trade." Between 1820 and 1860, the average forced migration of slaves from the Upper South to the Lower South was two hundred thousand per decade, or about ten percent of the Upper South's slave population. What these figures do not reveal were the countless untold stories of family separation and heartbreak endured by successive generations of slaves. The slave was forced to endure these cruelties based on market and financial trends, practiced without consideration or conscience by the planters. To the planter, it was business.

The slave markets of New Orleans were atypical with regard to the exceptionally heavy demand for strong young men, due to the intensive labor associated with sugar production. During the harvest season, sugarcane called for frenzied cutting, stripping, hauling, and boiling of the cane. For this type of harvesting, strength was needed, which meant adult male labor. The heavy work regime of the sugar plantations, and the diseases associated with the swampy areas of the sugar fields, resulted in high mortality and low birth rates among the laborers, thus creating the insatiable demand for new slaves. A system for replacing the loss of labor merely became a matter of practicality to the planters.

The conditions the slaves were forced to live and die under in the Louisiana sugar plantations persisted for some sixty years, and these conditions were equal to the conditions found in more recent slave camps, such as the Russian gulag, Pol Pot's Cambodian labor camps, Serbian leader Colonel Ratko Mladić's Omarska camp, the Xinjiang internment camps of western China, and Nazi Germany's death camps. The callous approach of the sugar planter to the loss of labor and the means of replenishing it is reflected in a letter to the London Times by Frances Anne Kimble, author of *Journal of a Residence on a Georgian Plantation in 1838-1839*.

> There was yet, however, another aspect of the question, which was that it sometimes clearly *not* the interest of the owner to prolong the life of his slaves; as in the case of inferior or superannuated labors, or the very notorious instance in which some of the owners of sugar plantations stated that they found it better worth their while to *work off* (i.e., kill with labor) a certain proportion of their workforce, and replace them by new hands every seven years, than work them less severely and maintain them in diminished efficiency for an indefinite length of time.[69]

With the importation of slaves from Africa made illegal by the 'Act to Prohibit the Importation of Slaves into any Port or Place Within the Jurisdiction of the United States' after 1808, any legal source of slave labor would have to be obtained from the propagation of those slaves already in North America. At the time, claims of planters purposely breeding slaves for the markets of the deep South, in particular New Orleans and the sugar growing regions of southern Louisiana, were considered abolitionist statements.

However, there is solid evidence that supports such a claim. Case in point, in the early 1830s, abolitionist Robert Finley wrote: "In Virginia and other grain growing states, blacks do not support themselves, and the only profit these markets derive from them is, repulsive as the idea may justly seem, breeding them, like other livestock for the more southern states."[70]

Another source that supports this conclusion is found in the writings of Joseph Sturge, an English abolitionist who visited the United States in 1841.

> The District of Columbia is the chief seat of the American slave trade; commercial enterprise has no other frequented slave mart in the world. The adjoining and once fertile and beautiful states of Virginia and Maryland, are now blasted with sterility, and ever-encroaching desolation. The cause of the first murderer rest upon the planters, and the ground will no longer yield to them her strength. The impoverished proprietors find now their chief source of revenue in what one of themselves expressly termed, their "crop of human flesh."[71]

By the 1830s, the Northern slave states, in particular Virginia and Maryland, had become dependent on the breeding and selling of slaves to the Deep South, as exemplified by the statement made in the Virginia Legislature by Thomas Jefferson Randolph: "Human flesh is now the great staple of Virginia."[72]

Additional testament from the time period further strengthens the brutal aspect of breeding in the Upper South. The following incident, related by Theodore Weld, an abolitionist and participant in the Creole Incident, not only establishes the strict oversight planters kept over their slaves, but reinforces the fact that slave breeding was a common practice.

> The following was told me by an intimate friend; it took place on a plantation containing about one hundred slaves. One day the owner ordered the women into the barn, he then went in among them, whip in hand, and told them he meant to flog them all to death; they began immediately to cry out 'What have I done Massa?' 'What have I done Massa?' He replied; 'D--n you, I will let you know what you have done, you don't breed, I haven't had a young one from one of you for several months.' They told him they could not breed while they had to work in the rice ditches. (The rice grounds are low and marshy, and have to be drained, and while digging or clearing the ditches, the women had to work in mud and water from one to two feet in depth; they were obliged to draw up and secure their frocks about their waist, to keep them out of the water, in this manner they frequently had to work from daylight in the morning till it was so dark they could see no longer.) After swearing and threatening for some time he told them to tell the overseer's wife, when they got in that way, and he would put them upon the land to work.[73]

These claims are based on eyewitness accounts and primary source observations. Yet, present day debate has refused to reach a consensus on the organized system of breeding in the Upper South. However, it seemed to be an obvious fact to those who were in the Virginia state legislature, circa 1830s. Professor Dew, president of the University of William and Mary in Virginia (1836-46), in his "Review of the Debate in the Virginia Legislature in 1831-32," stated: "A full equivalent being left in the place of the slave [the purchase money], this emigration becomes an advantage to the state, and does not check the black population as much as at first view we might imagine; because it furnishes every inducement to the master to attend to the negroes, '*to encourage breeding, and to cause the greatest number possible to be raised*'. Again, '*Virginia is in fact a negro-raising state for other states.*'"

The system of breeding as a staple of Virginia commerce was given further credence by statements contained in a speech of Mr. Goode of Virginia before the Virginia Legislature in January 1832: "The superior usefulness of the slaves in the South will constitute an effectual demand, which will remove them from our limits. We shall send them from our state, because it will be our interest to do so. But gentlemen are alarmed lest the markets of other states be closed against the introduction of our slaves Sir, the demand for slave labor must increase."

The reasoning used in explaining the fact of breeding was based simply on profit and the accepted lifestyle. Mr. Faulkner, in the Virginia House of Delegates in 1832, made this abundantly clear. "But he (Mr. James H. Gholson) has labored to show that the abolition of slavery would be impolitic, because your slaves constitute the entire wealth of the state, all the productive capacity Virginia possesses; and, sir, as things are, believe he is correct. He says that the slaves constitute the entire available wealth of eastern Virginia. Is it true that for two hundred years the only increase in the wealth and resources of Virginia has been a remnant of the natural increase of this miserable race? Can it be that on this increase she places her sole dependence? Until I heard these declarations I had not fully conceived the horrible extent of this evil. These gentlemen state the fact, which the history and present aspect of the commonwealth but too well sustain. What, sir, have you lived for two hundred years without personal effort or productive industry, in extravagance and indolence, sustained alone by the return from the sales of the increase of slaves, and retaining merely such a number as your now impoverished lands can sustain as STOCK?"[74]

The existence of breeding slaves for profit fostered and supported a seasonal trade in human cargo between the Chesapeake ports and New Orleans. The creation and organization of an inter-regional slave trade was firmly established by the 1820s. Created to fulfill the need for labor in the expanding regions of the lower South, and to allow older slave states opportunity to create wealth by selling off a number of their slaves, it was as regular and routine as the seasons of the year. This seasonal pattern of the trade was based on funds and credit made available when crops came to market. However, there is evidence that supports the trade flourished throughout the year based on the high demand for slaves in the sugarcane fields of the Lower South.

The inter-regional slave trade supported a very organized system of buying, transporting, and selling of the human machinery of the South.[75] Although the majority of the slaves shipped south was done overland, by means of human cattle drives called "coffles," there also existed an established inter-coastal slave trade between the Chesapeake ports and New Orleans.

The ships used in the inter-coastal trade required particular design factors, both common and uncommon. Built in the Chesapeake region, the majority of the brigs were specifically fitted to accommodate the shipping of slaves. One common example, due to the sand bars at the mouth of the Mississippi, is the shallow draft of the vessels so as to proceed over the bars without going aground. Another feature concerned the designs of the holds where the slaves were stowed. A separation between the forward hold and the aft hold was a significant feature in these coastal slave ships to provide the required separation of men and woman during transportation.

To accommodate the yearly shipping of slaves to the markets of New Orleans, there evolved in the Upper South an industry based on slave buying and selling. The highly selective demand for strong able-bodied slaves fostered urban slave collection centers. The large number of slaves in one location allowed the Lower South buyers the opportunity to inspect and purchase the strongest and ablest for the sugar markets.

Richmond, Virginia became the chief center for this trade and supported several agencies, called "speculators," who specialized in the inter-coastal trade. Beginning in mid-summer, speculators fanned out over Northern Virginia and distributed bills advertising their intention to buy slaves, usually between the ages of sixteen and twenty-four, for sale and shipment to Richmond. Often these bills specifically requested ". . . NEGROES suited for the New Orleans market." A typical bill might read:

Persons Having Suitable Negroes And Desiring To Dispose Of Them,

By Addressing A Line To
J. J. Toler
Fellows would Be Preferred With
Proper Certificate For The New Orleans Market[76]

Usually within the first weeks of September, after harvest, the speculators returned to make their purchases from the planters. The slaves were placed into coffle gangs—droves of slaves roped or chained together, increasing in numbers from plantation to plantation. The coffle gangs were then driven to the markets of Richmond and were frequently accompanied by music supplied by fellow slaves who could play a fiddle or banjo. This was an attempt to portray an image of the carefree, happy slave. At the same time, as the parade of slaves passed by, the crack of the whip and the clank of the chains ironically acted to reinforce a sense of security within the white community. The ability to keep a large number of slaves controlled and isolated from other slaves, thus avoiding the threat of an insurrection, was an overriding concern of the white community throughout the South. This spectacle of human misery was a common sight along the byways and roads of Northern Virginia during the antebellum period.

The destination of the coffles was the waterfront district of Richmond called Shockoe Bottom, where the slave markets were located. Although these markets furnished slaves for local buyers, their principal function was to provide slaves for traders from importing states, in particular the buyers from New Orleans. Some of the more prominent names in the business were Silas and R. F. Omohundro, J. J. Toler and the infamous Bob Lumpkin, whose slave pen was located on 15th Street, between E. Franklin and E. Broad Streets.

As a slave collection and reselling center, Richmond supported a number of facilities for the purpose of feeding, housing, and fixing up slaves prior to auction. Speculators would purchase in the counties near Richmond, but not having depots of their own, housed their slaves at holding centers in Shockoe Bottom. These depots were nothing more than holding pens, or jails, and became centers of activity as the coffles arrived at Richmond.

As may be imagined, the slaves are brought from all parts, are of all sorts, sizes, and ages, and arrive at various states of fatigue and condition; but they soon improve in their looks, as they are regularly fed and have plenty to eat.[77] —Ex-slave John Brown

In the summer of 1839, the business of the speculators was carried out with a dispassionate efficiency and coordination required of such an enterprise. With the posting of the bills, and speculators making their rounds of slave quarters on countless plantations in the Richmond area, a feeling of trepidation blanketed those slaves at the Johnston plantation who fit the profile for selling. The one sure fact was that, by mid-September, some would be gone.

It is conceivable the decision to run away and follow the North Star to freedom had been made by Madison Washington to avoid being sold South. Considering his age and physique, it was more than likely he would have been acutely aware that he was a prime candidate for the markets of New Orleans.

This may have been the reality Madison Washington faced on a cold snowy night, sheltered in an old farm shack on his way to Canada and freedom. His thoughts might have drifted back to a fateful summer day some four months earlier when the decision to runaway had been forced upon him.

Although his own safety and future were in jeopardy, the reality of being sold and separated from his family and friends was not the only dilemma that confronted Madison Washington. The decision to runaway concerned someone else, for Madison had recently taken a wife.

I had scarcely reached my twentieth year when I became acquainted with the angelic being who had since become my wife.[78] —Madison Washington

6

Susan

Lord, break them slavery powers—
Will you go along with me?
Lord break them slavery powers,
Go sound the jubilee. . .
there's a better day a coming [79]

T he records are not conclusive on her name and identity, but certain facts— some steeped in myth while others may have some basis in reality—have persisted over the years. In all the sources, there is agreement that she had blue eyes, long flowing black hair, light skin and went by the name of Susan.

William Wells Brown, a contemporary of Madison Washington and a fugitive from slavery from the Richmond area, wrote: "Though not tall, she yet had a majestic figure. Her well-molded shoulders, prominent bust, black hair which hung in ringlets, mild blue eyes, finely-chiseled mouth, with a splendid set of teeth, a turned and well-rounded chin, skin marbled with the animation of life, and veined by blood given to her by her master, she stood as a representative of two races. With only one eighth of African, she was what was called at the south an "octoroon." It was said that her grandfather had served his country in the Revolutionary War, as well as in both houses of Congress. This was Susan, the wife of Madison."[80]

Although there are few primary sources on Madison Washington's wife, the limited sources that exist share a striking similarity in their depiction of her as the daughter of the plantation owner.

She was the daughter of her master, and the blood of the white race predominated in several of her ancestors. Her eyes were blue, and her glossy dark hair fell in soft, silky ringlets.[81] —L. Maria Child

While she may have been the daughter of Judge Johnston, she could not escape the reality of her situation. Even if Susan could pass as white, the blood of Africa flowed in her veins, dictating her place in Southern society by the full force of law. If she ever fancied the idea that her father accepted her as his daughter, this wishful dream would never erase the imposed reality of her slavery. As to Judge

Johnston's perception of and responsibility toward his own progeny, there is little evidence that suggests any kinship was nurtured or displayed by the majority of the slave owners toward the offspring derived from such unions. It was an acceptable practice, and all too common for planters to show no remonstrance and feel no remorse at the seduction of their "property" to satisfy their licentious whims. Every male slave lived with the ever-present possibility of seeing his wife, sister, mother, and daughter abused at the hands of a planter.

> The annals of mankind do not afford a parallel, either in enormity, or extent, or continuance, to the degradation of the colored women in the United States. Despoiled of all protection; exposed to every indignity; obliged to submit to the brutal demand of any lawless white man; coerced to degradation by heartrending tortures; doomed to sacrifice the trendiest affections; scourged to conceal their instinctive sensibilities; and robbed of a husband's love, a father's guardianship, a son's aid, and a brother's endearment; they are merely human tools to pander to the sensuality, and to gratify the unclean desires of their inhuman task-masters.[82] —Reverend George Bourne

Though Susan's physical appearance and position may not conform to what is normally portrayed as a slave, the fact remained - she was a slave.

Yet, being the offspring of the master may have provided certain benefits not generally afforded to the common slave. One suggestion is that Susan may have fared better than most, and may have been educated to some degree.

> Accustomed to travel with her mistress, Susan had often been to Richmond, Norfolk, White Sulphur Springs, and other places of resort for the aristocracy of the Old Dominion. Her language was far more correct than most slaves in her position. Susan was as devoted to Madison as she was beautiful and accomplished.[83] —William Wells Brown

These statements suggest Susan may have spent her formative years working in the big house. If, indeed, she was the daughter of the owner, Judge Johnston, there is the further possibility that she may have been educated beyond her position as a mere slave, with opportunities normally not associated with the common domestic. As the daughter of the owner and resembling what would pass as "white," she may have received enough education to do simple math, read, write, or even be schooled enough to recite Shakespeare.

As for Madison Washington, there is some speculation as to whether he could read or write. Henry Highland Garnet, Robert Purvis, and Hiram Wilson, all leading abolitionists and reported acquaintances of Madison Washington, praised his intelligence and erudition. In William Wells Brown's *The Black Man: His Antecedents, His Genius, And His Achievements*, it is stated that Madison learned to read and write during his time in Canada. "His leisure hours were spent in learning to read and write, and in this he seemed to take the utmost interest."[84]

This again may be a glorification of the noble slave. However, there are documented instances of a favored slave receiving varying degrees of education.

Although educating slaves was against the law throughout the South, it was not unheard of. A favored slave was frequently educated in certain disciplines so as to assist and take on related responsibilities within the plantation. For example, the case of Frederick Douglass, who was a slave from the same time and area as Madison Washington, reveals how he received basic instruction. We know at first his mistress/owner taught him to read and write. However, she soon became apprehensive and paranoid about seeing a slave educated, and hardened her heart against further education.

Another example of a slave receiving instruction is told by ex-slave Harriet Jacobs, in her book, *Life of a Slave Girl.* "As a child, I love my mistress; and, looking back on the happy days I spent with her, I try to think with less bitterness of this act of injustice. While I was with her, she taught me to read and spell; and for this privilege, which so rarely falls to the lot of slaves, I bless her memory."[85]

Other than these rare benevolent instances of a white person educating a slave, there were other opportunities afforded a slave where he or she might surreptitiously receive instruction. This was provided through a father, mother, sister, brother, husband, or wife who had contact with the big house and all that it afforded a slave in that position. If the individual who worked in the big house had access to instruction, either from the owner or his children or by observation, it was not only conceivable, but a common situation where a slave could obtain a basic education.

The possibility that Susan and Madison were owned by Judge Johnston and raised on the same plantation did not guarantee the same upbringing. On the contrary, their worlds may have been very separate, considering that Madison was a field hand, while Susan was a privileged domestic. These two worlds guaranteed a separation that would provide only incidental or brief encounters.

The job of a field hand required rising before dawn, preparing a meal, caring for the livestock, and getting to the fields before sunrise. If late, the usual discipline was the overseer's whip. Even at a young age, a field hand worked at menial tasks such as carrying buckets of water to men in the field or holding a planter's mount on the occasions when he inspected the fields. Upon reaching a certain age, a hoe was put into the slave's hands and he (or she) now was required to do a full day's labor. The regime was never-ending and not gender-specific, for both men and women were field laborers whose sole purpose was to function as the machinery of agriculture in the South.

At the opposite end of the social spectrum within the slave community was the domestic, considered the plantation elite. It was not uncommon for the white community to view the field hand as beneath the domestic, therefore establishing a class system within the slave community. In certain instances, the domestic's constant contact with the white planter gave them the moniker "Sambo." The term Sambo is largely attributable to antebellum Southern literature, wherein there were three common slave characters portrayed: Jack, Nat, and Sambo.

John W. Blassingame, one of the preeminent scholars on slavery, explained the characteristics of Nate and Jack.

Jack "worked faithfully as long as he was well treated," Nat was the rebellious slave and "Sambo was inevitably a clown and congenitally docile."[86] These identities fostered and legitimized racial differences and continue to stereotype certain communities: immigrants from Central America, Muslims, and Jews—as well as African-Americans. The residual effects of slavery are still with us and continue to plague the civic and civil structure of American communities.

Although a field hand often worked sunup to sundown, a house slave fared no better. A domestic's work required being at the beck and call of the white family, night and day. A house slave slept on the floor, in closets, at the foot of a bed, or outside a bedroom door of the planter and his family, so as to be on call, twenty-four/seven. In a journal penned by Frances Anne Kemble, she related her account of such practices. "The young woman who performs the office of lady's maid, and the lads who wait upon us at the table, have neither table to feed at nor chair to sit down upon themselves. The boys sleep at night on the hearth by the kitchen fire, and the woman upon a rough board bedstead, strewed with a little tree moss."[87]

The mature house slave, in particular a male slave, was not allowed to sleep in the big house and was relegated to the same accommodations as the field hands.

[I] never was on a Southern plantation, and I never heard of one, where any of the slaves were *allowed* to sleep under the same roof with their owner.[88]
—Frances Anne Kemble

Being in close proximity to their owners, a domestic was under continuous scrutiny. Any whim of the residents of the house that needed venting due to frustration, or a frivolous desire of sadism or vengeance, often found its direction aimed at a house servant. Theodore Dwight Weld relates such an incident from his 1839 book, *American Slavery as it Is*.

Among the servants waiting was a young negro man, whose beautiful person, obliging and assiduous temper, and his activity and grace in serving made him a favorite with the company. The dinner lasted into the evening, and the wine passed freely about the table. At length, one of the gentlemen, who was pretty highly excited with wine, became unfortunately incensed either at some trip of the young slave, in waiting or at some other cause happening when the slave was within his reach. He seized the long necked [sic] wine bottle, and struck the young man suddenly in the temple, and felled him dead upon the floor. The fall arrested for a moment, the festivities of the table. 'Devilish unlucky,' exclaimed one. 'The gentleman is very unfortunate,' cried another. 'Really a loss,' said a third, &c &c. The body was dragged from the dining hall, and the feast went on; and at the close, one of the gentlemen, and the very one, I believe, whose hand had done the homicide, shouted in bacchanalian bravery, and *southern generosity,* amid the broken glasses and fragments of chairs, 'LANDLORD! PUT THE NIGGER INTO THE BILL.'[89]

Susan's role as a domestic held an additional scourge of slavery.

Generation after generation of the southern females, have witnessed their

fellow creatures, even the children of their own fathers and husbands, living as the mere tools of unbridled lust, and often violated with a savage barbarity, of which the legal annals of crime afford no parallel.[90]
—Rev. George Bourne

Being blue-eyed, young and attractive, the possibility of forced indiscretion, if not outright rape, was a constant threat. For Madison Washington and Susan, these realities were a part of their everyday lives. The only solace they might find in their situation was in each other and the dream that one day they would be free.

How and when Madison Washington met and fell in love with his wife can only be conjecture based on a general overview of the social life of the slave community in the mid-1830s. Considering the respective ages of Susan and Madison, a chance meeting would have been a moment in time for a young woman of eighteen and a young man of twenty to meet and fall in love.

7

Corn Husking

All dem purty gals will be dar,
Shuck dat corn before you eat
Dey will fix it for us rare,
Shuck dat corn before you eat
I know dat supper will e big,
Shuck dat corn before you eat
I think I smell a fine roast pig
Shuck dat corn before you eat [91]

The ability to identify and research individual slaves is difficult; to recover private musings of slaves is all the more improbable. Any civil records of births, marriages, deaths, any diary or recollection of a life lived were unlikely in the life of a slave. The idea that a common slave would have such emotions was foreign to planters of the antebellum South.

The one source that serves as a record of emotion and art that has survived to the present is music. The songs created and sung in the slave community of antebellum America express a range of emotions, from songs of survival and freedom, to feelings of those lost, to selling or death, to a dissemination of information as to the goings-on of the plantation and intelligence that supplied advantageous opportunities of escape. And always, the songs of love.

Examples that survive to the present times are "*Wade in the Water*," "*Roll Jordon Roll*," "*Swing Low Sweet Chariot*," and countless other songs that are part of the American musical lexicon. The contributions to twentieth century music have been immense in the form of jazz, classical, country, blues, rock and roll, and spirituals, from Armstrong to Ellington, Gershwin to the Beatles. All can be traced back to African-American roots.

Music not only gave voice to promise and pain, it also explored the more tender propensities of the heart.

The practice of courtship in the slave community not only existed, but flourished, for the language of love is universal. Many romances depicted in European society—from Sampson and Delilah, Shakespeare's Romeo and Juliet, the Bronte's brooding characters of northern England, and Jane Austin's clever banter, to the Americana expression of love denied in *The Scarlet Letter* and the mischievous and innocent yearnings of Mark Twain's Tom Sawyer and Becky Thatcher—have a common theme: love. These same expressions of love and fidelity were expressed in the slave community with the same intensity of discovery, longing, heartbreak, and passion.

The instances of romance in the slave community were not unlike those courtships that transpired between any boy and girl, albeit under slavery, courtship may not have been as sophisticated or as leisurely. Regardless, the act of falling in love was as prevalent and meaningful in the slave community as in any other society.

Using a blend of American ritual and African folklore, the slave community of North America developed a unique form of courtship. Borrowing from West African traditions that survived the Middle Passage, the use of poetry and storytelling were common devices of courtship used by a young man to win the heart of a young woman. John W, Blassingame, a leading Yale historian on American slavery, concisely related, "The slaves believed that in order to win a mate, a young man or woman had to 'know how to talk.'"[92]

The ability to "talk" referred to a style of verbal dueling between a male and female that practiced a rhetorical approach. This established a person's availability for courtship with the intention of a romantic liaison. Metaphor was the banter between boy and girl, with flattery a constant on the part of the male. This verbal duel was frequently in practice on those occasions when slaves gathered socially, usually associated with a common work detail. Such gatherings acted as a catalyst for a young man to test his powers of persuasion and charm on a young lady. The most common of these gatherings, that were both work and social, were cornhusking bees.

In both slave and farming communities, cornhusking bees were social events where romance flourished. During harvest, neighboring farms and plantations made arrangements to combine labor so as to derive the greatest productivity. What entertainment was afforded the slave was practiced and participated at such gatherings—music, dance, and oral storytelling.

Mr. Bryant, in his 'Letters of a Traveler,' describing a corn-husking scene of which he was a spectator, in South Carolina, says: "When the work of the evening was over, the negroes adjourned to a spacious kitchen, one of them took his place as a musician, whistling, and beating time with two sticks upon the floor. Several of the men came forward and executed various dances, capering, prancing, and drumming with the heel and toe upon the floor, with astonishing agility and perseverance, though all of them had performed their daily tasks, and worked all evening, and some had walked from four to seven miles to attend the corn-shucking."[93]

One form of entertainment at these gatherings that existed from the earliest colonial period was the oral tradition of "Telling of Tales." Preserved and retold over successive generations, these folktales were a link to a long-forgotten culture and reflected the oral traditions of African societies. As well as being entertainment, the tales gave voice to a desire to overcome the chains of bondage. Stories of conjures—the ability of the oppressed to overcome great odds by means of voodoo and other magical spells—and the use of anthropomorphism were common devices used in these tales. One example is the Brier Rabbit series of tales. In these stories the smaller and weaker animal outsmarts the stronger and larger animal. The one constant in many of these tales is the ability of the oppressed to overcome great odds, and seek retribution for the injustices perpetrated on them.

The constant control and interference into the lives of slaves caused many to seek relationships from adjoining plantations. A slave would desire such a relationship so as not to be a witness to the ill-treatment of a spouse, or the forcible rape of one's wife, by the owner. Former slave, John Anderson, gave testimony to this very situation when he stated, "I did not want to marry a girl belonging to my own place, because I knew I could not bear to see her ill-treated."[94]

Planters, however, strongly discouraged marriages between slaves belonging to different plantations. Left to legally clarify property rights while maintaining a good neighbor policy, a planter took into consideration the loss of property from children conceived between such unions. The owner of a female slave would benefit by accruing any offspring of such a union, while the owner of the male slave saw a loss of future production and profit. In the mindset of a planter, slavery equated wealth and was treated as such—and the main consideration of a Southern planter was profit. If there was to be a union of slaves from differing plantations, often times, one planter would purchase either one or the other of the slaves.

Marriage did exist between slaves, but only with the consent and knowledge of the owner. Whether they were allowed to marry, whom they married, and if they stayed together in marriage, or instead were sold separately, was the prerogative of the slave owner. A male slave had little say regarding the disposition of his family. It was the domain of the planter-owner to approve or disapprove of relationships between slaves. Frequently, these decisions were based on the effect such pairings would have on the value of a slave as property.

There were actual slave marriage ceremonies, but more often than not the two began married life by moving into a single cabin. The ritual of "jumping the broom," was more for the entertainment of the owners and was thought to originate in Wales. The bride, and then the groom, jumped backward over a broomstick about a foot off the ground. If one or the other fell while jumping the broom, the one who succeeded in clearing the hurdle would rule the house. If both cleared the obstruction, then harmony would exist in the union. The term "jumping the broom" amongst slaves was more an expression of marriage than the actual act of jumping.

The one threat that hung over the slave family, like the Sword of Damocles, was the possibility of separation through the sale of the husband, wife, parent, or child. In Michael Tabman's book, *Speculators and Slaves*, his in depth research into this issues is clearly stated with the following; "Because the typical slave woman . . . would have been married by about the age nineteen, and most males by about age twenty-four, buying policy again had the effect of striking hard against the Upper South marriages."[95]

It is a testament to the defiance shown toward the oppressive nature of slavery that many made the decision to run away, knowing full well they ran the risk of never seeing loved ones again. The one positive aspect of the decision was the hope that someday, somehow, some way, there was a possibility of reuniting in freedom.

The age and physique of an individual slave—coupled with the approaching selling season and the threat of being sold south—were harsh realities of plantation life in Northern Virginia. To a newly married Madison Washington, these circumstances would have been heavy on his soul. News of speculators coming around would have acted as a catalyst for a young man with a new wife to make the fateful decision to run away.

8

In Bondage

O Gracious Lord
When shall it be
That we poor souls
shall be free . . .
—Slave song

The majority of surviving records of those in slavery relate to a person's, age, height, gender, and color. However, based on a cumulative record of primary source materials from the time and place where Madison Washington is reported to be from, a realistic portrayal of life within the institution of slavery and the conditions of plantation life can accurately be summarized.

For example, the narrative of ex-slave Lunsford Lane tells of his early childhood on a tobacco plantation at the time and place Madison Washington would have experienced similar circumstances.

My infancy was spent upon the floor, in a rough cradle, or sometimes in my mother's arms. My early boyhood in playing with the other boys and girls, colored and white, in the yard, and occasionally doing such little matters of labor as one of so young years could. I knew no difference between myself and the white children; nor did they seem to know any in turn. Sometimes my master would come out and give a biscuit to me, and another to one of his own white boys; but I did not perceive the difference between us.[96]

Over time, the difference would become pronounced and imposed, both on the White free child and the Black slave. Children of African descent would be raised to be slaves in a world devoid of freedom—regulated, regimented, and controlled in every aspect—from where he could or could not go, what he ate, what time he awoke and what time he went to bed. His beliefs in a God, whether he was to be informed or educated in any manner, whom he or she was to marry, and the disposition of his slave family was at the behest and permission of his owner. This imposition upon a slave was enforced with the constant threat and actual application of corporal punishment to elicit submission to the authority of the White master.

The white child, however, would be filled with a sense of superiority that would lead him to deny any aspect of equality or recognition of a slave as anything more than a farm implement. The white child would be allowed to enforce his superiority with a variety of harsh measures so as to control his unfree property. From the whip to the denial of a slave's erudition, to the arbitrary sale of an individual, the white child would be raised to be the master of the black child.

The type of controls varied to some degree, but the basic precepts of slavery were common throughout the South. Over the two hundred plus years the institution existed, the vast majority of slaves spent their entire lives knowing only the land they worked and the labor they gave under the brutality of the institution. Many never had opportunity to travel more than a few miles from the slave quarters where they lived and the fields where they worked.

One important factor within the slave community was access to the everyday goings-on of the plantation—the news of an impending sale of a fellow slave, or slaves, as well as intelligence regarding when the master would be absent from the plantation. This intelligence would aid and facilitate any decision that concerned the timing of an escape.

Considering Madison Washington's age, physique and gender—coupled with the common practice of Virginia plantation owners selling off a portion of their slaves to the intercoastal slave speculators—there is little doubt he may have been keenly aware of his potential sale.

Another consideration concerning Madison's possible sale to New Orleans speculators was his attitude and possible lack of compliance. The fact that he led the largest successful slave rebellion in North America during the existence of slavery suggests a propensity for freedom and a defiant attitude against the oppressiveness of the institution. This all but guaranteed his being "sold down the river" and shipment to the deep South, as was the common practice for removing the rebellious from a slave community.

The dangers of running away and the possibility of never seeing loved ones again weighed heavy on those who considered the attempt. If it was just himself, the decision would be easy, but now, any thought of running involved Susan and the hardship it would bring to her as well.

Yet, there was little choice. The threat of being sold sealed their fate. The dream of freedom could not be delayed, for if they hesitated it would become a dream deferred. These were the realities facing Madison Washington as he came to the inevitable decision to follow the North Star to freedom.

Any help Madison derived from his wife's position as a house slave would have been invaluable. One common aid that the domestic provided for those who were prepared to run, was the lending, borrowing, or stealing of supplies that greatly augmented the rations distributed to slaves in the quarter. Meals allocated to the slaves were meager at best, proportioned to provide basic nourishment for the maintenance of production. The slave diet was farinaceous and for the field hand, usually consisted of two meals a day, the first eaten at noon, the other eaten after their labor was over.

Josiah Henson, who spent thirty years on a plantation in Montgomery

County, Maryland before escaping and becoming a Methodist preacher and abolitionist, recalled such conditions in his memoirs published in 1849:

> The principal food of those upon my master's plantation consisted of corn-meal and salt herrings; to which was added in summer a little buttermilk, and the few vegetables which each might raise for himself and his family, on the little piece of ground which was assigned to him for the purpose, called a truck-patch. In ordinary times we had two regular meals in a day: breakfast at twelve o'clock, after laboring from daylight, and supper when the work of the remainder of the day was over. In harvest season we had three.[97]

In a similar recounting ten years earlier and farther south, Francis Ann Kemble gave this observation of a slave meal on her husband's plantation in Georgia: "They go to the fields at daybreak, carrying with them their allowance of food for the day, which toward noon, *and not till then*, they eat, cooking it over a fire, which they kindle as best they can, where they are working. Their second meal in the day was at night, after their labor was over, having worked, at the *very least*, six hours without intermission of rest or refreshment since their noonday meal."[98]

As these and many other sources reveal, the system and practice of slavery was applied universally throughout the South. The unfortunate individuals who faced the oppression of slavery came together as a solid community to buffer the cruel realities of their bondage. Any opportunity to ease the burdens of slavery and provide a better life for oneself were readily taken and shared throughout the slave community. One example of this common bonding afforded to the slave, both as a solace and a form of control, was religion and religious teachings.

In the time of slavery, white planters constantly endeavored to instill in their chattel the virtues of obedience and an acceptance of one's lowly status in life. Some of the more ironic practices used by the planters in communicating lessons of submission were in the form of religious teachings, wherein examples of Christian values were used to reinforce obedience to a master.

Although religion was accessible to the slaves, it was believed that conversion by baptism would weaken the dominion of the planters over their chattel. The consensus among Southern planters for denying baptism was centered on the theory that a religious conversion would cause a slave to become unmanageable, even rebellious. Any recognition of a Negro as anything more than a slave threatened the institution, for slavery could only work if a Negro was set aside and made different from white society. Religious acceptance of a Negro as a brother in Christianity would create a sense of equality, thus fostering demands for freedom.

On those occasions when slaves were allowed to be baptized, it was made clear the slave did not achieve parity with white Christians. Planters went so far as to establish into law the guarantee that a slave remained a slave, regardless of salvation through baptism. As early as 1667, the Virginia Colony established that the act of baptism did not free a slave from slavery, and the idea was adopted into state and municipal codes throughout the South.

Even the afterlife would not end slavery. The right to a heavenly reward was reserved for whites only, and if there were blacks in heaven, their role would not vary from their position on earth. The following conversation between a three-year-old white child, a white nurse, and a black slave named Mary, from Frances Anne Kemble's, *Journal of a Residence on a Georgia Plantation, 1838-39*, confirms the common belief of white Southerners concerning the afterlife:

> "Some persons are free and some are not; do you know that, Mary?"
> "Yes, missis, here," was the reply. "I know it was so here, in this world."
> Here my child's white nurse, my dear Margery, who had hitherto been silent, interfered, saying: "Oh, then you think it would not always be so?"
> "Me hope not, missis."
> "I am afraid, E—, this woman actually imagines that there would be no slaves in heaven; isn't that preposterous, now, when, by the account of most of the Southerners, slavery itself must be heaven, or something uncommonly like it?"[99]

Not only baptism, but the choice of Biblical teachings preached to the slaves were censored and controlled. The white Southern preacher interpreted passages in the Bible that supported the claim of racial dominance and superiority of the white race. Slaves were told that their masters and mistresses were God's overseers. The Biblical stories of Jewish slavery and rebellion against their Egyptian overlords was censored, along with early concepts of Christ's teachings on equality. Peter Randolph, who grew up in slavery in the 1830-40s, gave testament to the type of message commonly delivered by white preachers in support of slavery:

> In Prince George County there were two meeting-houses intended for public worship. Both were occupied by the Baptist denomination. These houses were built by William and George Harrison, brothers . . . that their slaves might go there on the Sabbath and receive instruction, such as slave-holding ministers would give. The prominent preaching to the slaves was, 'Servants, obey your masters.' Do not steal or lie, for this is very wrong. Such conduct is sinning against the Holy Ghost, and is base ingratitude to your kind masters, who feed, clothe and protect you . . .[100]

Racial inequalities preached by white clergy and the inaccessibility of religion to a majority of slaves did not preclude a form of Christian worship from developing separately in the slave community. Each type of Christianity, white and slave, varied from the other in its function and purpose. Couched in innuendo that alluded to equality and freedom, a form of slave Christian worship surreptitiously evolved that rejected white Christian teachings of obedience. This in turn gave rise to the black preacher, one of a few slaves in a given area who could read and write, and who was an individual of strong character and personality. He possessed oratorical skills that mixed Christian faith and African folklore into a message of hope. Closely watched and continually censored in what he could and could not preach, he often disguised references within his sermons to the slave's plight and the always-prevalent desire to be free. Forced to teach obedience to the planter to avoid the lash, he was adept at the use of the double entendre. If left to his own, he invoked his flock to believe, "... there's a better day a-coming," and that the mighty hand of God would smite those who oppressed his people. Through his preaching he envisioned salvation and freedom, both in the hereafter as well as the here and now.

> She built a nice church with glass windows and a brass cupola for the blacks and a yellow man [light-skinned black man] preached to us. She had him preach how we was to obey our master and missy if we want to go to Heaven, but when she wasn't there, he come out with straight preachin' from the Bible.[101] —Litt Young, enslaved in Mississippi and Texas

Religious praise meetings attended by slaves acted as a cohesive social center for the slave community. The services varied from their white counterpart, distinguishable not only in message but also in the style of delivery. The call-and-response and the singing found in black services were in stark contrast to the staid and conservative white religious church gatherings.

Outside of approved and censored slave religious gatherings, there were clandestine religious meetings, held in slave cabins, swamps, or other locations not readily accessible to a white planter or overseer. These meetings brought together the slave community for a short respite from the burdens of their suffering. The religious teachings of freedom and the lessons taught to young slaves acted to counter the planter's indoctrination of white superiority. The place and time of such meetings were carefully transmitted from person to person in the slave quarters; broken branches bent in the direction of the meeting, and stones piled or laid in a particular fashion were common devices used to guide the faithful to the location of the services.

Ex-slave Peter Randolph, from the *County of Prince George*, Virginia, relates his own experiences of such a gathering.

> Not being allowed to hold meetings on the plantation, the slaves assemble in the swamps, out of reach of the patrols. They have an understanding amongst themselves as to the time and place of getting together. This was often done by the first one arriving breaking boughs from the trees, and bending them in the direction of the selected spot. Arrangements are then made for conducting the exercises. They first ask each other how they feel, the state of their minds, etc. The male members then select a certain space, in separate groups, for their division of the meeting. Preaching in order, by the brethren; then praying and singing all round, until they generally feel quite happy. The speaker usually commences by calling himself unworthy, and talks very slowly, until, feeling the spirit, he grows excited, and in a short time, there fall to the ground twenty or thirty men and women under its influence.
>
> The slave forgets all his sufferings, except to remind others of the trials during the past week, exclaiming: 'Thank God, I shall not live here always!' Then they pass from one to another, shaking hands, and bidding each other

farewell, promising, should they meet no more on earth, to strive and meet in heaven, where all was joy, happiness and liberty. As they separate, they sing a parting hymn of praise.[102]

These meetings allowed for old acquaintances to be renewed, information to be passed, and the leadership of the slave community to be recognized. Issues that concerned the slave community were addressed, but more important, the spirits of those attending were instilled with a higher purpose—a renewed belief that someday freedom would become reality.

The importance of the black church, particularly in the South, is a tradition that exists to present times. Black churches organized protests, sit-ins. and marches that attacked Jim Crow and segregation—the last vestiges of institutionalized slavery. Along with playing an active role in the civil rights movements of the 1950s and '60s, black churches provided leadership that gave the nation great voices in the Civil Rights Movement and American history: Dr. Martin Luther King, Malcom X, John Lewis, Andrew Young, James Meredith, and countless others.

This tradition traces its roots back to praise meetings where self-esteem, the concept of liberty, and the desire for freedom were a constant. The countless affidavits and interviews of former slaves have one common thread—the desire to be free.

> From my earliest recollection freedom had been the object of my ambition, a constant motive to exertion, an ever-present stimulus to gain and to save.[103] —Josiah Henson, 1849.

Although the idea of freedom played a significant role in a slave's resistance to bondage, there existed a harsher reality that motivated a slave to resist: the sale of a family member. This was the cruelest blow suffered under slavery. The desires and dreams for freedom could no longer be ignored in the face of an impending sale. It was the major motivating factor that caused a slave to run away.

The act of running away not only functioned as an escape from slavery, it became a form of protest. If successful, there was freedom, but if caught the consequences were swift and sure. Disfigurement to mark runaways and other malcontents—the breaking of bones, floggings, castrations, and even death were the consequences of a failed attempt. The most common was whipping. Based on research derived from; *The Slave Community, Plantation Life In The Antebellum South*, by John W. Blassingame and countless slave narratives, over fifty percent of the slave population in the South was flogged on a yearly basis .[104]

> Flogging—though often severe and excruciating in Maryland, is not practiced with the order, regularity and system, to which it is often reduced in the South. On the Potomac, if a slave gives offence, he is generally chastised on the spot, in the field where he is at work, as the overseer always carried a whip—sometimes a twisted cow-hide, sometimes a kind of horse-whip, and very often a simple hickory switch or gad, cut in the adjoining woods.

For stealing meat, or other provisions, or for any of the higher offences, the slaves are stripped, tied up by the hands—sometimes by the thumbs—and whipped at the quarter—but many times, on a large tobacco plantation, there is not more than one of these regular whippings in a week . . . though on others, where the master happens to be a bad man, or a drunkard . . . the back of the unhappy Maryland slave, is seamed with scars from his neck to his hips.[105] — ex-slave Charles Ball

Although these measures were brutal, the greatest punishment was the fear of being sold South and the inevitable separation from family and friends.

[t]he idea of being conveyed to the far South, seemed infinitely worse than the terrors of death."[106] —Lunsford Lane

A slave running away was one of the greatest liabilities a planter faced, and great lengths were taken by slave-owners to secure the machinery of the South. There were (what some have suggested as benevolent) measures taken by planters to establish control over the slave population. These consisted of slave marriages, developing monogamy, allowing religious practices that preached obedience to white planters, and the fostering of a family structure—when compatible with the needs of the planter. Although these measures seem less than harsh, a planter's underlying motivation for all actions taken toward their bonds people never had kindness in mind. A planter based his actions on two paramount considerations: (1) profit and the calculated effect on the growth and output of his industry and (2) the control of a large, unfree population.

Behind these carrots of benevolence existed a large and brutal stick. The use of curfews enforced by patrollers—community volunteers who patrolled the roads for strays and runaways—was one measure taken by the planters to control the slaves. It also added a layer of security against the threat of runaways or worse, insurrection. If a slave was out past curfew, or in an area where one did not belong, he would be jailed and upon being bailed out by his owner, had only the lash to look forward to. Punishment was one of the few guarantees in the system of slavery.

The measures of control practiced by the planters—the selling of family members, the use of slave women as concubines, disfigurement, floggings, castrations, and death—acted to guarantee the subjugation of the slave population. When slaves did revolt, the resulting backlash was swift and brutal.

In September of 1739, the Stono Rebellion near the Stono River in South Carolina was a gruesome example of a planter's harsh retaliation against any breach of his authority. The captured rebels were executed by beheading, and their heads placed on poles that lined the roads for miles. The effect of this gruesome display strongly discouraged slaves from making any future attempts at organized resistance.

The one positive African Americans encountered under the institution of slavery was the family, while at the same time it was ironically the strongest hold the planter held over his slaves. The effects of a sale of a family member manifested itself in many forms: depression, indifference, suicide, anger, and violence. Few families escaped or avoided this reality, which was a constant in the plantation system of the antebellum South.

> I never knew a whole family to live together till all were grown up in my life. There was almost always, in every family, some one or more keen and bright, or else sullen and stubborn slave, whose influence they are afraid of on the rest of the family, and such a one must take a walking ticket to the south.[107] —Lewis Clarke, ex-slave. 1841

In the antebellum South, it was not uncommon to find slaves who were not blood-related being raised under the same roof. If a mother was a field worker, she would have little time or energy to devote to a young baby, especially after a day of intense physical labor. Although a new mother was allowed a few weeks off to nurse her newborn, she was soon forced back to a full work regime. At first, a mother would take her newborn into the fields, nursing as she worked, but as the child grew, the burden and responsibility would become too much. The narrative of Margaret Ward, a slave from a tobacco plantation in Maryland, relates the experience of a fellow slave who found herself pregnant after she was sold to a new master.

> He then put her in the hands of a brutal overseer, with directions to work her to the extent of her ability on a tobacco plantation, which command was enforced up to the day of the birth of her child. At the end of one week she was driven again to the field and compelled to perform a full task, having at no time any abatement of her work on account of her situation, with exception of one week. It was the custom on the plantation to establish nurseries, presided over by old, broken down slaves, where mothers might leave their infants, but this privilege was denied to Margaret. She was obliged to leave her child under the shade of a bush in the field, returning to it but twice during the long day. On returning to the child one evening, she found it apparently senseless, exhausted with crying, and a large serpent lying across it. Although she felt that it would be better for both herself and child if it were dead, yet a mother's heart impelled her to make an effort to save it, and by caressing him and careful handling she resuscitated it.[108]

In cases where there was a mother and father, the relationship was often monogamous. In part, this was due to the gender ratio in the Southern slave states where the ratio of male to female slaves was near equal. This contributed to the stability of the family structure against the backdrop of bondage and separation. In turn, this significantly aided the traditional function of child rearing, which became the centerpiece of the slave family. The support and training a child received from his or her family provided the knowledge, sympathy, and counsel that helped shelter a young person from the dehumanizing effects of slavery. Both the surrogate mother and the actual mother told stories based on the oral traditions of their ancestral African societies. Adopted from African folklore, these parables enlightened generations of those in bondage about whole nations populated by African people and great African leaders. The stories instilled an identity and a sense of culture that was missing in the main slave society, and brought awareness of a heritage that buffered the oppression of slavery.

A serious impediment that affected the structure of the family was the practice of using female slaves as concubines. One result of this open indiscretion was the obvious outcome of children of mixed race. Although part white, the fact remained, instituted by law, that any person with black parentage was considered a slave.

Another result of these indiscretions was the white divorce rate in the South. White woman often found these liaisons between their husband and his concubines to be more than they cared to overlook. Loren Schweninger, Professor Emeritus, University of North Carolina at Greensboro, wrote of the nature of these liaisons.

> In fact, in every section of the state, from the Mountains to the Piedmont to the Coastal Plain, racial issues lurked under the surface or rose to become the primary cause of divorce.[109]

But it was not only men who partook of their slaves for their own gratification. Victoria E. Bynum wrote in *The Politics of Social and Sexual Control in the Old South* that, ". . . although wives were often forced to endure abusive spouses, 'not a single woman received a divorce solely on the grounds of having been beaten by her husband.' Bynum observed that the state supreme court, led by Chief Justice Thomas Ruffin (1833-1852), denied most cases on appeal but showed that the superior courts in the three studied counties granted far more divorces than they denied. In a study of black men charged with raping white women, Diane Miller Sommerville argues that a number of these interracial sexual relations were consensual."[110]

The actual process of obtaining a divorce by either member of a white plantation family was not easy. It was paramount to maintain the appearance of a stable family to project an image of authority to the enslaved population. The maintenance of order, and the reinforcement of the owner's authority, took precedence in maintaining control.

Other than divorce, a form of revenge practiced by white woman stemming from the husband's infidelity was the sale of the offending black woman, or the sale of part of her family. Ex-slave, William Thompson, who was born eighteen miles from Richmond and was interviewed by Benjamin Drew who published the narratives of es-slaves in Canada in 1856, relates such an incident.

> I knew a man at the South who had six children by a colored slave. Then, there was a fuss between him and his wife and he sold all the children but the oldest slave daughter. Afterward, he had a child by this daughter, and sold mother and child before the birth. This was nearly forty years ago. Such things are done frequently in the South.[111]

It is one of the ironies of slavery wherein plantation owners promote monogamy in the slave family, while indulging sexual proclivities with slaves.

> In the house of slave-holders, you behold young ladies elegantly attired and attended by their colored sisters, children of the same father, and yet slaves.[112] —George Bourne

These were the conditions a twenty-year old Madison Washington faced during the summer of 1839.

9
North Star

And it won't be long,
And it won't be long,
And it won't be long,
Poor sinner suffer here.
We'll soon be free . . .[113]

Slaves were beaten for singing this song. Georgetown, South Carolina.

F or slavery to survive and flourish over the 250 years of its existence, the slave had to be kept in a state of ignorance and physical degradation.

With a fatigued body and a dispirited mind, broken with incessant labor, tamed by a constant privation of every comfort, and often lacerated with severity unmingled with mercy, the slave can feel little anxiety to devote any part of that time which is indispensable to rest his worried and tortured frame, to the care of his soul.[114] —Reverend George Bourne

The isolation of the slave quarters found in the plantation system fostered a separation of the white population from the slave communities, as well as slaves from slaves. Some slave owners went so far as to build tunnels so the slaves could come and go out of sight, as was the case at Thomas Jefferson's Monticello.

On a plantation of average size there may have been several quarters, each situated near fields where the slaves worked each day. An individual would live a lifetime knowing only the slave quarters, the fields where they toiled, and the surrounding lands of a particular plantation. The quarter generally consisted of a cooper and blacksmith hut, the slave driver's hut, an overseer's house, a cookhouse, the cabins of the slaves, and an infirmary. Lest one imagine the slave owner provided medical care to his bondsmen, the infirmary, usually one to a plantation, was nothing more than a squalid, dirty building with no beds or blankets, where slaves who had labored their entire life for the wealth of the planter were brought to either recuperate or die.

The infirmary was a large two-story building . . . and contains four large rooms . . . The floor (which was not boarded, but merely the damp hard earth) was strewn with wretched women, who, but for their moans of pain, and uneasy, restless motions, might very well each have been taken for a mere heap of filthy rags; the chimney refusing passage to the smoke from the pine-wood fire, it puffed out in clouds in the room.[115] —Frances Anne Kemble

The cabins, or huts, provided for the slaves were often less than stables and could never be considered adequate housing. Cold and drafty in the wet winters, smoky and hot during the summer months, these dwellings were home to generations of slaves.

We lodged in log huts, and on the bare ground. Wooden floors were an unknown luxury. In a single room were huddled, like cattle, ten or a dozen persons, men, women, and children. All ideas of refinement and decency were, of course, out of the question. We had neither bedsteads, nor furniture of any description. Our beds were collections of straw and old rags, thrown down in the corners and boxed in with boards; a single blanket the only covering. Our favorite way of sleeping, however, was on a plank, our heads raised on an old jacket and our feet toasting before the smoldering fire. The wind whistled and the rain and snow blew in through the cracks, and the damp earth soaked in the moisture till the floor was miry as a pig-sty. Such were our houses. In these wretched hovels where we penned at night, and fed by day; here were the children born and the sick-neglected.[116] — Ex-slave, the Rev. Josiah Henson

Theodore Dwight Weld, a prominent abolitionist, wrote of his firsthand knowledge of such dwellings in his 1839 book, *American Slavery as it Is*: ". . . go at night, view their means of lodging, see them lying on benches, some on the floor or ground, some sitting on stools, dozing away the night;—others, of younger age, with a bare blanket wrapped about them; and one or two lying in the ashes. These things I have often seen with my own eyes."[117]

Another description of the slave huts finds little variance:

These cabins consist of one room, about twelve feet by fifteen, with a couple of closets, smaller and closer than the staterooms of a ship, divided off from the main room and each other by rough wooden partitions, in which the inhabitants sleep. They have almost all of them a rude bedstead, with the gray moss of the forests for mattress, and filthy, pestilential-looking blankets for covering. Two families (sometimes eight and ten in number) reside in one of these huts, which are mere wooden frames pinned, as it were, to the earth by a brick chimney outside, whose enormous aperture within pours down a flood of air, but little counteracted by the miserable spark of fire which hardly sends an attenuated thread of lingering smoke up its huge throat. A wide ditch runs immediately at the back of these dwellings, which was filled and emptied daily by the tide. Attached to each hovel, was a small scrap of ground for a garden, which, however, was for the most part untended and uncultivated.[118] —Frances Anne Kemble

Furnishings were manufactured by slaves on their own time—utensils carved from wood, a crude bench, a makeshift bed made of straw-covered boards or a mattress made of corn shucks sewed up in a crude blanket. The few material goods found in the quarters were communally shared, with thievery being rare amongst slaves.

A camaraderie existed to blunt the impact of their shared bondage. Strong, able-bodied members of this community came to the aid of the weaker and less fortunate, giving solace and physical comfort. An example of this group solidarity is evident in Frederick Douglass's depiction of the loyalty of slaves to each other: ". . . as true as steel, and no band of brothers could have been more loving. There were no mean advantages taken of each other. . ."[119]

Demand for able-bodied young men put a premium on young slaves throughout the Chesapeake Bay area. The production capability of a slave was based on physical type and age. Males between the ages of eight and fourteen made up twenty-five percent of the sales to the Lower South, based on the fact that at this age, a young slave was entering the period of his greatest productivity, guaranteeing a longevity of production from the investment.

The net earnings capacity, based on the amount of cotton an individual could pick, was directly correlated with gender and age. The sale of females between the ages of twelve and fifteen was a conscious decision made by the planters since females mature quicker and are taller than male slaves at this age. For fieldwork, this favored girls of that age range because they could pick all of the cotton due to their height and reach. The result was that young girls were frequently sold as single units, away from family, which resulted in permanent separations.

The number one category comprising the trade, however, was males between eighteen and twenty-five. They were rarely, if ever, sold as a family unit or with a wife, and the planter felt little remorse at any hardship caused by the selling of a slave. The inevitable separations and countless family tragedies that resulted underline the tragic dimensions of the intercoastal slave trade.

Ex-slave Lewis Clarke said, "Generally there was but little more scruple about separating families than there was with a man who keeps sheep in selling off the lambs in the fall. On one plantation where I lived, there was an old slave named Paris. He was from fifty to sixty years old, and a very honest and apparently pious slave. A slave-trader came along one day, to gather hands for the South. The old master ordered the waiter or coachman to take Paris into the back room pluck out all his gray hairs, rub his face with a greasy towel, and then had him brought forward and sold for a young man. His wife consented to go with him, upon a promise from the trader they should be sold together, with their youngest child, which she carried in her arms. They left two behind them, who were only from four to six or eight years of age. The speculator collected his drove, started for the market, and, before he left the state, he sold that infant child to pay one of his tavern bills, and took the balance in cash . . ."[120]

The frustration of being powerless to stop the separation of mother from son, husband from wife, father from daughter, took its toll on the psyche of a slave, and black men saw an erosion of their ability to exercise their role as the head of the family. It was the white planter who determined the amount of care and attention a female slave would be provided with while pregnant and the treatment her infant received. There was no participation by the male slave in these decisions. One result of this loss of authority by the male slave was the expanded role of the female in the slave community, and this created a sharing in the raising of children by the entire slave community. Regardless of the circumstances and the makeup of the slave family, whether broken or whole, the education of the children to life under slavery was a primary role of the family.

Part of that education consisted of lessons on freedom and the real circumstances involved in fleeing to the North. The decision to run away and go north, with the reality of leaving loved ones behind, was never an easy choice, and the actual running was fraught with peril. The dread of being hunted and caught by the overseer's dogs was chillingly recounted in former slave Margaret Ward's narrative:

> Margaret had been lying in the woods on the bank of a river, intending to start again as soon as it was dark, when she was startled by the whining and nervous motions of old Watch, and listening, she heard the hoarse ringing bay of a blood-hound. Although she had expected she would be hunted with dogs, and recalled over and over again the shocking accounts related by Overseers to the slaves, of fugitives overtaken and torn in pieces by the savage Spanish blood-hounds, she had not, until now, realized the horrors of her situation.[121]

Slave owner J. R. Long relates his methods of punishment of a fugitive who was captured and returned: "I gave him a real whipping and hand sawing[122] and he had been a fine negroe ever since. I told him he might run off if he chosed [sp] and I would knock out one of his jaw teeth and brand him and I intend to stick to my promise."[123]

Branding, disfigurement, the knocking out of front teeth, the wearing of a steel collar with long lengths of metal that came up and out from the collar with bells on the end, crippling by breaking a leg or foot, amputation of a foot, selling to the deep South, and in some cases, death, were cruel realities that existed in the slave regions of the United States. From the New Orleans Commercial Bulletin of September 30, 1841, we find further evidence of these practices:

> Ranaway from the subscribers, on the 15th of last month, the negro man, Charles, had had the upper lip of his right eye torn, and a scare on his forehead; speaks English only, and stutters when spoken to; had on when he left an iron collar, the prongs of which he broke off before absconding . . .[124]

Or in the case of the runaway described below:

> Ranaway from the residence of Messrs. F. Duncom & Co., the negro Francois, aged from 25 to 30 years, about 5 feet 1 inch in height; the *upper front teeth are missing;* he had *chains on both of his legs,* dressed with a kind of blouse made of sackcloth. A proportionate reward will be given to whoever will

bring him back to the bakery, No. 74, Bourbon street.[125]

Yet, many still ran. The promise of freedom created a steady flow of fugitives that followed the "drinking gourd," a reference to the North Star, north to Canada.

These were the realities Madison Washington faced as he came to the inevitable decision to follow the North Star to freedom. If it was just himself, the decision would have been easy. Yet, there was little choice. The first step Madison and Susan would have taken in their preparations for freedom would be to contact those who could provide assistance. There were those in the slave community who had knowledge of how to make such a contact, or who were actually a part of the underground.

In the final decision, either for practical reasons that ensured the best chance of success, or circumstances we are not privy to, Madison would make his way north to Canada on his own. Once in Canada, it was reported that his intentions were to either raise the funds to buy his wife's freedom or to find the means to smuggle her out of Virginia. His overriding goal was freedom for both himself and Susan.

The Creole Incident

THE BEGINNING OF THE END OF SLAVERY

BOOK III: THE RADICALS

10
The Burned-Over District

The Burned-Over District derived its name from the practice of having large 'revival fires' at the camp meetings. The area of the district encompassed the part of New York State from the west, the shores of Lake Erie up to Buffalo; the north shore of Lake Ontario and the St. Lawrence River to Rooseveltown (this was where the border between Canada and the United States leaves the St. Lawrence and follows the land division), then a straight line south to the Pennsylvania border to form the eastern border, the southern border follows the Pennsylvania, New York border to Lake Erie.[126] —Milton C. Sernett

As Madison Washington traveled north in late 1839, he was assisted by a loose coalition of men and women who believed slavery was a sin against humanity. Many of these people were actively involved in social, religious, and political organizations that demanded an end to the South's peculiar institution. Some went even further in their fight against slavery.

One of the more effective and immediate acts of defiance against slavery was accomplished by those who operated the Underground Railroad. Although organized to a certain degree, the Underground Railroad was essentially improvised. In the 1899 book, *The Underground Railroad from Slavery to Freedom* by Wilbur H. Siebert, we are given an insight into the way it operated:

> Much of the communication relating to fugitive slaves was had in guarded language. Special signals, whispered conversations, passwords, messages couched in figurative phrases, were the common modes of conveying information about underground passengers, or about parties in pursuit of fugitives. These modes of communication constituted what abolitionists knew as the grape-vine telegraph.[127]

The type of person who participated in the Underground Railroad firmly believed in their cause and displayed great courage on a daily basis. Both the fugitive and the conductors faced threats in varying degrees. Conductors risked property, reputation, and at times their lives to assist fugitive slaves. The runaway constantly feared capture, either by patrollers in the slave states or bounty hunters in the free states. Until a fugitive from slavery reached Canada, he or she was never safe, and relied on and trusted those who aided along the journey.

Neighbors hid their activity from neighbors, never sure of their politics. A recollection by a resident of Westfield, New York, a community along the Underground Railroad in western New York State, typified the Railroad's clandestine activity:

> I had never seen any black people . . . and here in this immense kitchen, seated in a row around the entire wall, were from twenty to thirty, old and young men and women . . . I entered and seeing me standing there dazed and wondering, came towards me with a finger on her lips and after getting my message said, 'Keep what you have seen here a secret, tell it to no one but your mother . . .'[128]

The abolitionist conductors came from all strata of society: the wealthy and the poor, city folk and farmer, young and old, white and black, non-believers and preachers of varying denominations. Many of the leading voices for abolition found their calling in the great revival meetings that took place in an area of western New York State that has come to be known as the Burned-Over District.

Throughout American history there have regularly occurred resurgences of Christian fundamentalism. So it was in the late 1820s when such a religious awakening took place in the Burned-Over District. The district extended from New York's shore of Lake Erie, north to Lake Ontario, east to the St. Lawrence, then south to the Pennsylvania border. In this area preachers held large religious revivals that lasted several days. Great bonfires burned as people came from miles around to hear the preaching and take part in rural revival meetings. The residual aftermath from the two- to three-day gatherings were large, scorched areas where bonfires had burned simultaneously with the intensity of the preaching. Thus, the term Burned-over District.

The religious phenomena of the Burned-Over District contributed to an awakening of a crusade that sparked the fire for emancipation and freedom for all Americans. The radical concepts fostered in the revivals were the catalyst for the growth of benevolent organizations that evolved into anti-slavery societies. Many of the leading abolitionists traced their roots back to the Burned-Over District, including Charles Grandison Finney, the Tappan brothers, Theodore D. Weld, George Bourne, Theodore S Wright, Elizur Wright, and Henry Highland Garnet.

Another aspect directly attributable to the Burned-Over District was the experimentation with communes, and the establishment of centers of learning and theology. These centers were open to segments of society that had been previously denied participation in higher education. One example was the Oneida Institute that enrolled African Americans, a practice not generally accepted by the mainstream community. One of its early presidents, Beriah Green, demanded that he be allowed to do more for the cause of black freedom and education than had previously been allowed.

"I am assured," Beriah Green wrote Elizur Wright, Jr., "that Africa shall lose nothing in the exchange of stations I am urged to venture on. I am even assured that the Trustees [of Oneida Institute] would help me in my efforts to strike the chains from colored limbs."[129]

The above phrase, "Africa shall lose nothing," referred to colonization societies that proposed freed slaves be returned to Africa or other regions thought to be amenable to their lifestyle. Many in these colonization societies based their intentions on the precept that the returning ex-slaves would act as missionaries, with the expectation of Christianizing Africa.

Not all abolitionists agreed with this approach, and by the late 1830s many within the anti-slavery movement strongly disagreed with the concept of colonization. The issue of removal and colonization became such a bone of contention that it eventually contributed to a schism in the anti-slavery societies in America. Those who opposed colonization interpreted the trend toward colonization as perpetuating—rather than putting an end to—the great iniquity of slavery.

Many abolitionists who favored the idea of colonization failed to grasp the concept that black Americans were as generationally invested in America as most white Americans. Abraham D. Shadd, the grandson of a white German soldier and a free black woman, strongly opposed colonization and frequently spoke out against it. He recognized that people of African descent were as American as those of European descent. "We are natives of the United States; our ancestors were brought to this country by means over which they had no control; we have our attachment to the soil, and we feel we have rights in common with other Americans."[130]

The call for the abolition of slavery by those of African descent can be traced back to 1619, with the introduction of people from Africa into the early settlement of Jamestown. With regard to white abolitionism, by the 1830s many had found their calling in the struggle for emancipation during the great religious revival of the late 1820s.

The path from religious revivals of the Burned-Over District to the establishment of anti-slavery societies took a circuitous route that was interconnected with the growth of benevolent organizations. Two of the organizations associated with the religious revival of the 1820s were the Anti-Mason Party and the American Seamen's Friends Society. Although one was political and the other strictly a temperance and religious organization, members of both became associated with the inception and growth of anti-slavery societies.

Roots of the Anti-Mason Party can be traced to an incident that occurred in the same area of Western New York where the Burned-Over District was located. In 1826, ex-Mason William Morgan revealed the secrets of Freemasonry to the world, violating the Masonic oath of secrecy. The consequence of such an act was "to have my throat cut across, my tongue torn out by the roots, and my body buried in rough sands of the sea, at low water mark."

Members of a Masonic Lodge in Western New York sought their revenge. Morgan was arrested by a Masonic sheriff on a questionable charge, imprisoned, and then released to a hostile mob. Sometime later a badly decomposed body thought to be Morgan's was found floating in the Niagara River.

This incident sparked an Anti-Masonic movement. From this inconspicuous beginning, the Anti-Mason Party formed into an established political party that became a stepping-stone to the establishment of a party platform that called for the abolition of slavery. President Millard Fillmore had his start in the party, and in 1833 ex-president John Quincy Adams was asked to run on the Anti-Mason ticket as the Massachusetts gubernatorial candidate. One innovation of the Anti-Mason Party that is still with us today is the legacy of the first nominating convention.

The Anti-Mason party eventually melded with the Whig Party and became the Liberty Party. The final stage of this political metamorphosis was the evolution into the Republican Party and its ascendancy to power with the election of Abraham Lincoln as the first Republican president in 1860. Many of the same names associated with the creation of the Anti-Mason Party later participated in the founding of abolitionist societies in the 1830s: Joshua Leavitt, Theodore Weld and James Gillespie Birney, along with the greatest Anti-Mason of them all, the arch-evangelist and reformer, Charles G. Finney. All of these men were members of a benevolent organization called the American Seamen's Friend Society.

The American Seamen's Friends Society, although a very different organization from the Anti-Mason Party, proved to be as much of an asset to the abolitionist movement as the Anti-Mason Party. This society, established in January of 1826, focused on bringing religion to merchant sailors by means of distributing Bibles, holding temperance meetings, establishing reformed boardinghouses for sailors, and placing preachers in foreign ports. The interaction with merchant seamen along the Eastern Seaboard allowed members of the ASFS to become acquainted with a variety of people associated with the maritime industry and the social and legal aspects of the shipping business. Connecticut State University Professor Hugh H. Davis, one of the nation's premiere scholars of slavery in American history, wrote the following about the American Seamen's Friends Society.

> During the 1830s the number of men employed in the whaling industry and the foreign and coastal trade increased rapidly, approaching 100,000 late in the decade. Equally important, during this period the ethnic and racial composition of the crews became increasingly heterogeneous.[131]

Through the program of placing preachers in foreign ports, the American Seamen's Friends Society expanded its influence and reach throughout the world. This network of preachers in both foreign and domestic ports were relied upon to act as invaluable agents in doing the work and promoting the goals of the society.

Another facet of the ASFS was a familiarity with maritime law. This knowledge, derived from numerous litigations, aided the endeavors of future abolitionist societies with regard to both the transatlantic slave trade and the intercoastal slave trade. For example, during the Amistad trial that involved a revolt on a Spanish flagged ship by individuals who had been kidnapped into slavery, it was the Seamen's Society that was instrumental in locating sailors who spoke the native tongue of the Africans being held. The society's role in obtaining information about events that surrounded the insurrection and its aftermath on board the brig *La Amistad* contributed to the successful outcome of the trials and appeals that were eventually heard before the United States Supreme Court.

The first major abolitionist society, founded in 1833, gave witness to the individual ties of those in benevolent societies. Established as the American Anti-Slavery Society, the following names appeared as signatories on the Declaration of the Anti-Slavery Convention assembled in Philadelphia on December 4, 1833: Joshua Leavitt, editor of the *New York Evangelist*; Elizur Wright; Peter Williams; Theodore S. Wright; Samuel Cornish; Dr. Bartholomew Fussell; Abraham D. Shadd; William Goodell, editor of the *Genius of Temperance*; Charles W. Denison of the *Emancipator*; the Tappans; and the Rev. George Bourne, editor of the anti-Catholic Protestant *Vindicator* and an early immediatist.

Immediatists were the opposite of those who espoused colonization. They believed slavery needed to be abolished instantly, and by force if need be. Needless to say, many of these founding members were extremely radical.

Elizur Wright wrote that the newly formed society "must put on the muscle and transfuse the warm blood and breathe into it [the movement] the breath of life."[132]

At first, early abolitionist's societies relied on the pulpit, and were based on a strict religious focus to achieve their goals. However, as time went on it became evident to some that a means beyond prayers and preaching were required to end the sins of slavery. While some in the societies insisted on a purely religious approach, others preached a more radical approach by soliciting and recruiting members of Congress. They wished to carry the fight of emancipation into the very heart of government.

The American Anti-Slavery Society eventually splintered over matters of colonization, the participation and rights of women, and immediate abolition. The portion of the society led by William Lloyd Garrison, a leading abolitionist and the founder of the American Anti-Slavery Society and his Boston adherents, supported to some extent by the Philadelphia circle, a branch of the American Anti-Slavery Society, fought for the abolition of slavery through conventional means. But those who sought a more radical approach broke from Garrison in the spring of 1840 and formed the American and Foreign Anti-Slavery Society. This faction of Anti-Slavery abolitionists went its own way, and drew strength from those in the organization who originally established the society in the 1830s—the Tappans, wealthy merchants of New York, James Gillespie Birney, Henry Stanton, George Bourne and the leading legal authority on abolition, Theodore Weld.

One approach both anti-slavery societies took was to petition Congress with regard to slavery's legal status in the District of Columbia. Many in the anti-slavery societies believed a constitutional confrontation over slavery in the District could prove to be a viable path toward emancipation. As we have witnessed, the significance of challenging slavery in the District of Columbia was based on the fact that Congress, a federal body, governed the District. The existence of slavery in the District of Columbia created an incongruity. Some argued an attack against slavery should be based on the question: "Under what authority does Congress condone slavery in the District of Columbia?"

As to the Southern view, there could be no greater threat to slavery. They argued that any attempt to regulate or abolish slavery in the District of Columbia was to be construed as a hostile affront to their very way of life.

Yet, attacks by Northern anti-slavery members continued unabated. In 1836 the Southern members of Congress answered with the enactment of the Gag Rule with the hope of ending the flood of petitions against slavery. The solid phalanx of Southerners who defended their peculiar institution caused many in the North to step back from the issue of abolition in the District of Columbia.

Historian Samuel Flagg Bemis captured the hesitancy of the North when he wrote the following:

> The serious concern of patriotic men of good will was that too much immediate pressure for abolition might break up the Union. They feared that rather than accept abolition of slavery in the nation's capital, some of the Southern states, especially South Carolina, would secede—before the North had grown strong enough to prevent secession. Southern leaders exploited this fear at every turn in order to defend and extend the outworks of their system. To them the District of Columbia was both a citadel and a symbol for the defense of slavery in Federal territories and in their own states.[133]

Even John Quincy Adams, the leading voice against the Gag Rule, was reluctant to attack slavery in the District.

> There are three reasons, Adams informed the good Friend [Moses Brown, Quaker], why he could not support emancipation in the District of Columbia; (1) he did not think the inhabitants of one state competent to petition the legislature of another state, or even Congress acting for the District of Columbia, on matters so deeply affecting the interests of that state or District; (2) he was averse to stirring up ill blood between the Northern and Southern sections of the Union; (3) he believed he was acting in accordance with the opinion of a great majority of his own constituents.[134]

The South felt the Gag Rule provided the dikes that would contain the rising tide of anti-slavery sentiment, until either slavery was written into the Constitution, or, if forced, they could enact a legal secession of slave states from the Union. The Southern members' one voice, united against the scattered, self-serving interests of the North, guaranteed their hold on the direction of government. This was not only evident in the legislative branch, but in the other branches of government as well.

John Quincy Adams spoke of this when he said, "Its practical operation has been to give the balance of power in the house, and every department of the government, into the hands of the minority of numbers. For particular results look to the present composition of your government in all its departments. The President of the United States, the President of the Senate, the Speaker of the House, are all slaveholders. The Chief Justice and four out of the nine Judges of the Supreme Court of the United States are slaveholders. The commander-in-chief of your army, and the general next in command are slaveholders. A vast majority of all officers of your navy, from the highest to the lowest, are slaveholders. Of six heads of the executive departments, three are slaveholders, securing thus, with the President, a majority in all cabinet consultations and executive councils. . . As to the House itself, if an article of the constitution had prescribed, or a standing rule of the House had required, that no other than a slaveholder should ever be Speaker, the regulation could not be more rigorously observed than it is by the compact movements of the slave representation in the house. Of the last six speakers, including the present, everyone has been a slaveholder . . ."[135]

It was evident that the Gag Rule gave an advantage to the Southern representation and provided an opportunity for total domination of the government. Adams and his supporters in Congress avoided a vote on slavery and its legality concerning its existence in the District. This was based on an apprehension that a constitutional showdown would bring about a predictable result in favor of the South. A means of circumventing the Gag Rule, beyond the issue of the District of Columbia, would have to be found if the Southern stranglehold in Congress was to b broken.

Until such a means could be found, the work of the anti-slavery societies continued to confront slavery, from petitions to aiding runaways. The Underground Railroad sought to achieve abolition, one freed person at a time. Every individual who escaped from slavery was a victory for the cause and a step toward the ultimate goal of a Union where slavery no longer existed.

11

The Reverend George Bourne

In the year 1776, the United States stood, in fact, seven free to six slave colonies, for the slaves north of Maryland, are unworthy of notice. Since that period, six additional slave states have been added to the Union, and only three free states. For Vermont and Maine being then settled as now, are not numbered in this relation. Now the states instead of reckoning seven to six on behalf of freedom, are truly thirteen to eleven in favor of Slavery. This has given to the slave states in the Senate of Congress, the power of coercing all the legislation of the United States; so that all hope of deliverance from that source is a mere idle dream.[136] —George Bourne, 1834

One of the leading radical voices in the anti-slavery movement was the unremitting call for abolition by the Reverend George Bourne. He came from a lineage of reformers, his maternal grandmother a descendant of the Reverend John Cotton, the first Puritan minister of Boston. On his father's side "he reckoned the martyr James Johnston, who suffered death at the Cross of Glasgow . . . in defense of 'the Covenant and work of Reformation . . .' No wonder that he stemmed the tide of slave-holders' opposition for seven years in Virginia without fear."[137]

Bourne arrived in New York from his native England in 1804 at the age of twenty-four, accompanied by his wife. He worked as a journalist and local politician, and after several tumultuous years moved to the Harrisonburg area of the Shenandoah Valley in Virginia where, in 1809, he became pastor of a Presbyterian church. As a young preacher in Virginia, he came face-to-face with the realities of slavery.

Theodore Bourne, the son of George Bourne, recounts this experience in an article he wrote in the Methodist Quarterly Review titled: *Rev. George Bourne; The Pioneer Of American Antislavery.*

> While in Rockingham County [Va.] he came directly in contact and conflict with the system of American slavery…and his whole soul revolted at the injustices and iniquities which he constantly witnessed. Believing himself to be ordained to preach the truth, he failed not to denounce the evils of the

system publicly and privately.[138]

These encounters with the machinery of the South left a lasting impression on Bourne. He resolved to fight the iniquities he encountered and rededicated the remainder of his life to the struggle for emancipation. He began by simply preaching against the evils of the system from his pulpit in Virginia, and published several ardent protests against slavery. Among his writings is a small volume titled *The Book and Slavery Irreconcilable*, in which he addressed all who professed to be members of the Christian faith. Bourne wrote that he could discover no palliative suitable to alleviate the evil of slavery except total and immediate emancipation. He vigorously and repeatedly urged the "immediate and total abolition" of slavery, and warned his contemporaries of the consequences of continuing the system until by its growth, it should endanger the Union.

> The period has arrived, when slavery must be entirely abolished. To tolerate its abominations for one hour, extends a pestilence throughout the union, adds fuel to the volcano which is ready to burst forth in all its devastating fury upon the republic . . .[139]

For his protestations he was persecuted and driven from Virginia. Not unlike those for whom he sought to find justice, he and his family were forced to flee north.

As he became ever more radical, he sought ways to involve himself politically in the struggle. In 1833 he became a founding member of the American Anti-Slavery Society. It was during this period that Bourne came in contact with several radical abolitionists. One person with whom he established a working relationship was Hiram Wilson.

In *The Letters of William Lloyd Garrison, Volume II: A House Dividing Against Itself: 1836-1840*, edited by Louis Ruchames, it is clear Bourne and Wilson were acquainted with each other.

> In May of 1839 at the annual meeting of the American Anti-Slavery Society, of which Hiram Wilson was a member, it was resolved . . . that George Bourne, Charles W. Denison, Wm. Lloyd Garrison, . . . and Hiram Wilson, be a committee . . .[140]

However, by 1839 Bourne and several others became dissatisfied with the complacent approach of the American Anti-Slavery Society toward ending slavery. Bourne made this evident when he wrote;

> The system was so entirely corrupt that it admits of no cure but by a total and immediate abolition. For a gradual emancipation was a virtual recognition of the right, and establishes the rectitude of the practice. If it be just for one moment, it was hallowed forever; and if it be inequitable, not a day should it be tolerated.[141]

Bourne's demand for immediate emancipation denotes him, even within the anti-slavery societies, as a radical. He could no longer justify raging against slavery from the pulpit as the sole means to accomplish emancipation. He and others in the American Anti-Slavery Society believed the true course of action toward total emancipation was through the halls of Congress. They began to advocate by petitioning Congress for the abolition of slavery in the District of Columbia. This, they believed, was where the battle for emancipation was to be fought and won.

> A beginning must be made. The efforts already commenced, by petitioning Congress for the abolition of slavery in the District of Columbia, must be repeated, with renewed vigor, with enlarged numbers, and in a more thundering tone. The Federal legislation is controlled by the kidnappers . . .[142] —Reverend George Bourne

When a schism occurred in the anti-slavery movement over this radical approach, Bourne and several others formed the American and Foreign Anti-Slavery Society. Bourne, along with other members of the Foreign and American Anti-Slavery Society, clearly understood the one major impediment to free expression in Congress on the issue of slavery was the Gag Rule.

> Slavery alone was the chief, if not the sole cause of all the agitations which now perplex and disturb the body politic. Its peculiar demands are so utterly adverse to all the best interests of our citizens, and so totally incompatible with all that constitutes national prosperity and harmony; that no permanent concord among the different portions of our country, and no lasting security for the stability of our national institutions can rationally be anticipated, as long as that direful curse shall exist.[143] —Reverend George Bourne

Bourne, along with the other members of the newly formed American and Foreign Anti-Slavery Society, truly believed that if the Gag Rule was allowed to stand, the nation and its Constitution were in jeopardy. Bourne stated; ". . . slavery exercises its ruthless despotism over the United States of America. It controls all our congressional legislation."[144]

Ironically, in 1841 a flaw in the institution of slavery would be fortuitously discovered that could conceivably end the scourge of the Gag Rule.

12

Leavitt

The whole nation shares in the disgrace of slavery, in the guilt of introducing and perpetuating it, and in the danger which threatens our free institutions, our national union, and our friendly intercourse with other nations.[145] —Joshua Leavitt

One of the key players involved in the Creole Incident was a bright, but at times caustic, lawyer named Joshua Leavitt. Fiery and impatient, Leavitt viewed himself as altruistic and benevolent, where others sometimes considered him arrogant with a hasty temper.

Born on September 8, 1794, in Heath, Massachusetts, Leavitt grew up to lead a diverse and philanthropic life. He was a graduate of Yale College and Yale Divinity School; the editor, general agent, and corresponding secretary of the American Seamen's Friends Society; a leading radical abolitionist; the publisher of several anti-slavery publications; and a founding member of the American and Foreign Anti-Slavery Society. Leavitt was a driven man.

After graduation from Yale, he set up a successful legal practice in his hometown. In 1823, during the religious revivals that took place in the Burned-Over District, Leavitt returned to Yale to attend classes at the newly established theological seminary. He completed his training after a year and was offered a position at the First Congregational Church in Stratford, Connecticut, where he first began to speak out publicly against slavery.

Initially, the position at Stratford fulfilled Leavitt's ambitions, but within a short period of time he became restless. With the growth of benevolent societies, it was common for young clergymen to look beyond their immediate area for career growth. Such an opportunity presented itself to Leavitt when the American Seamen's Friends Society offered him the secretary and general agent's position. In October of 1828 Leavitt accepted the position and moved his family to New York City.

Although the American Seamen's Friends Society initially had ceased operations due to financial problems, in 1828 it had been revived with the appointment of Smith Thompson to its presidency. An associate justice of the Supreme Court and former secretary of the navy, Thompson served as president of the society until 1831. With Thompson's association, the society received a minimum of funding that sustained the organization. Leavitt's appointment brought youth and a fiery idealism that guaranteed a continuance.

Shortly after joining the society, Leavitt became the editor in chief of *The Sailor's Magazine* and sat on the executive committee of the society. These positions not only introduced Leavitt to the world of benevolent societies, but to seafaring and commerce. His position took him on speaking tours throughout the Northeast and as far south as Richmond and Norfolk, where he was required to address clerical conventions, meet with contributors, and attend gatherings of other benevolent groups. Along with these duties it was also common to see Leavitt and Lewis Tappan, a life director of the American Seamen's Friend Society, spending several hours each week distributing tracts and Bibles to sailors along the wharves of New York City. These outings gave opportunity for Leavitt to establish a familiarity with many of the captains and sailors in port.

As well as distributing Bibles, holding temperance meetings, and establishing reformed boardinghouses for sailors, Leavitt considered the placement of Seaman's chaplains in foreign ports to be as important as his domestic activities, and made it a leading goal of the society. This and his other responsibilities within the society gave Leavitt a broad understanding of maritime operations and greatly expanded his contacts with merchant seamen around the world.

Leavitt's legal background proved to be an asset. Conversely, the work within the ASFS presented Leavitt with opportunities to become familiar with a broad spectrum of maritime law and legal issues, from naval regulations, interstate commerce, and shipping to jurisdictions with regard to crimes committed on the high seas. Along with the variety of contacts that included the common sailor, captains, and shippers, Leavitt also became familiar with many established politicians in government.

In 1830, Leavitt visited Washington on behalf of the American Seamen's Friend Society where he attended meetings with President Jackson and met with several legislators and high-ranking naval officers. The society fought for and won the repeal of the grog or rum ration on all United States naval vessels. Suffice to say, these encounters greatly broadened his experience, understanding, and perception of maritime law, as well as the give and take of Washington government and politics.

Another major advantage to his association with the American Seamen's Friend Society was the opportunity to become acquainted with the intercoastal shipping of slaves. His familiarity with the interstate commerce of humanity, the seasonal aspect of the trade from the Chesapeake Bay ports to the markets in New Orleans, and the particular type of ships used in this trade was extensive and thorough. In January of 1834, Leavitt had occasion to visit the slave trading facilities of Franklin and Armfield, located in Alexandria, Virginia. There he was given an extensive tour of the auction house, pens, and docks, and was informed by one of the principals of the business about the number of slaves carried from the district last year and the expectations for an increase in trade in the new year. Leavitt noted that Franklin and Armfield expected to ship between eleven and twelve thousand slaves in the coming year.

Leavitt was then given a tour of the type of vessel owned by Franklin and Armfield that was presently employed in the carrying of slaves to New Orleans during the season.[146] Leavitt wrote about his firsthand look at these ships.

> The Captain of Franklin and Armfield's *Tribune* [a brig, as was the *Creole*. a.n.] . . . very obligingly took me to all parts of the vessel. The hold was appropriated to the slaves, and is divided into two compartments. The after-hold will carry about eighty women, and the other about one hundred men. On either side [of the hold] were two platforms running the whole length; one raised a few inches, and the other half way up the deck. They were about five or six feet deep. On these the slaves lie, as close as they can be stowed.[147]

He was told that it was not uncommon to let the slaves up on deck during the day for exercise on the voyage South, but at night or during stormy periods they were kept chained and locked in the holds. During the voyage, the slaves were well fed, so as to give a sellable appearance upon their arrival at the slave markets of New Orleans.

Leavitt's knowledge of the routine of the intercoastal slave ships, segregation of male and female slaves in separate holds, supplying of ships on their passage from Chesapeake ports to New Orleans, the route and the assorted other duties of the crews would prove to be invaluable. He also learned about the threats and dangers associated with shipping slaves on board the intercoastal slavers.

While visiting the slave center, the recent case of the brig *Comet* was discussed. The *Comet* had been carrying 160 slaves bound for the slave markets of New Orleans. Leavitt was informed that the ship, owned by Franklin and Armfield, had gone aground in 1831 at Abaco Island, part of the Bahamas chain governed by the British. The island was a logical and convenient stop where fresh water could be secured on the way to New Orleans.

Of particular note to Leavitt were actions taken by the colonial government. The British colonial authorities had allowed the slaves to go free, although English colonies had yet to emancipate their own slaves. It would not be until 1834 that England would no longer recognize slavery in their colonies and have a general emancipation.

It was also during the tour that Leavitt was made aware of the threat of revolt by slaves while in passage to New Orleans and of measures taken to secure the cargo while in passage. The possibility of revolt was not that uncommon. An ex-slaver, Nathan Ross, who was familiar with Leavitt, reported the following incident in 1830:

> The schooner *Lafayette*, with a cargo of slaves from Norfolk, Virginia, for New Orleans, narrowly escaped being captured by them on the voyage. They were subdued after a considerable difficulty, and twenty-one of them were bolted down to the deck, until the arrival of the vessel at New Orleans.[148]

Leavitt's accumulated knowledge of seafaring and the business of commerce while a member of the Seaman's Society gave him a unique insight into the legalities of the intercoastal slave trade. For example, the concept of territorial law superseded by international law and state law superseded by federal law on the high seas and their relationship with interstate commerce. Leavitt applied this knowledge deftly against the intercoastal slave trade. In a speech before the British and Foreign Anti-Slavery Society, only a few months after the Creole Incident, Leavitt said: "As he understood the principle of general law, it was this- that the law of slavery is confined in its force to the territorial jurisdiction of the state which establishes it."[149]

It was during his time at the American Seaman's Friend Society that Leavitt became drawn into the debate over slavery. His tenure with the society gave him opportunities to become acquainted with other preachers who had evolved out of the Burned-Over District and moved to New York to pursue their individual calling.

In 1829, Leavitt, Lewis, and Arthur Tappan, in association with Charles Finney, founded the First Free Presbyterian Church, which was open to all classes of people. The desire to spread the revival and to convert the city to God led to the next step, the establishment of the *Evangelist*, a paper dedicated to spreading the concepts of benevolence. By December of 1831 Leavitt had assumed full editorial responsibilities of the paper and was closely associated with the Tappans and Finney.

Leavitt and other religious reformers believed their mission in life was to cleanse the nation of sin, and the greatest sin the nation faced was the scourge of slavery. At first, Leavitt sought to rectify the slavery question by adopting the colonization scheme. As noted earlier, not all agreed with the idea of colonization. Elizur Wright, Beriah Green, Theodore Weld and George Bourne were the leading voices against colonization and preached a doctrine of immediatism.

Theodore Weld wrote his feelings and thoughts on immediate emancipation in his treatise *American Slavery as it Is*.

> Emancipation would be safe. I have had eleven winters to learn the disposition of the slaves, and am satisfied that they would peaceably and cheerfully work for pay. Give them education, equal and just laws, and they will become a most interesting people. Oh, let a cry be raised which shall awaken the conscience of this guilty nation, to demand for the slaves immediate and unconditional emancipation.[150]

By the summer of 1833, Leavitt had reached the same conclusion. He was now convinced that the total abolition of slavery was the primary agenda for Christians. Further, he no longer found solace in a purely religious approach toward ending this national curse. He came to the realization that if total abolition were to be accomplished, the means to bring about the end of slavery would have to be accomplished through an active role in secular matters.

By the end of the decade, Leavitt left no doubt that the focus needed to achieve this goal must be directed in the halls of governance. In a letter to Myron Holley on July 12, 1839, Leavitt clearly stated his intentions. "We want to set forth the issue and evil of slavery, its character as a political apostasy, its arrogance, usurpation, continued encroachment, danger, etc. Also the duty of American citizens to meet it in the very citadel of power, vis., in politics. I am convinced its peculiar power is here, rather than in the church, i.e., it is resistless in the church because it is resistless in the State. We are eminently a political people."[151]

One of the major inspirations for Leavitt's conversion to immediate emancipation was based on recent developments in England. In 1833, Parliament passed the Emancipation Act, which ended slavery in the British Empire effective August 1, 1834. Much of the struggle to bring about this change was due to the efforts of the British and Foreign Anti-Slavery Society. With the coming abolition of slavery in the British West Indies by act of Parliament, those in the States were inspired to form their own anti-slavery societies.

"Let us imitate our British brethren and open the flood gates of light on this dark subject," one abolitionist journal demanded.

John Quincy Adams testified to this fact with observations noted in his diary, Aug. 11, 1835: "There is a great fermentation upon this subject of slavery at this time in all parts of the Union. The emancipation of the slaves in the British West Indies Colonies; the Colonization Society here; the current of public opinion running everywhere stronger and stronger into democracy and popular supremacy contribute all to shake the fetters of servitude."[152]

The abolition movement triggered a strong response from the South, as well as negative reactions by many Northern business and political leaders based on a combination of racism and economic ties with the South. Incidents and threats against abolitionist societies increased as the rift over slavery came to the forefront in American communities. The first general meeting of the American Anti-Slavery Society was met with hostility. The location of the meeting was New York City, the leading American port for cotton exports. Not only did New York merchants and businessmen view abolitionist activity as a threat to their livelihood, but the common workers in New York also condemned any talk of emancipation based on a belief that emancipation would bring a flood of cheap labor that would threaten their own jobs. On October 2, 1833, the original location of the meeting, Clinton Hall, was changed to Chatham Street Chapel due to an apprehension of mob violence incited by Tammany Hall, the Democratic party organization that had influence in City Hall through patronage, graft and gangs that enforced Democratic Party prerogatives. New York City was the commercial center for the cotton trade and the idea of the abolition of slavery was deemed as a threat to cotton commerce and profit.

The American Anti-Slavery Society met again in Philadelphia on December of 1833 where it formed the leadership of the society headed by William Lloyd Garrison. Leavitt was appointed to its executive committee along with Elizur Wright; Peter Williams; Theodore S. Wright; Samuel Cornish; William Goodell, editor of the *Genius of Temperance*; Dension of *The Emancipator*; and the Reverend George Bourne.

At an 1834 meeting of the society, William Lloyd Garrison and his fellow abolitionists were threatened with mob violence by plug-uglies[153] in New York City. It was George Bourne who held the mob at bay while Garrison and the others safely escaped. The bravery displayed by Bourne at that meeting secured for him a reputation as a man with calm nerves and strong character.

When Elijah P. Lovejoy was murdered in Alton, Illinois in 1837 for publishing anti-slavery materials, many in the anti-slavery movement could no longer rely on simple reason or the power of prayer to achieve their goals. Some began to agitate for a radical approach.

Within the society a rift occurred between the followers of William Lloyd Garrison and those members led by the Tappans, who took a more strident stance that called for an involvement in the political process to achieve the end of slavery. In May of 1840, at the annual meeting of the American Anti-Slavery Society, held in New York City, it became apparent that the ongoing feud with Garrison and his adherents over the direction of the abolition movement would not be resolved. Earlier in the meeting, several of Leavitt's closest associates, along with three hundred other abolitionists, walked out over issues of a political, versus a church-oriented approach toward abolition and the role of women in the American Anti-Slavery Society. Leavitt decided to stay at the meeting as a member of the executive committee with the hope of resolving differences. However, after a series of votes that ended up voting him off the committee, Leavitt left the hall and the society.

Leavitt could no longer compromise his approach to abolition. He concluded that William Lloyd Garrison's cautious, religious approach toward ending slavery was no longer viable.

Henry Mayer concisely relates this fact in his book, *All on Fire: William Lloyd Garrison and the Abolition of Slavery*.

> For Garrison, politics had to be understood in a moral framework, and the abolition movement had to remain a religious enterprise that opened hearts to the imperatives of Christian love.[154]

That May, after the walkout from the American Anti-Slavery Society, Leavitt, the Tappan brothers, James G Birney, Elizur Wright, the Reverend Henry Highland Garnet, and the Reverend George Bourne, along with several other radical abolitionists, met and formed the American and Foreign Anti-Slavery Society. In direct variance with the outmoded anarchy and political abstention of William Lloyd Garrison and his followers, the newly formed American and Foreign Anti-Slavery Society (AFASS) quickly became a radically politicized organization. They would stop at nothing short of total abolition and attempted to persuade, intimidate, exhort, convince, coerce, and cajole those in power to fall in step with their radical views.

Leavitt became the editor of *The Emancipator*, the official publication of the newly formed American and Foreign Anti-Slavery Society, and proclaimed for immediate emancipation no matter the cost. He lectured, chided, and harangued those in Congress who were opposed to slavery to forgo all other agendas—except the agenda of total abolition. "There is no object but slavery that can serve our turn . . . It is the dictate of sound wisdom to make opposition to slavery the leading object of public policy."[155]

One example of this radical rhetoric came from the Reverend George Bourne, who strongly attacked those in public office who deviated from the path of immediate emancipation, and even suggested that voters who elected such officials were just as responsible. "Every voter for public office who will not destroy the system, is as culpable as if he participated in the evil, and is responsible for the protraction of the crime . . ."[156]

The politicized approach toward total emancipation excited those of like mind and attracted new alliances with other societies. The newly formed society quickly established strong ties with its English counterpart, the British and Foreign Anti-Slavery Society. By 1840, the American and English societies had come together on a series of issues that were dedicated to ending slavery. Joseph Sturge, leader of the British and Foreign Anti-Slavery Society, traveled to the United States in 1840 with the intended purpose to ". . . promote an entire unity of action and co-operation between the British and Foreign Anti-Slavery Society and the American and Foreign Anti-Slavery Society."[157]

One of the concerns of the American and English anti-slavery societies involved the illegal transportation of slaves from Africa into the markets of the Caribbean. Sturge became familiar with the Caribbean region during a tour of the West Indies in 1836-1837. Over seven months, he and several other members of the British Anti-Slavery Society observed and reported on the conditions of the newly freed slaves within the British Empire.[158]

England had not only abolished slavery in its colonies, it had outlawed the importation of slaves from Africa to the New World as early as 1807, and in 1808 the United States followed suit. England then negotiated treaties with several countries about the right to search upon the high seas for contraband (slaves). John Quincy Adams signed such a treaty in 1824, when he was Secretary of State in the Monroe administration, but the Senate rejected the treaty. The Southern members of Congress were particularly sensitive to any infringement on the jurisdiction and continuation of slavery, particularly when the threat came from a foreign power.

However, the prohibition of the importation of slaves from Africa became law in March of 1807 with the passage of the "Act to Prohibit the Importation of Slaves into any Port or Place Within the Jurisdiction of the United States, From and After the First Day of January, in the Year of Our Lord One Thousand Eight Hundred and Eight."

The United States further increased pressure on those who were found to be involved in the illegal slave trade by making it a crime of piracy to participate in the importation of slaves from Africa. In May of 1820, during the Monroe administration, Congress amended an existing federal statute against piracy. The amended Act now declared:

> And be it further enacted, That if any citizen of the United States, being of the crew or ship's company of any foreign ship or vessel engaged in the slave trade, or any person whatever, being of the crew or ship's company of any ship or vessel, owned in the whole or part, or navigated for, or in behalf of, any citizen or citizens of the United States, shall land, from any such ship

or vessel, and, on any foreign shore, seize any negro or mulatto, not held to service or labour by the laws of either of the states or territories of the United States, with intent to make such negro or mulatto a slave, or shall decoy, or forcibly bring or carry, or shall receive, such negro or mulatto on board any such ship or vessel, with intent as aforesaid, such citizen or person shall be adjudged a pirate; and, on conviction thereof before the circuit court of the United States for the district wherein he may be brought or found, shall suffer death..[159]

However, enforcement of the statute lagged and it wasn't until 1862 that the United States brought to trial Captain Nathaniel Gordon of Portland, Maine for the illegal importation of slaves from Africa. He was found guilty and hanged.

The American and British societies were also concerned with the possible dissemination of slavery on the North American continent, in particular, the westward migration of slavery into the newly formed Republic of Texas. The two anti-slavery societies realized Texas could remain an independent republic or—a more likely scenario—become part of the United States. The concern shared by both societies was the possibility of Texas being admitted into the Union as several slave states, which would proportionately increase the number of Congressional representatives from the area.

To date, a balance of free versus slave states had been maintained based on a series of compromises forged in Congress. With the expected admittance of Texas as several slave states, without a counterbalance of free states, the status quo would quickly collapse and favor the South. Based on the three-fifths clause in the Constitution at that time, the South stood to obtain a commanding number of new representatives who would strongly advocate for slavery.

As early as 1833, Adams stated that the conditions of representation of the Southern states with regard to the three-fifths vote of the number of slaves, gave "the entire control of the national policy, and, almost without exception, the possession of the highest executive office of the Union . . ." to the South.

Now, with the Gag Rule in place, the ability to debate the status of a state's admittance to the Union as either free or slave favored the South, since the subject of slavery was no longer allowed to be petitioned. To further solidify their position, in 1840 Southern members of the House adopted the strongest Gag to date:

> Resolved, That no petition, memorial, resolution, or other paper praying the abolition of slavery in the District of Columbia, or any State or Territory [emphasis added], or the slave trade between the States or Territories of the United States in which it now exists, shall be received by this House, or entertained in any way whatever.

Referred to as Rule 21, this gag rule acted to control the debate about the status of new territories being considered for statehood. If successful, states created from territories where slavery already existed would precipitate a preponderance of Southern representation in both houses of Congress, giving Southern slaveholders total legislative control. This, in turn, would secure for the

South the needed votes to legislate slavery into the Constitution of the United States.

Those in Congress who opposed any reinterpretation of the Constitution understood the position they would be in if this came to pass. The unchecked growth of Southern representation in Congress would not only commit the United States to an agrarian-based economy, but would threaten the continued existence of the United States as a free, democratic union.

The immediate goal of abolitionists on both sides of the Atlantic became obvious—a way must be found to allow petitions on slavery to be accepted in the House and Senate—in particular, those that sought the abolition of slavery in federally controlled territories. This would stop the threatened takeover by Southern Representatives and begin a reversal of fortunes that favored the North. A precedent had to be found that would override the gag. The challenge was to formulate a legal precedent to establish some form of federal authority over the disposition of an enslaved person, while at the same time, not recognize the institution of slavery to exist under federal jurisdiction. If federal jurisprudence could be established over any aspect of slavery, a legal precedent would then exist that would allow the subject of slavery to be again discussed and debated in the federal House and Senate. If this could be accomplished, the Gag Rule would, for all intents and purposes, would cease to exist.

Leavitt and Adams understood that slavery, being an abridgment of the natural rights of man, can exist only by force of positive municipal law and is necessarily confined to the territorial jurisdiction of the power that created it.[160] The two different interpretations of law, one being positive law and the other natural law, can co-exist at the same instance. Consider the basis for equal justice under the law, wherein one is given the tenant "that all men are created equal, that they are endowed by their Creator with certain unalienable rights, that among these are life, liberty and the pursuit of happiness." Although this is a declaration rather than a statutory law, a law created by legislation, referring to Parliament, or law imposed by the state, the ideas expressed in natural law form the basis for all law and are thus anterior and superior to positive law. For example, the 13th amendment to the United States Constitution, making slavery illegal, is a positive law that is based on the natural law that states, "all men are created equal."

With regard to the situation facing the nation, slavery was an imposed positive law created by legislation in certain states and municipalities. It was reasoned that the federal government did not recognize the institution of slavery, and in turn did not condone its existence in circumstances under the jurisdictions of federal control.

As in the case of the District of Columbia, if it was decided that slavery existed under the jurisdiction of federal law, it would greatly facilitate the argument for it being constitutionally accepted and protected. This fact alone would solidify Southern dominance of the government and would for all intents and purposes be a *fait accompli* concerning the planters' agenda to restore and reform the Constitution into an image that reflected an agricultural slave society.

At the same time, there was reluctance on the part of many in government to attack slavery in the District. The apprehension was based on the unknown aspect as to the outcome over the question of slavery in the District of Columbia. Both North and South were tentative in bringing the issue to a vote.

Adams set forth his reasoning for avoiding a showdown in the District by describing "stirring up ill blood between the Northern and Southern sections of the Union."

His reluctance to question emancipation in the District was well founded, since each side of the issue could not be assured that the question would be settled in favor of one side or the other. As for the South, with the Gag Rule in place they could sidestep the issue entirely. This left no other choice but to find an alternative issue that involved slavery under federal rather than state jurisdiction.

In February of 1841, a possible remedy presented itself to Adams and Leavitt.

The Creole Incident

THE BEGINNING OF THE END OF SLAVERY

BOOK IV: ORPHEUS

13

Canada

What are the duties of colored men in these Provinces, who have been forced here from American despotism and oppression? We shall answer this question as frankly and at the same time, as sincere (sic) as we think its importance demands. Well then! we live in a government that knows no caste in its political organization. All men stand on the broad platform of equality before the laws, and are alike cared for by Her Majesty's government. It is as true now as it was when Curran spoke those immortal words. No matter what complexion incompatible with Liberty, an Indian or an African man may have burnt upon him, the moment he sets his foot upon British soil he is free. —Voice of the Fugitive, March 12, 1851

Madison Washington's escape to Canada can be authenticated, to some degree, as to when, where and how it took place. Without a doubt, he made his way north, and was reported to have entered Canada in late 1839. Although there may never be a definitive answer, this suggests he left Virginia sometime after harvest.

Fugitive slaves from the time period and the area of Virginia where Madison was from (the easterly counties adjacent to Richmond) would have made their way north along similar routes. Based on these known routes of the Underground Railroad and on the affidavits and narratives of runaways and conductors at that time, it may be deduced, with a degree of accuracy, what routes and experiences Madison may have encountered.

It has been stated that Madison had contact with Robert Purvis of Philadelphia, Henry Highland Garnet of Troy, New York; and finally, Hiram Wilson of St. Catharines, Canada. This is the same Hiram Wilson who was acquainted with both George Bourne and Joshua Leavitt from his association with the American Anti-Slavery Society.

The location of each of these individuals suggests the particular route north that was commonly used by fugitive slaves and is mentioned in Wilbur H. Siebert's 1899 book, *The Underground Railroa: From Slavery to Freedom.*

Frederick Douglass, who was familiar with this Albany route during the period of his residence in Rochester, describes it as running through Philadelphia, New York, Albany Rochester, and thence to Canada; and he gives the name of the person at each station . . . Hiram Wilson, St. Catharines, Canada. The Rev. Charles B. Ray, a member of the Vigilance Committee of New York City . . . knew a regular route stretching from Washington, by way of Baltimore and Philadelphia, to New York, thence following the Hudson to Albany and Troy, whence a branch ran westward to Utica, Syracuse and Oswego, with an extension from Syracuse to Niagara Falls.[161]

The final leg of this trip found Madison on the American side of the Niagara River in Buffalo, New York. A narrow stretch of land at the foot of Ferry Street and Black Rock Canal, called Broderick Park, was the location of the Black Rock ferry crossing. It was a common gathering spot where fugitive slaves made the final leg of their journey to Canada and freedom.

It was common to attempt the crossing into Canada at night, with the hope of avoiding bounty hunters. Whenever possible, the Black Rock ferry was used, but if bounty hunters were in the area, slaves rowed across to freedom.

Every runaway knew that the moment he or she acted on the desire to be free the potential for capture and return to slavery became a constant threat. Until the fugitive set foot on Canadian soil, the possibility of capture haunted the runaway's every step. There are countless stories from the annals of the Underground Railroad where fugitive slaves were hounded all the way to the Canadian border by bounty hunters, and in many unfortunate cases, caught as they attempted the final step of a long, arduous journey, just short of the border.

The pursuit by bounty hunters was a matter of economics, based on the amount of reward the planter-owner posted for the return of their property. The justification for such an expense went beyond mere financial considerations. The return of fugitive slaves was a strong form of control over the enslaved population of the South. It was important to instill a hopelessness in any who contemplated escape. Not only would the body be broken, but also the spirit. Seeing an individual who had attempted freedom returned to slavery left a lasting impression, and added to the psychological chains that held millions in bondage.

Yet, the river of refuges from slavery continued to flow north. Regardless of the consequences, the opportunity to reach Canada and freedom was the dream of countless generations of those enslaved. It far outweighed the consequences of failure.

On a cold, clear December night in 1839, a group of fugitives prepared to quietly shove off from the icy shore of the Niagara River. Huddled together on the riverbank, shivering from cold with hands tucked deep into pockets, occasionally withdrawn to blow a steamy breath into them, the fugitives stared silently at the opposite shore as if it was a mirage. The reality of traveling this far, while enduring the hardships of escape from the chains of slavery, seemed surreal, as if they might awaken from a dream and find themselves back on a plantation far to the south.

Yet, they knew that on the far side of this river was freedom. The only discernible sound was the crunch of a thin film of ice beneath their feet at the river's edge as they carefully made their way into a waiting skiff. Crowded into the boat, huddled against the cold, they looked around nervously as they awaited the command. If they needed to speak, they did so in whispers.

After what seemed an eternity, the skiff pushed into the river and glided out into the stream. The men sat still as statues, dark figures against the cold night, not daring to row until the current carried them to the middle of the river.

As Madison and the others drifted in the river's current, their fears began to disappear as one shore slipped farther away while the opposite shore inched closer. Once the skiff was well clear of the shore, the men set the oars and began to row toward the opposite side, the oars slicing into the cold dark waters. No one spoke; the only sound was the dipping of the oars and the creaking of the oarlocks. They had all crossed so many rivers and streams on their way north that it seemed surrealistic that this river meant the difference between slavery and freedom. Yet, the importance of the moment wasn't lost on those in the skiff. The next dry land on which they would walk, they would walk as free men.

They neared the opposite shore, and the conductor called out in a loud whisper for the men to stop rowing. Although they were some distance above the falls, the current quickly carried them downstream. The escort stood carefully in the skiff and opened a small door on the lantern he was holding, and then, just as quickly, closed it; allowing a brief second of light to escape. From the opposite shore, some fifty yards downstream, another light blinked on and off. The conductor sat down carefully and with an even voice said, "Row, men. Your journey comes to an end."

The men set to rowing with renewed vigor, as the shore of the United States faded while Canada and freedom drew near. As the boat came to the shore, the guide turned toward those in the boats and said, "You are free."

There followed a silence and stillness as those in the skiff sat with anticipation and disbelief that the words "you are free" pertained to them.

When the skiff rode up on the shore, the men splashed onto the land, and lined up facing the river and where they had come from. No one moved as the realization swept over them, that for the first time in their lives they were free men. Some began to smile; some had tears in their eyes. One spoke in the dark: "Thank God almighty, free at last." Then they began to laugh, dance, and cry.

More than likely, Madison and the others were taken to Bertie Hall in Fort Erie, Ontario. Owing to the drift of the current and its location on the Canadian side of the river, Bertie Hall was ideally located for housing fugitives upon their arrival. Their next move probably was to nearby Hamilton, where they spent their first full day of freedom.

As they entered Hamilton on a snowy day, the atmosphere was festive with the Christmas spirit. As falling snow swirled around the newly arrived fugitives, their penniless, ragged, homeless, helpless, hungry, forlorn, and above all, lonely condition was a common sight to residents of Hamilton.

Nonetheless, for the first time in his life, Madison Washington walked down a street as a free man. This one simple act that so many took for granted made the winter night less cold, the hunger less demanding, and added a dignity to his ragged appearance. He was a free man, no longer stalked and hunted, no longer enslaved. Yet, part of him was still in slavery. He could only imagine how Susan would react to being free. How their lives would be changed. The thought of being with his wife where they both would be free brought a smile to Madison's face. At the same time, the reality of Susan back in Virginia intruded upon his reverie with the realization that his quest would never be complete until he could bring his wife to freedom.

Madison stayed at the home of the Reverend Hiram Wilson, the missionary abolitionist who provided assistance to newly arrived fugitive slaves in Canada. Wilson had a settlement in the St. Catharines area of Canada where his ministry aided newly arrived fugitives with food, shelter, and clothing. The church of Reverend Hiram Wilson was established in conjunction with the British and American Manual Labor Institute for colored children. Since 1838, this organization not only schooled children of refugees from slavery; it also aided those recent arrivals with securing shelter and employment. As late as 1855, Wilson aided fugitives on their arrival in Canada as witnessed by the abolitionist Benjamin Drew:

> I have seen the negro—the fugitive slave, wearied with his thousand miles of traveling by night, without suitable shelter, meanwhile for rest by day, who had trodden the roughest and most unfrequented ways, fearing, with too much cause, an enemy in every human being who had crossed his path; I have seen such arrive at Mr. Wilson's, bringing with him the subdued look, the air of sufferance, the furtive glance bespeaking dread, and deprecating punishment; I have seen such waited on by Mr. and Mrs. Wilson, fed and clothed, and cheered, and cared for. Such ministrations give a title to true greatness, a title recognized by Divine wisdom, and deriving its authority from revelation itself; "Whosoever would be great among you let him be your minister."[162]

Well known and active in anti-slavery societies, Wilson had a wide range of contacts within the societies. Joseph John Gurney, a member of the British and Foreign Anti-Slavery Society, toured the United States and Canada in 1839 and spoke of Wilson and his work in Canada:

> At Toronto I was glad to form the acquaintance with Hiram Wilson, the excellent agent of the American Anti-Slavery Society, who was watching over the interests of the negroes in Canada. About one hundred slaves per month were at that time making their escape into this land of freedom. It gave me pleasure to aid him in promoting the formation of schools for the Christian education of their children.[163]

Further, Wilson was an associate of Charles Finney, who was instrumental in helping Wilson establish the British and American Manual Labor Institute for colored children in St. Catharines. The networking between abolitionists was not isolated amongst a few regional societies. On the contrary, anti-slavery societies worked closely together over vast distances. In May of 1839, at the annual meeting of the American Anti-Slavery Society, of which Hiram Wilson was a member, it was resolved, ". . . that George Bourne, Charles W. Denison, Wm. Lloyd Garrison, . . . and Hiram Wilson, be a committee to declare a Declaration, which shall announce the judgment of the American Anti-Slavery Society, concerning the common error that our enterprise is a POLITACAL [sic], and not a religious character."[164]

This established Wilson's involvement in the American Anti-Slavery Society and his close acquaintance with the Reverend George Bourne. It also reveals Wilson's and Bourne's propensity toward a political means, rather than a religious path, to end slavery.

Coincidently, a fellow abolitionist from the St. Catharines area where Wilson lived was the Reverend Pelham Stanhope Aldrich. In March of 1841, Reverend Aldrich left Canada and traveled to Nassau, Bahamas, to work side-by-side with Reverend Poole, the company chaplain at the garrison of Nassau. Whether by design or coincidence, both Poole and Aldrich would play a crucial role in the Creole Incident.

The weeks following Madison's arrival in Canada were occupied with getting settled in a new land. Wilson aided Madison in securing work, and in so doing became acquainted with Madison and his capabilities. Many of the ex-slaves, being adept farmers from their years of labor on plantations, found ample employment on the farms of eastern Canada. With the aid of Wilson, Madison found shelter and employment on the farm of a Mr. Dickson. For over a year he labored on the farm and in the logging industry.

> He traveled only in the night, and by careful management, after a good deal of hardship, he reached the Northern States and passed into Canada. There he let himself out to work on the farm of a man named Dickson.[165]
> —L Maria Child

Once employed, Madison wasted little time in implementing his plan to raise the needed funds to buy his wife out of slavery. However, there is no record of Madison's further involvement in the Underground Railroad or abolition societies after his arrival in Canada. But it was not uncommon for abolitionists to recruit newly freed slaves for speaking tours that promoted the ideals of emancipation. What better way to show equality and the need for emancipation than to showcase an individual who was bright, articulate and a former slave.

One well-known example of this was another former slave who sought freedom in the north, Frederick Douglass. Douglass's escape from slavery in Baltimore on September 3, 1839, the same time as Madison Washington, is chronicled in his book *Narrative of the Life of Frederick Douglass*, published in 1845. The experiences Douglass relates in his book were not uncommon to those escaping slavery. Douglass went on to become an abolitionist and a popular speaker on the abolitionists' speaking tours and at anti-slavery conventions. After the Creole Incident, on more than one occasion, he spoke of Madison Washington and his heroic exploits, and even wrote a fictional account of Madison's odyssey titled *The Heroic Slave.*

But such praise was yet to come. During Madison's stay in Canada, his future was unsettled and uncertain. The distance and time away from Virginia and Susan left Madison with a troubled heart. He longed for any word or correspondence from Susan. It was not uncommon to send and receive a letter or message along the Underground Railroad. Although the vast majority of those in slavery were not schooled in reading or writing, letters were sent, both north and south. Archived and accessible, these poignant letters are a portal into that harrowing time.

As the days turned to weeks, then months and then a year, a discontent came over Madison. The time and money needed to secure his wife's freedom did not seem to be any closer to reality than the day he first arrived in Canada. As his second winter in Canada began to slowly fade, the coming spring brought on a restlessness as the memory of the woman he had left behind continued to haunt him.

In the spring of 1841, Madison reached a fateful decision. He believed that if he were to ever see Susan again, he would have to return South and attempt to rescue her. Dickson tried to dissuade Madison, and found reasons to postpone the departure one more week, one more day. As spring wore into summer, Madison plotted his return to Virginia. He had been in contact with Hiram Wilson and word was making its way south along the Underground Railroad that Madison Washington was returning to Old Dominion to rescue his wife.

In a letter written by a fugitive slave in Canada, the heartfelt desire to be reunited with his wife speaks to the exact situation Madison faced in the spring of 1841.

Toronto, May 7, 1854

Mr. W. Still

Dear Sir—I take this opportunity of writing you these few lines and hope when they reach you they will find you well, I would have written you before, but I was waiting to hear from my friend, Mr. Brown. I judge his business has been of importance as the occasion why he has not written before. Dear sir, nothing would have prevented me from writing, in a case of this kind, except death.

My soul is vexed, my troubles are inexpressible. I often feel as if I were willing to die. I must see my wife in short, if not, I will die. What would I not give no tongue can utter. Just to gaze on her sweet lips one moment I would be willing to die the next. I am determined to see her some time or other. The thought of being a slave again is miserable. I hope heaven will smile upon me again, before I am one again. I will leave Canada shortly, but I don't name the place that I go, it may be in the bottom of the ocean. If I had known as much before I left, I would never have left until I could have found means to have brought her with me. You have never suffered from being absent from a wife, as I have. I consider that to be nearly superior to death, and hope you will do all you can for me, and inquire from your friends if nothing can be done for me. Please write to me immediately on receipt of this, and say something that will cheer up my drooping spirits. You will oblige me by seeing Mr. Brown and ask him if he would oblige me by going to Richmond and see my wife, and see what arrangements he could make with her, and I would be willing to pay all his expenses there and back. Please to see both Mr. Bagnel and Mr. Minkins, and ask them if they have seen my wife. I am determined to see her, if I die the next moment. I can say I was once happy, but never will be again, until I see her; because what is freedom to me, when I know that my wife is in slavery? Those persons that you shipped a few weeks ago, remained in St. Catharines, instead of coming over to Toronto. I sent you two letters last week and I hope you will please attend to them. The post-office is shut, so I enclose the money to pay the post, and please write me in haste.

I remain evermore your obedient servant,

I. Forman.[166]

14

Orpheus

*So he resolved again to take no counsel either on the one hand or
the other, but to go back to Virginia and rescue his wife if possible.*
—Frederick Douglas [167]

Like Orpheus, who descended into the netherworld to rescue his wife
Eurydice from eternal damnation, Madison Washington returned to Old
Dominion to lead his wife from the hell of slavery. Considering the
distance traveled, the time of year, and the documented events that followed
Madison's trip south, it may be safe to assume that by the end of August 1841,
Madison left the security of Canada and set out on his fateful journey back to
Virginia.

At each stop along the way, Madison reconnected with agents on the Underground Railroad who had assisted him on his way north in the winter of 1839.
Those who remembered him as a fugitive, escaping the brutality of slavery a
year-and-a-half earlier would barely recognize the man who now stood before
them. A figure of strength and prosperity, freedom had been kind to Madison
Washington. In place of the worn brogan boots wrapped in rags, he now wore
new leather bluchers. His trousers were not worn or patched, and his full-length
greatcoat, referred to as a "bang-up," had all the buttons and the cuffs pressed
and turned back. His diet had improved greatly in Canada, and he no longer had
the famished look of someone who was hunted. His face reflected a vitality and
calmness that reassured all he met. One lasting impression, both going north
and returning south, was his intelligence. Here was an individual that in other
societies and in different circumstances would have been successful in whatever
endeavor he chose.

Dignified, calm, and unaffected features that announced at a glance that
he was one endowed with genius, and created to guide his fellow-men.[168]
—William Wells Brown

The late George Hendrick, along with his wife, Willene Hendrick, in their
book, "*Black Refugees in Canada: Accounts of Escape During the Era of Slavery,*"
write of Madison's stay in Rochester, New York.

As he retraced his route south, it is reported that he stayed in Rochester, New York:

> Washington left Canada in 1841 and headed for Virginia, taking the Underground Railroad in reverse. He arrived at a station in Rochester, New York, operated by Lindley Murray Moore, a Quaker teacher. Moore collected money for him and gave the fugitive $10, suggesting Washington was traveling by public transportation.[169]

His next known stop was in Troy, New York at the home of Henry Highland Garnet. In 1824, Garnet, along with his family, had left Maryland and escaped slavery. Early in his life he had been a merchant sailor and sailed from the Chesapeake ports to the Caribbean, acquainting himself with the same shipping routes used by the intercoastal slave trade. He was highly educated and a graduate of the Oneida Institute. In 1840, along with Joshua Leavitt and the Reverend George Bourne, Garnet was one of the original founding members of the American and Foreign Anti-Slavery Society. A leading abolitionist of African descent, Garnet believed not only in a political means to achieve emancipation, he also strongly advocated for slave rebellions to end slavery, believing a call-to-arms against slavery was the only language the Southern planter understood.

During Madison's stay in Troy, Garnet tried to dissuade him from returning to Virginia. He suggested patience and a return to Canada until a way could be found to bring Madison's wife out of slavery. Frederick Douglas wrote that Madison;". . .arrived in Troy where he met with Garrett [Garnet]; a highly intellectual black man, who admonished [him] not to go, it would be perfectly fruitless."[170]

Once it became obvious that Madison could not be persuaded from his attempt to rescue his wife, one can easily imagine Garnet encouraging Madison to organize other runaways in the area of Virginia to, "strike for liberty, ready for war to the knife and knife to the hilt."[171]

Madison was well aware of the dangers that lay ahead. The very real possibility of capture and being sold farther south could not be ignored. Yet, he remained steadfast in his plan to free his wife—or die trying.

His next reported stop on his way south was in Philadelphia, where he stayed at the home of Robert Purvis. Frederick Douglass spoke of Madison's sojourn at the home of Purvis during an address delivered in New York City several years later. Douglass recalled how Madison would not be deterred by Purvis's entreaties to delay his attempt to rescue his wife.

> He [Madison Washington] went to Virginia, against the entreaties of friends, against the advice of my friend . . . He left Canada to make an effort to save his wife . . . he arrived at Troy where he met with Mr. Garnet . . . He went contrary to the advice of another . . . Robert Purvis was the man: he advised him not to go, and for a time he was inclined to listen to his counsel. He told him it would be of no use for him to go, for that as sure as he went he would only be himself enslaved, and could of course do nothing towards freeing his wife. Under the influence of his counsel he consented not to go;

but when he left the house of Purvis, the thoughts of his wife in Slavery came back to his mind to trouble his peace and disturb his slumbers. So he resolved again to take no counsel either on the one hand or the other, but to go back to Virginia and rescue his wife if possible.[172]

It is noteworthy that in 1841, Robert Purvis commissioned the artist Nathaniel Jocelyn to paint a portrait of Cinque, the leader of the revolt on board *La Amistad*.[173] The painting hung in the study of Purvis home in Philadelphia, and was a subject of discussion between Purvis and Madison. Purvis believed that the portrait and the discussion with Madison regarding the Amistad affair contributed to the revolt on the brig *Creole*.[174]

After Philadelphia, Madison made his way south, retracing the path of his escape north two years earlier. By early October, he found himself in the area of Northern Virginia where he was raised. The familiar woods and surrounding area near the Johnston plantation provided known hideouts where Madison sought refuge. When Madison first escaped he secluded himself in these hiding places, referred to as maroons; small hidden camps which held up to several dozen runaways or as few as two or three. These encampments provide a safe refuge from the patrollers and often times were staging areas for raiding and plundering plantations. Maroons were a constant threat to the planters, undermining their authority as 'master' and were a beacon of hope to runaways. Several large scale uprisings, such as the Nate Turner revolt in 1831, were based out of maroons. Many of the more permanent maroons became integrated with local Indian tribes. The largest of these types of maroons were those associated with the Seminole Indians of Florida and the organized resistance by runaways referred to as 'The Seminole Wars' that persisted until 1865.

These familiar woods of only a few short years ago heightened Madison's desire to be reunited with Susan. He settled in and began to plan the rescue. During the day, he remained concealed in one of the old hideouts. At night he ventured forth, foraging for food. He sat for hours along the side of a road as he acquainted himself with the routine of the patrollers. Considering that his return to the area coincided with selling season, the patrollers would have been frequent, and on heightened alert for runaways.

Although he wanted to rush directly to Susan's cabin, he had been warned by those in the underground just how closely Susan and her cabin were watched. He needed a plan, and a way to get a message to her. The fact that a prize field hand had run away would have been a blow to the bottom line of any plantation. To capture such a slave would not only benefit the bottom line, but reinforce the sway and power of the slave owner over his charges. During selling season, an individual who had the characteristics of a Madison Washington would have brought top dollar at auction in Richmond.

When it came to recapturing a runaway, there were certain methods employed by the planters. The first was for the overseer to release the dogs and begin the hunt. If the desired capture was not accomplished, then the owner would make announcements by placing ads in the personals of local papers.

Local authorities were informed, and supplied with a description of the individual that was missing.

If the slave was valuable, further attempts at his recapture were made. The planter might hire bounty hunters. These hunters of humans became familiar with the terrain and hiding places of fugitive slaves, and were adept at tracking runaways. Unlike Northern farmers, Southern men considered it sport to be avid hunters and horsemen. The culture of the South and its gentleman class lent itself to the pursuit of leisure, augmented with the ability to ride, shoot, and hunt—and were personified as part of the aristocratic sway of the Southern gentry class.

The Southern propensity for horsemanship was evident in the years during the Civil War, when the Southern Confederate cavalry was far superior to its Union counterpart, in large measure due to experience in equestrian pursuits. The Union soldier's experience was limited; relegated to the back end of a large farm horse he followed behind on foot with a plow. The Southern gentlemen's pursuit of an aristocratic lifestyle included dueling, a particularly Southern practice that played a significant role in establishing one's manhood in the face of an insult. It became so prevalent that it was outlawed between members of Congress in the 1830s.

Another peculiar pursuit of Southern gentlemen was the aberrant proclivity they practiced with regard to slave concubines. A mythical belief among Southern men was the interpretation of Negro women as especially passionate. A popular verse commonly found in print in the South expressed an attitude prevalent among white Southern men toward black women:

> *"Next comes a warmer race,*
> *from sable sprung,*
> *to love each other . . . to lust each nerve is strung;*
> *These sooty dames,*
> *well vers'd in Venus's school,*
> *make love an art,*
> *and boast they kiss by rule."*[175]

The stereotype, "these sooty dames," coupled with ownership of property to do with as one pleased, allowed a *carte blanche* attitude of the planter to follow freely his lecherous desires. He excused his actions, proclaiming, "How could a normal male deny himself the pleasures presented by such a sexual being?"

The American historian and professor, Winthrop Donaldson Jordan, in his book, "*The White Man's Burden, Historical Origins of Racism In The United States,*" wrote; "Not only did the black woman's warmth constitute a logical explanation for a white man's infidelity, but, much more important, it helped shift responsibility from himself to her."[176]

These attitudes played a role in the capture and return of runaways. An effective method in apprehending a runaway was to use family and loved ones as a lure. The planter maintained a surveillance of the runaway's family, hoping the fugitive would return to either find food and shelter, or attempt to rescue a loved one from bondage.

In the scant records of Madison's attempt to rescue Susan, all relate the fact that she was in the big house. Considering Susan's age and beauty, and the practice of the planter to use family or loved ones as a lure, accounts of her being in the big house are not out of the realm of reality. When Madison purportedly found Susan in the house, the realization that his wife was being used in such a manner added to his fury and his desire to rescue her.

William Wells Brown, in his book *The Black Man: His Antecedents, Genius, and His Achievements* gives a detailed account of Madison Washington's return to Virginia and his attempt to rescue his wife. Brown tells of Madison hiding during the day and forging at night, and his chance encounter with a group of slaves on their way to a cornhusking. It was from these slaves that Madison learned of Susan's situation at the Johnston plantation.

There is a very similar account of Madison's return south to free his wife in a book written by Lydia Maria Child, *The Freedmen's Book*. In this book, Child also relates how Madison hid out near the Johnston plantation and how, one night, he fell in with slaves going to a corn shucking:

> As they passed up the road he came out from the woods and joined them. There were so many of them that the addition of one more was not noticed. He found that they were slaves from several plantations who had permits from their masters to go to a corn shucking.[177]

As to the details of these events as they relate to Madison Washington, we know little as to the sources. William Wells Brown lived at the time of Madison and would have been privy to such stories and would have known many a fugitive who had returned south to make just such an attempt to free a loved one from bondage. Brown's depiction places Susan in the big house. When Madison attempted to escape with her, he was discovered and a struggle ensued:

> Fearful that if he waited until a late hour Susan would be asleep, and in awakening her she would in her fright alarm the household, Madison ventured to her room too early in the evening, before the whites in the "great house" had retired. Observed by the overseer, a sufficient number of whites were called in, and the fugitive secured ere he could escape with his wife; but the heroic slave did not yield until he with a club had laid three of his assailants upon the ground with his manly blows; and not then until weakened by loss of blood. Madison was at once taken to Richmond, and sold to a slave trader, then making up a gang of slaves for the New Orleans market.[178]

Lydia Maria Child's telling of that night is similar to Brown's. Child's information with regard to Madison could have been derived principally through her participation with the Underground Railroad and her position on the American Anti-Slavery Society's executive board. Her acquaintances with both Bourne and Leavitt, who played a significant role in the Creole Incident, may have provided her with primary source material on the story of Madison Washington. In her retelling, Madison found Susan in the big house, asleep:

He was afraid to tap at her window, after all the people in the Great House were abed and asleep, for, as she supposed he was in Canada he thought she might be frightened and call somebody. He therefore ventured to approach her room in the evening. Unfortunately, the overseer saw him and called a number of whites who rushed into the room just as he entered it. He fought hard and knocked down three of them in his efforts to escape. But they struck at him with their bowie knives till he was so faint with loss of blood that he could resist no longer. They chained him and carried him to Richmond where he was placed in the jail.[179]

These depictions are so similar, they could have been written by the same person. Brown published his account in 1863 and Child's published in 1866. It is plausible that Child borrowed heavily from Brown, to the point of plagiarizing, especially since there is an absence of annotation of source material and research.

However, what was there to gain? The published dates, 1863 and 1866, are at a time when slavery was either on its deathbed, or deceased. Romanticizing the plight of the heroic slave was a moot point, due to the fact that the institution of slavery was dying an agonizing death.

Regardless, the indisputable fact is that, in the fall of 1841, Madison Washington left Canada and returned to Virginia with the expressed intention to rescue his wife from slavery. While attempting the rescue, he was caught, sold to speculators, sent to Richmond, and auctioned to a trader in the intercoastal slave trade.

His fate was now in the hands of providence—and a radical group of abolitionists.

15

Lumpkin's

See the wives and husbands sold apart,
their children's screams will break my heart,
There's a better day a coming
will you go along with me,
there's a better day a coming
Go sound the jubilee
—Sung by slaves sold south to the New Orleans market.

Eastern Maryland and Northern Virginia were in the middle of an Indian summer in the autumn of 1841. The days were lazy and hot as the distant hills shimmered in the midday sun. For several weeks throughout the area, speculators were busy conducting their business of making rounds, doing their buying, and forming up coffles[180] to be marched to the slave markets of Richmond.

For those who witnessed the approach of such a procession, a cloud of dust was first discernible, kicked up by chained feet tramping down back-country roads. The procession lacked any spirit; an aimless shuffling gait moved this body of humanity to its destination. As it slowly meandered along, music drifted on the lifeless air as it accompanied the sad parade, a fiddle and tambourine attempting to convey a festive air inside the column of chained slaves. Instead, it only added a surreal aspect to the trudging coffle. The clank of the chains and occasional snap of the whip mixed with the cadence of the music suggested more of a funeral march.

Approximately fifty men, women, and children, young and old, were strung together, all moving as one. Their ragged clothes coated in dust, dampened with their exertions, their faces streaked with the mixture of dust and sweat. From the shaded porches of estates, from taverns along the way, and the fields of small tobacco farms, people stopped for a brief moment to stare at the procession of wretched souls passing by, their escorts half asleep on their mounts on either side of the column, jerking awake every so often as they yelled commands to "look lively there, keep up," followed by the crack of the whip.

As a slave collecting and reselling center, Richmond, Virginia, and the Chesapeake ports were indelibly linked with the New Orleans and Louisiana slave markets. Shockoe Bottom in Ricmond provided a convenient, systematic means of purchasing slaves from an abundant and easily accessible stock. Its primary function was to supply labor to the expanding cotton regions, and to resupply labor for the sugar-growing regions of the South. Richard Follett, Deputy Pro Vice Chancellor and Associate Vice President at the University of Sussex and a professor of American slavery eludes to this aspect of Louisiana sugar planta-tions in his book *The Sugar Masters.*

> Extreme work and undernutrition taxed the bondswoman throughout most of the year, while disease and death eroded the adult slave population further. Despite importing thousands of slaves a year to the sugar region, Louisiana was unique among the slave states in having a natural decrease in its population.[181]

Although conditions related to sugar production were difficult on their own, the added effect of brutality inflicted by the sugar masters significantly added to the death rate:

> When other slaves failed to measure up to the incessant pace of work, planters beat and occasionally tortured them. Daffney Johnson, for instance, recalls that slaves were stripped to the waist before cats were released to claw and scratch 'de blood out of our backs.' Others had their ears cropped and faced brutal disfigurement.[182]

Another contributing factor that fueled demand was the practice of the owners to "work off" their labor. As noted earlier, rather than adequately nourish, house, and care for the slaves in the sugar cane fields, it was economi-cally more feasible to work off, or more concisely, work to death, one's labor and replenish it with new labor.

By the 1840s, the slave markets of Richmond flourished to accommodate the growing demand for labor in the sugar fields. Richmond was home to a large number of speculators, traders, and auctioneering firms that catered to the intercoastal slave trade: Hodges Ray & Pulliam, R. H. Dickinson and Brothers, Johnson and Apperson, and Sidnum Grady were a few of the major firms. Regarded as respectable, established businesses, many leaders of these concerns held prominent positions in the community.

The business of buying and selling humans operated in an efficient and profitable manner, similar to present day commodity markets. The process had an established routine, practiced with a callous efficiency. Profit, production, and the accumulation of wealth were the main considerations, evident in the numbers associated with the trade. For example, in 1840 the sale of slaves to the intercoastal slave trade was equivalent to twenty percent of the staple-crop production in the region, the money exchanged in Richmond alone was $6.24 million.

Speculators went to individual plantations in the area, and advised clients when to hold slaves until a more advantageous price could be made at auction.

Then, right before buying season, they distributed fliers that specified the type of labor for which they were in the market, and when they would be in the area for buying. A typical flier advertised, "NEGROES suited to the New Orleans market."

After harvest, and in the spring, speculators fanned out over the counties of northern Virginia to begin the process of buying and herding slave coffles back to Richmond. As the slaves arrived in Richmond from the outlying countryside, speculators placed them in depots prior to being sold to long-distance traders. A large number of traders, like J.J. Toler, who purchased in the surrounding counties of Richmond, did not have depots of their own. They relied on specialists in "Negro accommodation," who provided lodging for the slaves. These accommodations, which were nothing more than jails or holding pens, were commonly referred to as "barracoons."

Bob Lumpkin, known as the "bully trader," ran the most infamous barracoon in Richmond. It was commonly referred to as "Lumpkin's slave jail," or "the devil's half acre" and was located on Birch Street between Franklin and Broad in Richmond's Shockoe Bottom. Prior to the fall of Richmond to the Union Army in April of 1865, Bob Lumpkin, still in business, tried to escape the capital of the Confederacy with over fifty slaves chained together. He failed in his attempt to board a Confederate supply train, and returned to his barracoon to await the arrival of Union soldiers. After the fall of Richmond, Lumpkin's devil's half acre became a school for liberated African-Americans. This eventually evolved into Virginia Union University, a school that still promises a limitless future.

But in 1841, the business of Lumpkin's was the buying and selling of slaves.

> The barracoon was centered upon a large court. On one side of the court was . . . a large open tank for washing . . . Opposite was a long, two-story brick house, the lower part fitted up for men and the second story for women. The place, in fact, was a kind of hotel or boardinghouse for Negro traders and their slaves. I was invited to dine at a large table with perhaps twenty traders, who gave me almost no attention, and there was little conversation. They were probably strangers to one another.[183] —A description of Lumpkin's from a visiting Northerner, Otis Bigelow, 1850

During the season, Shockoe Bottom was a beehive of activity with buyers and sellers actively pursuing their business in human bondage. The recent construction of the new Exchange Hotel, with its bay windows set in a brick edifice separated by ionic columns, was often fully booked with traders from New Orleans and the cotton regions of the deep South. The arrival of another coffle stirred little notice, other than an occasional glance from a perspective buyer, as the coffle passed on its way to Lumpkins, a few blocks away on Franklin Street. The coffle next passed Bell Tavern, the main auction house in Richmond, across the street from Lumpkin's.

Madison Washington's coffle probably arrived at Lumpkin's in mid-October of 1841—fatigued, dirty, and dispirited. Regardless of their condition, they soon improved in their looks. The goal was to present slaves in the best condition so as to command the highest price at auction. Upon arrival, they were set into a general routine, beginning each morning with a washing, then hair combed, and faces shaved. The pulling of gray hairs, and the dying of hair on those who were too gray to be plucked without making them look bald were part of the process of preparation for auction. After the grooming, slaves were fed a breakfast of bread, bacon, and coffee. It was mandatory that each slave receive an ample amount to plump them up so as to give a healthy, sleek appearance.

Slaves were also dressed in a particular uniform. The male slave's uniform consisted of a fashionably shaped black, fur hat; a roundabout that was a short, close-fitting jacket; and trousers of coarse corduroy velvet of the type worn by Irish laborers. The women were dressed in neat calico frocks, white aprons, and caps or fancy kerchiefs tied around their heads.

The demand for this specialized clothing supported a small cottage industry of tailors and clothiers in Richmond. The tailor Lewis B. Levy, located at 4 Wall Street below the City Hotel (Bell Tavern), the major slave auction site, ran the following add:

LEWIS B. LEVY, No. 4 WALL STREET, RICHMOND, VA
Under the City Hotel,
Manufacture of all kinds of
SERVANT CLOTHES
Persons bringing their servants to the city for hire or
sale, can be supplied on reasonable terms.
References: R. H. Dickinson & Bro.,
N. B. & C. B. Hill,
Pullman & Slade,
Benjamin Davis.[184]

At the time of Madison's incarceration there was a mulatto assistant named Eddie who worked at Lumpkin's. His job was to instruct the slaves on how to show themselves for buyers. He commanded the slaves to line up: males on the right side of the court, females extending along the left. The slaves were then formed into companies, according to size. Those who were nearly the same height and build were put into separate lots. Men, woman, and children of both sexes were divided and separated.

The narrative of ex-slave John Brown describes the "sizing up" and the inevitable separation that follows:

As soon as we are roused in the morning, there was a general washing, and combing, and shaving, pulling out of gray hairs, and dying the hair of those who were too gray to be plucked without making them look bald. When this was over-and it was no light business-we used to breakfast, getting bread and bacon, and coffee, of which a sufficiency was given us, that we might plump up and become sleek. Bob [a "mulatto" assistant of the trader] would then proceed to instruct us on how to show ourselves off, and afterwards form us into companies, according to size; those who were nearly the same height and make being put into separate lots; the men, the woman, and the children of both sexes, being divided off alike. In consequence of this arrangement, the various members of a family were of necessity separated, and would often see the last of each other in that dreadful showroom . . .[185]

This inevitable separation dealt the cruelest blow to the slave. There was no relief, no sanctuary, no shelter from the evils of slavery when confronted with the pain of separation. The ex-slave Moses Grandy, spoke of seeing his wife carried off in such a manner. When he was asked about the incident, even after many years had passed, the pain still haunted his words:

> My heart was so full that I could say very little . . . the speculator, however, brandished a pistol, refused all conversation except at a distance . . . I have never seen or heard from her from that day to this. I loved her as I love my life.[186]

After the slaves were sized out and formed into companies, they were made to stand at attention as buyers approached to inspect them. When spoken to, they were expected to answer every question quickly with a demurring ignorant tone. Solomon Northup, auctioned and sold from Virginia in the 1840s from the Freeman pens in Richmond, gave this account of being viewed by customers before being sold:

> Customers called to examine Freeman's 'new lot.' The latter gentleman was very loquacious, dwelling at much length upon our several good points and qualities. He would make us hold up are heads, walk briskly back and forth, while customers would feel of our hands and arms and bodies, turn us about, ask us what we could do, make us open our mouths and show our teeth . . . Sometimes a man or a woman was taken back to the small house in the yard, stripped and inspected more minutely. Scars upon a slaves back were considered evidence of a rebellious or unruly spirit, and hurt his sale.[187]

The humiliation did not stop there. Slaves were also forced to perform a series of maneuvers so the buyer could ascertain if there were stiff joints, broken bones, infirmities, or other physical maladies. All the while, the slave was required to display a happy, childlike persona of deference.

> I do not think that anyone could describe the scene that takes place . . . The companies, regularly 'sized out', are forced to stand up, as buyers come up to them, and to straighten up as stiffly as they can. When spoken to, they must reply quickly, with a smile on their lips, though agony is in their heart, and a tear trembling in their eye. They must answer every question, and do as they are bid, to show themselves off; dance, jump, walk, leap, squat, tumble and twist about, that the buyer may see they have no stiff joints, or other physical defect.[188] —The narrative of ex-slave, John Brown.

At ten in the morning, the auctions commenced with the raising of a crimson flag. The buying and selling proceeded with uncaring efficiency until one p. m.   During this time slaves, sitting about in their respective companies, remained ready for inspection until placed on the auction block. At one o'clock, they were fed a repetition of the morning meal, varied with vegetables and, on occasion, a little fruit. After the afternoon feeding, slaves were compelled to walk, dance, and kick about in the yard for exercise. Eddie often produced a fiddle and played jigs as the companies danced, either to the music or the crack of the whip. When the exercise was over, slaves were sized out again, ready for the afternoon sale, which commenced at three and ended at six p. m. After the final sale, slaves were allowed tea, and were then ordered into the pens, until Eddie rang them off to bed.

This was the routine in the barracoons of Richmond, Virginia during the autumn of 1841. Madison Washington was enduring the final insult of slavery—the degrading auctioning of one's self to the highest bidder, having no say whatsoever in the process. His station in life had become less than that of a beast of burden. The very essence of humanity was stripped away as he was left exposed to the world as a mere commodity, to be bought and sold at the will and whim of others.

As for the majority of buyers, they observed no individual as a person, but rather as a machine or a tool for the production of goods in the industry of the South. One ironic factor in Madison's favor: the fresh bruises and cuts, evidence of the recent struggle that could not be hidden on his body, drove down his price since these telltale signs equated a rebellious nature. His scars, worn like medals, were a non-too subtle *caveat emptor*. At the same time, this made it all too obvious to other slaves that here was a man who was not easily subjugated and who strove to be free. Although his sale at auction was probably delayed until his injuries had a chance to heal, the fact remains: he was sold.

Madison Washington was purchased at auction by a New Orleans trader named Thomas McCargo. There is no known record as to the amount for which he was sold, or the exact date he was sold. However, according to the ship's manifest, Madison was put on board the brig *Creole* on October 20, 1841. The manifest listed Madison as "black, age twenty-two, five feet nine and one-half inches tall, male."

The agony Madison felt over his failure to bring Susan to freedom haunted his soul. Although he had endured the cruelest separation, he hadn't given up all hope. He decided to bide his time, for there still might be a chance for freedom. It would not be easy, for it was strictly forbidden for slaves to communicate with each other for fear of a rebellion, or the planning of an escape. They were watched over constantly, and any pretense at communication found the overseer's whip quickly enforcing the code of silence. Yet, the resourceful slave always found a way to give and receive information. A quick whisper while passing each other in line at mess, or the occasional recognition of someone with just the slightest nod of the head or the cryptic, slave slang that conveyed what was to come and what had happened to others—all were all employed as a means of giving and receiving information.

It is possible, that while in Richmond, Madison began to actively recruit others for an attempt to break free. One factor that suggests he began to formulate a plan in Richmond is evident with regard to certain names that appeared on the brig *Creole's* manifest. The following slaves were known to be in Richmond at the same time as Madison and were placed on board the *Creole* with Madison between October 20–25, 1841, all for shipment to New Orleans:

Name	Color	Age	Height
Elijah Morris		23	5' 5 1/2"
Phil Jones		17	5' 6 1/2"
Doctor Ruffin	brown	25	5' 6"
Peter Smallwood			
Ben Blair	brown	15	4'11 1/2"
Robert Limpley			
Horace Beverly	black	19	5' 9 1/2"
P Smallwood	brown	23	5' 10 1/2"
Andrew Bunkind	black	25	5' 7"
Addison Tyler	"	23	5' 5 1/2"
Willy Glover	"	22	5' 5 1/2"

These were eleven of the eighteen individuals who would instigate the mutiny on board the *Creole*. Madison Washington, Elijah Morris, Ben Blair, Andrew Bunkind and Willy Glover were all purchased by the same trader; Thomas McCargo.

And, as we shall see, while in Richmond, Madison Washington may have been surreptitiously contacted by a man who represented himself as a buyer. This man (or men), would have visited several auction houses, carefully recruiting slaves being shipped South on board intercoastal slave ships with the intention of instructing them on how to revolt and seize a brig as it made its way on the open sea, bound for New Orleans.

The Creole Incident

THE BEGINNING OF THE END OF SLAVERY

BOOK V: THE GROWING THREAT

16
Omne Trium Perfectum:
Everything That Comes in Threes is Perfect

The weird sisters, hand in hand
Posters of the sea and land.
Thus go about, about:
Thrice to thins, and thrice to mine
And thrice again, to make up nine,
Peace! The charm's wound up.
—William Shakespeare, Macbeth (Act 1, Scene 3)

In early 1841 three events occurred in all three branches of government: judicial, executive, and legislative, that had a profound influence on those who wished to put an end to gagging. In the judicial, John Quincy Adams presented arguments in the Amistad case before the United States Supreme Court.

THE UNITED STATES, APPELLANTS, V. THE LIBELLANTS AND CLAIMANTS OF THE SCHOONER AMISTAD, HER TACKLE, APPAREL, AND FURNITURE, TOGETHER WITH HER CARGO, AND THE AFRICANS MENTIONED AND DESCRIBED IN THE SEVERAL LIBELS AND CLAIMS, APPELLEES.

SUPREME COURT OF THE UNITED STATES

—40 U.S. 518; 10 L. ED. 826

The case involved a Spanish flagged ship, *La Amistad*, seized off Long Island by the US brig *Washington* on August 24, 1839. On board were fifty-three Africans who had revolted and taken possession of the ship with the intent of sailing it back to Africa and freedom. In actual fact, the course plotted by the surviving Spaniards was a meandering tack that eventually ended when the USS *Washington* intercepted *La Amistad*. The *La Amistad* was then towed into New Haven, Connecticut, where the Africans were jailed on charges of mutiny and murder.

The original criminal charges were dropped since the incident occurred in international waters, outside the jurisdiction of Connecticut courts. Although the criminal phase of the proceedings was decided, civil litigations began in earnest.

In court, the Spanish government claimed possession of the Africans as slaves. The owners of the *La Amistad*, along with the governments of Spain and the United States, and the crew of the USS *Washington*, based on maritime salvage law, filed a writ of attachment to regain possession of the ship and the Africans, claiming both as property. The owners of *La Amistad* and Spain based their claim on the treaty of 1795, continued in 1819 and ratified in 1827. The ninth article stated; "[t]hat all ships and merchandise, of what nature soever, which shall be rescued out of the hands of any pirates or robbers, on the high seas, shall be brought into some port of either state, and shall be delivered to the custody of the officers of that port, in order to be taken care of and restored entire to the true proprietor, as soon as due and sufficient proof shall be made concerning the property thereof."[189]

However, the lower court found the Africans were illegally imported as slaves into non-English colonies. Slaves on board *La Amistad* had been transported to Cuba, sold in the slave markets of Havana, and shortly thereafter, were placed on board the brig *La Amistad* for shipment to Guanaja, Cuba. It was during this voyage, in July of 1839, when the captured Africans arose in revolt, killed several of the crew, and took possession of *La Amistad*.

Although *La Amistad* with its crew and cargo were found in American waters, *La Amistad* was a Spanish-flagged ship. Spain insisted that the ship and its possessions were protected by international law. In a letter from Mr. Calderon de la Barca, envoy extraordinary and minister plenipotentiary of her Catholic Majesty the Queen of Spain, addressed to the honorable John Forsyth, Secretary of State of the United States, Calderon pleads his case.

> [N]o tribunal in the United States has the right to institute proceedings against, or to impose penalties upon, the subjects of Spain, for crimes committed on board a Spanish vessel, and in the waters of the Spanish territory.[190]

Spain put forth the argument that a ship from the country of origin was under the laws of said country, based on; the law of nations, the stipulations of existing treaties, and those good feelings so necessary to the maintenance of the friendly relations that subsist between the two countries, and are so interesting to both. One of the treaties cited by the counsel for Spain was Pinckney's Treaty, respecting the sanctity of a foreign ship, which had been reaffirmed by the Adams-Onis Treaty of 1819. Under these existing stipulations, Spain demanded the return of the cargo (the slaves) for trial in Cuba, based on property rights. In preparing their defense against these claims, the American Anti-Slavery Society established a committee, with Joshua Leavitt at its head, to facilitate legal counsel for the imprisoned Africans from *La Amistad*. Lewis Tappan, the brother of Arthur Tappan, both leading abolitionists, wrote in 1870:

> This committee, consisting of S. S. Jocelyn, Joshua Leavitt, and Lewis Tappan, were appointed at a meeting of the friends of liberty, September 1839, to procure legal counsel for the defense of forty or more native Africans, who had been seized the preceding month by the United States authorities, on a charge of piracy and murder on the high seas, and bound over for trial at the

United States circuit court at Hartford, Connecticut.[191]

Dwight P. Janes, a Connecticut abolitionist, also became involved with the plight of the Africans taken off *La Amistad* when they were held for trial on charges of murder and mutiny. It was at this time that Janes wrote to Joshua Leavitt requesting that he investgate the validity of *La Amistad's* papers in New York with regard to the Spaniard's claim of the slaves being Spanish subjects, rather than Africans. Janes again wrote to Leavitt, requesting Leavitt enquire if Roger Sherman Baldwin, a distinguished attorney who later became the governor of Connecticut and a future United States Senator, would take the case for the Africans.

Leavitt's association with the American Seamen's Friends Society proved to be an asset during the proceedings when he and Lewis Tappan searched out three African natives, merchant marines from New York, who were able to communicate with those from *La Amistad*. John Ferry, a native of the Kissi tribe and had spent some time in Mendi country in Sierra Leone, and James Covey, a native Mendian, were recruited later by the abolitionists to further aid in interpreting.

The lower court decided against the argument put forth by Spain. It stated that jurisdiction concerning the Africans and their fight for freedom was clearly established, since the whole affair had occurred on the high seas. Once jurisdiction was established, the court cited international law that stated the African slave trade was illegal. Spain, along with Great Britain and the United States, were signatory to the treaty. Based on this fact, the court proclaimed the Africans were neither slaves nor Spanish subjects and ordered the release of the prisoners. The decision of the lower court's civil and criminal decisions were appealed, and the case eventually made its way to the United States Supreme Court.

Leavitt, along with Lewis Tappan, sought out the council of John Quincy Adams and approached him with a request to represent the Mendi from *La Amistad* in front of the Supreme Court. Adams had shown an interest in the case earlier when he had introduced a resolution to have all correspondence of the executive department regarding the Amistad case submitted to the House of Representatives for review. House Document Number 85, as the correspondence request was labeled, clearly revealed the sympathies of the Van Buren administration and how relations between the United States and Spain had become strained over the incident.

At first Adams refused to take on the case, citing age and the fact that he had not argued a case before the Supreme Court since 1809. Although Adams initially begged off, Leavitt persisted. On November 17, 1840, Adams visited the Amistad Africans being held on charges of mutiny and murder at Westville, outside New Haven, Connecticut. After further consideration, he agreed to be one of the attorneys who would present arguments on behalf of the Africans before the Supreme Court. However, in his diary, Adams expressed his reservations regarding his ability and stamina to represent the case.

"I am yet to revise for publication my argument in the case of the Amistad

Africans, and in merely glancing over the Parliamentary slave–trade papers lent me by Mr. Fox, I find impulses of duty upon my conscience, which I can not resist, while on the other hand, the magnitude, the danger, the insurmountable burden of labour to be encountered in the undertaking to touch upon the slave-trade. No one else will undertake it. No one but a Spirit unconquerable by Man, Woman or Fiend, can undertake it, but with the heart of Martyrdom [. . .] to put down the African Slave trade—and what can I upon the verge on my seventy-fourth birthday, with a shaking hand, a darkening eye, a drowsy brain and with all my faculties, dropping from me, one by one, as the teeth are dropping from my head, what can I do for the cause of God and Man, for the progress of human emancipation, for the suppression of the African slave-trade."[192]

It was during this phase of the case that Adams began a close association and friendship with Joshua Leavitt. In January of 1841, Leavitt arrived in Washington to assist Adams with the presentation before the Supreme Court. Leavitt met with Adams several times over the following weeks as they prepared their legal arguments. Both Adams and Leavitt became aware of a wide variety of legalities associated with the transportation of slaves and the jurisprudence of such activity concerning international law and interstate commerce. Leavitt's knowledge of maritime law, acquired during his association with the American Seamen's Friends Society, encompassed maritime and international law as well as a background in ships and shipping. These experiences brought an expertise to the case that proved invaluable.

Adams made his presentation before the Supreme Court between the twenty-fourth of February and the first of March, 1841, during which time Justice Philip P. Barbour died, causing a minor delay in the proceedings. Leavitt attended each session and made extensive notes on the case. Hugh Davis, author of *Joshua Leavitt; Evangelical Abolitionist*, explains; "He (Leavitt) had been involved [Amistad] in the case from the moment that fifty-four Mendi Africans . . . were intercepted by a U.S. Navy cutter near the tip of Long Island . . . Not until he came to Washington in January of 1841 to attend the presentation of arguments before the Supreme Court and to consult with John Quincy Adams did he again become involved in the case. In the days before the hearing he met several times with Adams . . . Throughout the hearing in late February, (he) listened intently to both the government's arguments and those of Adams and Roger Baldwin . . . taking extensive notes."[193]

The final decision of the Court found for the Africans, based on the argument they had been illegally forced into slavery and, in seeking their freedom on the high seas, were not liable—or to be held for piracy. The court recognized the treaty wherein it stated that slave importation from Africa was illegal, thus securing the status of the Africans as individuals who could seek their freedom from their captives. They ordered the Mendi to be set free and returned to Africa.

The Amistad case was a victory for the cause of abolition, but more important, the case established the legal status of slavery outside a jurisdiction that had imposed slavery on them. The legal disquisition Leavitt was privy to during the

Amistad case presented a set of legal principles based on interstate commerce with regard to the transportation of slaves between states and upon the high seas. Although the case dealt with jurisdictions between nations, it raised a series of questions about federal versus state jurisdiction with regard to interstate transportation of slaves.

For example, as early as 1815, the case of *Forbes v. Cochrane* established legal precedent in English common law regarding the territorial jurisdiction of slavery. During the presentation of the Amistad case before the Supreme Court, Mr. Baldwin, the co-counsel along with Adams for the defendants, cited *Forbes v. Cochrane* to establish constitutional protections taking precedent over state and municipal law when a slave went beyond the territorial boundaries of a state.[194] From the records of *Forbes v. Cochrane* is the following citation:

> The law of slavery is a law *in invitum* [against the will of the subject,] and when a party gets out of the territory where it prevails, and out of the power of his master, and gets under the protection of another power, *without any wrongful act done by the party giving that protection*, the right of the master, which is founded on the municipal law of the particular place only, does not continue.[195]

In 1841, this was accepted common law. This legal argument, wherein, the institution of slavery is confined in its force to the territorial jurisdiction of the state that established it, begs the question of "once outside the territorial jurisdiction of the state that established slavery, was one held in bondage to be regarded as any other person?"

Could it be established that once a ship of the United States, flying the flag of the United States, while in the act of transporting individuals from one state to another upon high seas, goes outside state territorial waters, would it then be under the jurisdictional control of the federal government, based on interstate commerce?

Furthermore, would the laws and protections of the Constitution apply to such individuals if they came to be outside the jurisdiction of a state that enforced slavery? Would such individuals be held liable if they sought their freedom by taking control of a ship and sailed it to a port that would recognize their freedom?

The question then becomes: Does the ship come under the laws of the state it sailed from, or under Federal regulations, once upon the high seas?

As a competent lawyer, it is conceivable that Leavitt considered the legal ramifications of the interregional slave trade in the United States, particularly the trade that plied its goods between the Chesapeake ports and New Orleans. It is clearly evident that Leavitt, along with Adams, understood the role of federal law as it pertained to the intercoastal slave trade.

> As he understood the principle of general law, it was this—that the law of slavery is confined in its force to the territorial jurisdiction of the state which establishes it; so that the slave, as soon as by any means he gets beyond this limit, is to be regarded as any other man.[196] —Joshua Leavitt

And, "[T]he slave, as soon as by any means he gets beyond this limit, is to be regarded as any other man" was the crucial point. The Constitution did not recognize the institution of slavery and avoided using the term "slave." Instead, it used the term of "person" when referring to a *"person held to service or labor in one state, under the laws thereof."*[197]

It is important to realize that "persons" are entitled to the "blessings of liberty" established within the Constitution of the United States. Further, the Constitution was the supreme law of the land, as established in the Supremacy Clause.

So, federal jurisdiction, or state? There was in place at that time, and still today, a uniformed federal commercial law and also state common law development: Two bodies of law, federal and state, coexisting, side by side in the same jurisdiction. Established in the Constitution of the United States and upheld by several Supreme Court decisions prior to 1841, interstate commerce came under the jurisdiction of the federal government.

In Article 1, Section 8, Clause 3; the Constitution, states: ". . . Congress shall have power . . . To regulate commerce with foreign nations, and among the several States, and with Indian tribes."

The domain of the federal government over states in matters that deal with interstate commerce was further strengthened by the following Supreme Court cases: *McCulloch v. Maryland*, 1819 and *Gibbons v Ogden*, 1824. *McCulloch v. Maryland* dealt with the correlatives of federal and state sovereignty. The case was based on the constitutionality of the Second Bank of the United States and the right of a state to tax a federal institution. Chief Justice John Marshall stated in his opinion that ". . . government proceeds directly from the people themselves; consequently, it is, emphatically and truly, a government of the people, fully sovereign within the sphere of its authority." It followed that the states were not wholly sovereign, nor autonomous. Federal power thus need not "be exercised in subordination to the states."

The decision by the Supreme Court strengthened the implied powers of the federal government. This, in turn, allowed Congress to enact, regulate, and enforce laws that superseded and, in certain instances, made certain state laws invalid. This decision did not sit well with Southern leaders. The states not only viewed the decision as a consolidation of power on the part of the federal government, but more important, Southerners interpreted the decision as an implicit threat to the institution of slavery.

Gibbons v Ogden in 1824 also strengthened federal jurisdiction over interstate commerce. The case dealt with an issue of steamboat monopolies that operated between states. Specifically, it concerned the Commerce Clause, Article I, Section Eight of the United States Constitution. The decision was an important instrument in furthering principles of federal power over state sovereignty, and strengthened federal jurisdiction with regard to interstate commerce.

In the opinion of the Court, Chief Justice Marshall made clear where the authority lay with regard to inter-state commerce: "[T]he power over commerce with foreign nations, and among the several States, is vested in Congress as absolutely as it would be in a single government."[198]

The South believed individual state power over commerce equated to power over slavery.[199] The decision in *Gibbons v Ogden* reversed this concept and began an erosion of municipal codes and state laws based on interstate commerce.

In the argument of counsel for the steamboat monopoly, it was insisted that states had the authority to regulate commerce, with particular regard to navigation. In his decision, Chief Justice Marshall settled the issue with the following statement: "All America understands, and has uniformly understood, the word 'commerce,' to comprehend navigation. It was so understood, and must have been understood, when the constitution was framed."[200]

Marshall went further, touching on the statute regarding the prohibition of the importation of slaves by the federal government. Chief Justice Marshall made abundantly clear the extent of the power to regulate commerce by the federal government.[201]

> It is the power to regulate; that is, to prescribe the rule by which commerce is to be governed. This power, like all others vested in congress, is complete in itself, may be exercised to its utmost extent, and acknowledges no limitations other than are prescribed in the constitution.[202]

Prior to 1808, individual states could determine if they would import slaves from Africa, or restrict importation. However, after 1808 the question of importing slaves was regulated by the federal government. It was this phase of the decision that aroused the opposition of Southern statesmen; interpreted as a further consolidation of power at the national level. Marshall noted that the power of states over the importation of slaves did not extend beyond the year 1808 and that, by implication, state laws enacted after that date would be void.

> The act passed in 1803, 3 U.S.L. 529, prohibiting the importation of slaves into any State which shall itself prohibit their importation, implies, it is said, an admission that the States possessed the power to exclude or admit them, from which it is inferred that they possess the same power with respect to other articles. If this inference were correct, if this power was exercised not under any particular clause in the Constitution, but in virtue of a general right over the subject of commerce, to exist as long as the Constitution itself, it might now be exercised. Any State might now import African slaves into its own territory. But it is obvious that the power of the States over this subject, previous to the year 1808, constitutes an exception to the power of Congress to regulate commerce, and the exception is expressed in such words, as to manifest clearly the intention to continue the preexisting right of the States to admit or exclude, for a limited period.[203]

The jurisdiction of the federal government over individual states concerning interstate commerce was strengthened again in the Taney court. In *Proprietors of the Charles River Bridge v. Proprietors of the Warren Bridge* (1837) Chief Justice Taney's decision implied corporations are liable to the protection and restrictions of the Constitution as individuals. In *Bank of Augusta v. Earle*, Taney held that a corporation was "for certain purposes" a person in the eyes of the law. "A corporation is the creature of the law, and it is clothed with all the powers of a person." [204]

This supported a claim wherein the machinery of Southern industry, slavery, being an instrument of the business of production, was answerable to the law as individuals in relation to commerce, in particular interstate commerce. Chief Justice Taney further reinforced interstate commerce being the jurisdiction of the federal government when he concluded the following in his opinion on the *Charles River Bridge v Warren Bridge*:

> Borrowing . . . our system of jurisprudence from the English law; and having adopted, in every other case, civil and criminal, its rules for the construction of statutes; is there anything in our local situation, or in the nature of our political institutions, which should lead us to depart from the principle where corporations are concerned?[205]

This rhetorical question supports the claim that the machinery of the South, as a part of the corporation of the industry of agriculture, came under federal regulation in terms of interstate commerce by the fact that goods shipped from one state to another fall under the restrictions of interstate commerce, and thus under federal jurisdiction. The interstate shipping of slaves would then come under the regulation of interstate commerce. Once outside state territories, slaves would come under federal jurisdiction as established in the previous Supreme Court cases that acted to strengthen federal jurisdiction at the expense of individual states.

The growth of federal versus state's rights quickly became the juggernaut that threatened a fragile union of states. Many in the South came to the conclusion that the one option that would provide protection to Southern institutions was a reformation of the Constitution. To accomplish this, the South had to gain control of the government, in particular the legislative branch.

If that failed, another, more serious, option was being considered. Many in the South felt that if the trend toward a strong federal government continued, their participation in the Union would become restricted and would force them to consider withdrawing from the United States. They firmly believed this was not only a possibility but also a right guaranteed by the Constitution itself.

In the Southern planter's point of view in 1841, they would stop at nothing to protect their industry, even to the point of a legal separation from the Union through legislation, or if that failed, secession. To avoid such a decision, leaders of the South felt compelled to make a concentrated effort to gain control of the Federal government to establish protections that would recognize slavery as a Federal institution—with all the protections found in the Constitution concerning life, liberty and *property*.

A major step in this consolidation of power was the enactment of the Gag Rule. Leavitt clearly understood the implications of the Gag Rule. He had spoken out strongly for action against it in December of 1839, when he wrote in the abolitionist paper he edited, *The Emancipator*: "Let us rally under our own banner, and as soon as we have put in Congress men who do not care a straw for other questions in comparison with that of slavery . . . there [will be] an end to Gagging."

In September of 1840, as a featured speaker at the Ohio Anti-Slavery Convention in Hamilton, Ohio, Leavitt charged that while slavery had never been a vital interest to the nation, Southern domination, based on the three-fifths clause, shaped policies that created a "continual tax upon the products of free industry." Leavitt argued that if allowed to continue along the path toward Southern domination, slave interests would achieve a monopoly in Congress, threatening republican governance.

John Quincy Adams was of like mind. As early as June of 1830 he remarked in his diary after a conversation with Oliver Wilcott, who succeeded Secretary of State Alexander Hamilton, the frustration and deep concern he felt at the impending struggle for control of the government.

> The South Carolinians are attempting to govern the Union as they govern their slaves, and there are too many indications that, abetted as they are by all the slave-driving interest of the Union, the free portion will cower before them, and truckle to their insolence. This is my apprehension.[206]

By 1841, it had become apparent that drastic measures were needed to save the Union. Many felt the inevitable course of action would be a civil war. And, they believed if it should come to such a point when debate and compromise could no longer hold together a fragile Union, then succession should be made difficult, if not illegal.

In Section 8, Line 15 of the Constitution under the heading, "Powers Granted To Congress," it reads as follows: "To provide for calling forth the militia to execute the laws of the union, suppress insurrections and repel invasions." If dissolution could be legislated, it would not be construed as an insurrection and could not be answered by force, based on the structure of the Constitution. But if the South failed to legislate dissolution and left the Union illegally, the secession *could* be answered by force.

Adams had a premonition that the conflict between the free North and the slave South would lead to civil war. He also realized that if the South attempted to leave the Union, it must do so without the legal protections of the Constitution. There must not be a legal separation.

In February of 1820, during the Missouri Compromise, Adams's conversation with John C. Calhoun over the very question of a legal dissolution revealed the threat of foreign intervention on the side of the slave states:

> *February* 24, 1820. "I had some conversation with Calhoun on the slave question pending in Congress. He said he did not think it would produce a dissolution of the Union, but, if it should, the South would be from necessity compelled to form an alliance, offensive and defensive with Great Britain.
>
> I said that would be returning to the colonial state.
>
> He said, 'yes, pretty much, but it would be forced upon them'. . .[207]

Calhoun's statement, that the South would attempt to ally itself with a foreign state, could only be possible if the dissolution were legal. This, in turn, would legitimize the sovereignty of the newly created nation, allowing it to form treaties and alliances with other nations. However, if the dissolution were illegal, the legitimacy of a new nation would have to be resolved on the field of battle. Foreign countries would observe the conflict from the sidelines until the issue was settled, one way or the other.

Adams did not pursue the conversation further at the time, but mused on the possible consequences of the dissolution of the states.

> Slavery . . . is the great and foul stain upon the North American Union, and it is a contemplation worthy of the most exalted soul whether its total aboli-tion is or is not practicable: if practicable, by what means it may be effected, and if a choice of means be within the scope of the object, what means would accomplish it at the smallest cost of human sufferance. A dissolution, at least temporary, of the Union, as now constituted, would be certainly nec-essary, and the dissolution must be upon the point involving the question of slavery, and no other. The Union might then be reorganized on the funda-mental principle of emancipation. This object is vast in its compass, awful in its prospects, sublime and beautiful in its issue. A life devoted to it would be nobly spent or sacrificed.[208] —John Quincy Adams

Another factor that provided for and promoted the South's aim to reform the Constitution was the mounting pressure to admit the Republic of Texas into the Union as several states. The only guarantee the South had in terms of pro-tecting its institutions and its way of life was to either reform the Constitution to reflect the institution of slavery or legislate a legal separation from the Union. Either was possible as long as the Gag Rule stood.

As it turned out, the balance of power was further compromised in 1840. The upcoming presidential election year and events that followed bolstered the South's control over all three branches of government. Ironically, these same events made it clear to those who fought against slavery that immediate and drastic measures had to be taken to break the Gag Rule.

One thing was certain; time was running out.

17
Death of a President

This day was in every sense gloomy.
—Diary of John Quincy Adams, April 4, 1841.

I n the presidential election of 1840, considerably more time was allocated for the purpose of casting one's ballot than we experience today. America was mostly agrarian at that time and the population was not as centralized as it is in today's society. Although polling places were located in a variety of locations, from the county courthouse to store fronts, barns, saloons, churches, and private homes, they were not as accessible as our present polling locations. Due to distances traveled to the widely dispersed polling locations and the conditions, both weather-related and infrastructure in rural areas, polls remained open for an extended period of time. Travel, communication, information, and commerce moved to the technology of the times, and the expectation of results and correspondence corresponded to a more leisurely pace.

Thus, between October 30 and December 3 of 1840, Americans cast their ballots and elected William Henry Harrison the ninth president of the United States. Considered to be the first modern campaign with its slogan, "Tippecanoe and Tyler Too," campaign buttons, and stump speeches, the Harrison run for the presidency set a new standard for political electioneering.

Harrison also holds the distinction amongst all presidents to date as having served the shortest term of office. A dreary, cold, blustery inauguration day greeted the ninth president as he made his way to the east portico of the Capitol. The inaugural parade passed in front of the home of John Quincy Adams on F Street where Adams and Joshua Leavitt were ensconced in the front room. Neither man was impressed. Adams referred to the parade as "slowly-shabby" while Leavitt sniffed that it was a "small affair" compared to the many parades in New York.

The sixty-eight-year-old Harrison went on to deliver an hour-and-forty-five-minute speech in a driving snowstorm on Thursday, March 4, 1841. He stayed outside the entire time, greeting well-wishers, and later that evening attended many inaugural functions.

One month later, on April 4, 1841, Harrison died of pneumonia, and along with his passing, went the coalition that made up the Whig party.

Harrison's vice president and successor was John Tyler of Virginia. Picked as a running mate to balance the ticket, Tyler took the oath of office to become the tenth president of the United States on April 6, 1841. At age fifty-one, Tyler was also the youngest president to date. John Tyler was a slave owner and a strong states rights man, although he did not join Calhoun in advocating nullification. Despite that, Adams once referred to him as a "Virginia Nullifier."

Besides Tyler, one other person's political life was significantly impacted by the death of Harrison: Senator Henry Clay of Kentucky. In the election of 1840, Clay sought to create a candidate who would act as a unifier and at the same time be amenable, if not malleable, to his expansionist visions. Clay believed Harrison was someone who would veto legislation that would deny either side of the slavery issue an advantage, keep nullification from seeing the light of day, and at the same time sign legislation that would support the American system and westward expansion. Clay believed that Senator Calhoun and his drive to reform the Constitution would be held in check by Harrison, while at the same time, Clay would advise Harrison to support states right, recognizing the institution of slavery as a state or municipal code—thus, maintaining a status quo.

The American system depended on a legislative agenda where the federal government financed the building of roads and canals, regulated and enforced interstate commerce, and created a central bank to help consolidate the currency throughout the country. The strongest proponents of the American system were those who advocated for the westward expansion of the country, for their very existence relied on government support in securing and settling the west. The North supported this system, whereas in the South, use of federal money and regulation was interpreted as a form of imposition by the federal government on the sovereignty of the individual states.

Senator Henry Clay of Tennessee was the leading voice for the American system. A coalition of Adams, Webster, and Clay combined to form a national Republican Party, which later took the name "Whig,"[209] that championed a broad construction of the Constitution, and directed their efforts toward advocacy of high protective tariffs and liberal aid for internal improvements. The opposing party, the newly organized Democratic Party, which still clung to the name "Republican" for the time being, espoused the cause of state's rights and a strict construction of the Federal charter.

Although Clay had an early edge at the Whig convention in Harrisburg, Pennsylvania, he failed to garner enough support to get the nomination. When Harrison became the party's choice for president, Clay set aside his disappointment and added his support to the Harrison campaign.

The presidential campaign of 1840 saw these two parties compete for the White House, and in the process create the jingoisms and sound-bites that have come to be associated with present-day elections. William Henry Harrison, known to the public as "Old Tippecanoe," represented the common man and was seen as a friend of the West. With the successful election of Harrison to the office of president, the Whigs were in position to extol the virtues of the

American system to the American people as directed and scripted by Clay.

Clay had, in a sense, brought Harrison along, and was the controlling force behind his presidency. With Daniel Webster as Secretary of State and Clay pressing his American system in the Senate, all seemed united for the Whigs. Clay believed Harrison could be persuaded to use the veto with discretion, thus allowing Clay to push through Whig legislation in support of a national bank, high tariffs, and internal improvements. It was even thought, with Harrison in office, that pressure could be applied by the White House to do away with the Gag Rule, opening debate on the status of territories that were applying for statehood.

However, with Harrison's sudden death, Clay and the Whigs of Congress were left without a power base. It soon became evident that Tyler would not support a national bank or any Whig legislation. In fact, Tyler began his term by vetoing two bills Congress had passed to create a national bank. Calhoun wrote to James Henry Hammond on August 1, 1841, predicting ". . . the loss of the bank bill would probably break up the Whig Party and lead to a remolding of the cabinet."

Calhoun's assessment would prove to be prophetic. The original Cabinet, set up by Clay to advise Harrison, was referred to as "constitutional advisors" and was to guide the inexperienced Harrison in the concepts of "Whiggery." Tyler chose at first to keep the Cabinet, hoping to hold the Whig party together. However, in protest over the veto of the bank bill, the entire Cabinet resigned on August 11, 1841, except for Secretary of State Webster, who was urged by Adams to stay on in the hopes of keeping someone at the Cabinet level who would protect Northern interests. With the resignation of the Cabinet accepted by Tyler, Clay's last hope for any positive outcome concerning Whig legislation evaporated.

On Monday, September 13, 1841, Tyler presented to Congress the names of his new Cabinet for consideration.[210] The Senate quickly approved.

Although Clay was a slaveholder, slavery was not part of the agenda in Clay's American system. He believed that as long as the balance of power in the House and Senate remained intact, neither side could radically alter the direction of government.

The Whigs considered Tyler an unrepentant Democrat in Whig clothing. His liberal use of the veto killed any legislation that supported the American system, and in turn created a stalemate between the legislative and executive branches of the government. Adams weighed in on Tyler's ascendancy to the presidency, considering it a marked disadvantage for those in Congress who stood against state's rights and slavery. He wrote the following comments in his diary on the day Harrison died:

> Tyler is a political sectarian, of the slave-driving, Virginian, Jeffersonian school, principled against all improvements, with all the interests and passions and vices of slavery rooted in his moral and political constitution— with talents not above mediocrity, and a spirit incapable of expansion to

the dimensions of the station upon which he has been cast by the hand of Providence . . . This day was in every sense gloomy.[211]

To further complicate the issue, there was the increasing threat of foreign intervention with regard to the newly formed Republic of Texas. This was clearly evident regarding recent diplomatic forays by Texas with Belgium, the Netherlands, and England that resulted in a series of treaties for commerce and loans.

A growing concern of Southern members in both houses of Congress was the interest shown by the British and Foreign Anti-Slavery Society regarding the new republic.

Broad Street's view on this question were outlined, as early as August, 1839, in a letter from O'Connell to Sturge. Britain's aim, O'Connell observed, should be the establishment of a free republic on the borders of Mexico and the United States. Such a state would discourage further American expansion and would, like Canada, constitute an 'asylum for people of colour.'[212]

The threat of European powers seeking territorial acquisition on the North American continent heightened interest in Texas being admitted to the Union.

Another issue that contributed to a perceived power vacuum was the legal status of Tyler as president. This was the first time in the country's history someone had obtained the office of president without having been duly elected by either the people or the House of Representatives. There was no precedent. It was debated as to whether Tyler was a true sitting president or an interim or acting president until the next election—or if a special election should be called.

Adams visited Tyler at the White House on April 16, 1841, and made these comments about his interpretation about how Mr. Tyler should be treated.

I paid a visit this morning to Mr. Tyler, who styles himself President . . . and not vice-president acting as President, which would be the correct style . . . a strict Constructionist would warrant more than a doubt whether the vice-president has the right to occupy the President's house, or to claim his salary, without an Act of Congress. He moved into the house two days ago.[213]

The issue was settled on May 31, when the House gave its Congressional confirmation to Tyler as president. After a short debate between Representative Henry Wise of Virginia, a Tyler supporter, and John McKeon of New York, Wise made a motion that Tyler "would claim the position that he was, by the Constitution, by election and by the act of God, President of the United States."

In the Senate, Calhoun cleared up the issue that was verging on filibuster. Although the Constitution was ambiguous and may have considered the vice president as an acting president, Tyler had taken the oath of office. The Senate decided the issue by agreeing to refer to Tyler as the President of the United States.

For Adams, the ascendancy of John Tyler to the presidency was believed to portend not only the demise of the Whig coalition, but a threat to Union itself. The apprehension was based on the ability of the South to garner enough votes to reform the Constitution to recognize the institution of slavery or, if that failed, to enact a legal secession.

What became evident was a power vacuum in the leadership positions of government. Senator John C. Calhoun astutely recognized the situation and realized that the opportunity was at hand for his design to reform the Constitution to reflect Southern ideals. His view of the Tyler presidency reflected a personal belief that the new president was incapable of leading the South to a dominant position of governance.

In late 1841, Calhoun wrote to Dixon H. Lewis expressing his perception of Tyler: "He (Tyler) lacks the capacity & inflexibility, to say no more, to reform the Government and restore the Constitution."[214]

Prior to Tyler becoming president the situation had taken on a further ominous threat when Congress met in December of 1839. At the beginning of each new session of Congress, the parliamentary process of the House requires the rules of the House be reintroduced and voted on, as the rules of the House do not carry over from the previous session. Since 1836, the House had to vote a new Gag Rule with each new Congress.

In December of 1839, the 26th Congress convened at the same time the Whigs were holding their nominating convention in Harrisburg. Because some perceived the Whig Party to be made up of a sizeable membership of abolitionists, people felt a statement needed to be made to disavow the party of such affiliation. It was politically prudent to placate those in the South, as well as supporters of the institution of slavery in the North to avoid a loss in the upcoming presidential election of 1840.

On December 30, 1839, Mr. Henry Wise from Virginia's 7th Congressional district, at the time a member of the Whig Party, rose to introduce a resolution that the Gag Rule be made a permanent rule in the House. By making the Gag Rule a *permanent*, or standing rule of the House that need not be reintroduced and voted on with each new Congress, Mr. Wise called for a change in the standing rules of the House. This caused a delay in its acceptance as the House debated Wise's resolution. Representative William Slade of Vermont's 2nd Congressional district, took advantage of the lack of a gag to make a speech that condemned the resolution as an attack on the constitutional right of petition. Slade "... argued to show that the laying the question of reception on the table, did not lay the petition on the table, but in point of fact, put it back into the pocket of the member who presented it—that it amounted to a decision that they should not be received. It was in effect the abridgment of the right of petition."[215]

On January 28, after a full month of debate, counterproposals and amendments, William Cost Johnson of Maryland rose and presented a resolution that stated the following:

> *Resolved,* That, upon the presentation of any memorial or petition praying for the abolition of slavery or the slave trade in any District, Territory, or State of the Union, and upon the presentation of any resolution, or other paper touching the subject, the *reception* of such memorial, petition, resolution, or paper, shall be considered as objected to, and the *question of its*

reception shall be laid on the table, without debate or further action thereon."[216]

In short order, the Johnson resolution was voted on and became a standing rule of the House. Although Adams tried to postpone the vote on the question, it was prearranged that the resolution would come to a vote without further debate.

Mr. Adams moved a postponement of the question 'till the house was constituted; that is—'till the State of New Jersey is represented.

The CHAIR said this motion was not in order.

The question was taken on the resolution as amended, and decided in the affirmative--yeas 114, nays 108 . . .[217]

The severest gag to date was now a standing rule of the House of Representatives. Professor William Lee Miller, in his book; *Arguing About Slavery: John Quincy Adams and the Great Battle in the United States Congress*, makes clear the impact of the 1840 Gag Rule as a standing rule of the House.

The gag thus entered into the House rules went much further than the previous gag resolutions . . . most extensive form of the gag . . . no petition or memorial praying for abolition, "shall be *received* by the House, or entertained in any way whatever . . . The Johnson (Thompson-Wise) gag of 1840 really was a gag *rule*, where the others had been gag *resolutions*. It being planted in the house rules made it much harder to uproot."[218]

Time had run out. The death of President Harrison, the unraveling of the Whig coalition, the looming annexation of the Texas territories, the scattered interests of the North, coupled with the imposition of the Gag Rule as a standing rule of the House, created a perfect storm for Southern ascendancy. John Quincy Adams of Massachusetts, Joshua Reed Giddings of Ohio, William Slade of Vermont, Seth Gates of New York, John Mattocks of Vermont, Sherlock Andrews of Ohio, Nathaniel Borden of Massachusetts, and Francis James of Pennsylvania, along with Joshua Leavitt and later Theodore Weld, came together to form a select committee. Giddings referred to the committee as, ". . . a select committee about which little is said . . . but which in the future history of our government will fill a larger space than that of any other select committee of this or any former Congress."[219]

The select committee faced a daunting task. With the gag permanently in place, the South was primed to reform the Constitution to reflect Southern institutions. The additional representation to the House and Senate that would come from Texas territories would tip the balance of power in favor of the South as long as the Gag Rule stood.

Adams and Leavitt needed to find a way to break the gag before Texas came up for a vote of statehood. What they hoped to discover was a possible Achilles' heel in the South's design. One possibility came out of the recent Amistad case.

Based on the opinion delivered by the Court, Leavitt became aware of particular legal aspects that could be pertinent to the intercoastal slave trade. In the Amistad case, part of the opinion of the Court delivered by Justice Joseph Story referred to the ninth article of the Treaty of 1819 between the United States and Spain. The opinion read in part:

> [t]hat all ships and merchandise, of what nature soever, which shall be rescued out of the hands of any pirates or robbers, on the high seas, shall be brought into some port of either state, and delivered to the custody of the officers of that port, in order to be taken care of and restored entire to the true proprietor, as soon as due and sufficient proof shall be made concerning the property thereof.[220]

Justice Story further stated: ". . . [t]hat there has been a rescue of them (the slaves) on the high seas, out of the hands of pirates and robbers; which, in the present case, can only be by showing that they themselves are pirates and robbers."[221]

If those who took control of a ship followed Article Nine and delivered the ship "[t]o the custody of the officers of that port to be taken care of and restored entire to the true proprietor," then a charge of piracy could not be brought against those in control of the vessel if they did not retain possession of the ship. Furthermore, if individuals entered the said port unarmed, this would further substantiate their intention to not commit piracy, but rather, to seek sanctuary.

It was conceivable that an incident on the high seas outside a state's jurisdiction that involved slaves seeking their freedom while the vessel was conducting the business of interstate commerce, would place slaves on board under protection of the Constitution. This would put the incident under federal jurisdiction and attempts to re-enslave such people would not be supported under the Constitution. This would establish precedent under Federal jurisdiction, rather than state law or municipal codes, precedent that would circumvent the Gag Rule.

The question was, was it possible?

18

Stare Decisis: Decided

The U.S. Supreme Court described the rationale behind stare decisis as "promot[ing] the evenhanded, predictable, and consistent development of legal principles..." [222]

By 1840, Joshua Leavitt had made it clear to his friends and associates where he thought the struggle for emancipation would best be accomplished. "I am convinced in its peculiar powers is here, rather than in the church, i.e., it is resistless in the church because it is resistless in the State. We are eminently a political people."[223]

If an organization can claim guilt by association, it was the radical group of abolitionists who formed the American and Foreign Anti-Slavery Society. Although historians have referred to Leavitt and the other abolitionist who broke with Garrison as "conservatives," in fact these men were the extreme radical element of the abolitionist movement.

Charles Tappan had been involved with the Anti-Mason party, and his brother, Arthur, was life director of the American Seamen's Friend Society and a close associate of both the Reverend Bourne and Joshua Leavitt.

James Birney, a former Kentucky slave owner who had emancipated his slaves and taken up the mantle of abolition, was an able anti-slavery lawyer on constitutional interpretation and international law.

Henry Stanton was married to Elizabeth Cady [Stanton], a leading voice for women's rights. It is ironic in that one of the issues that perpetrated the schism and created the American and Foreign Anti-Slavery Society involved disagreements about women's rights. The Tappans and their followers, called Tappanites, believed the women's rights issue would dilute the effort to achieve the abolition of slavery.

Theodore D. Weld was a convert of Charles Finney, and traced his anti-slavery stand back to the Burned-Over District. Weld was a man unto himself who disdained meetings, ceremony, and most organized activities. His aloof and purposeful resolve strengthened the impression that the newly formed American and Foreign Anti-Slavery Society was an organization that would no longer rely on previous practices and philosophies to end slavery, but instead would take extreme measures to achieve the goal of emancipation.

Married to Angelina E Grimke,[224] Weld was considered one of the foremost legal experts in the organization. He was known for his research and interpretations on constitutional affairs, particularly those dealing with the struggle in Congress over the Gag Rule and was solicited by Leavitt and the select committee to research and create petitions for the purpose of breaking it. James Birney, the Tappans, Henry Stanton, Bourne, and Weld, were the sword of the radical anti-slavery movement, with Leavitt being the leading edge. Leavitt's drive to seek the total abolition of slavery defined who he was and was evident not only to those who opposed him but, at times, to those with whom he worked closest. This is made evident in an article written by Lawrence J. Friedman, titled *Confidence and Pertinacity in Evangelical Abolitionism: Lewis Tappan's Circle.*

> Weld once pointed out that Leavitt struck a deeper level of emotion than the Tappans ever did within the group. However, Leavitt was often blunt and tactless. In the 1840s he championed the Liberty Party over the church as the proper forum for antislavery operations with a fervor that disenchanted others. He was no group leader.[225]

Louis Tappan was one who felt the sting of Leavitt's stubborn disagreement. Leavitt and Tappan had developed a close relationship that began with their work in the American Seamen's Friend Society and the committee to assist the Amistad fugitives. Regardless, there were times when Leavitt disagreed with Tappan over the political approach to ending slavery, as well as Tappan's view of gender in the antislavery society; Leavitt supported women having an active role in antislavery societies as well as seeking equality in civil society.

> The hostility that arose between Louis Tappan and Joshua Leavitt over the propriety of political antislavery can be cited. So can the divergent views these men held on the propriety of female officers in the American Anti-Slavery Society.[226]

However, the American and Foreign Anti-Slavery Society was disciplined enough to not lose focus. It was the infamous Gag Rule that became the central issue. With the Gag Rule now a standing rule in the House of Representatives, the death of President Harrison and the assumption of John Tyler as president, plus the looming question of the Republic of Texas being annexed into the Union, it was crucial that a way be found to circumvent the gag. The threat of a government takeover by Southern slave interests in Congress was the overriding matter that concerned this group of radical abolitionists. Leavitt and the AFASS were desperately aware that time was running out.

> As a featured speaker at the Ohio Anti-Slavery Convention in Hamilton, [Sept. 1840] Leavitt charged that while slavery had never been acknowledged as a vital interest of the nation, southern domination of the national government, based on the three-fifths clause, shaped policies that created a "continual tax upon the products of free industry."[227]

The task of establishing a legal precedent to nullify the Gag Rule was daunting. The bulwark that protected the South's peculiar institution was in the capable hands of the Southern members of Congress. The one person Leavitt relied on for counsel with regard to the threat of the Gag Rule was John Quincy Adams. Both men clearly understood that the added Texas representation would bolster Southern aspirations. As early as February of 1833, Adams, in a speech on the House floor, illustrated those protections afforded the South via the three-fifths clause:

> There were on the floor at that time upwards of twenty members who represented what in other states had no representation at all, the 'machinery of the South.' Elected by those who owned the machinery, not the machinery.[228]

"Was this not protection?" Adams asked.

This protection, he claimed, ". . . took millions of money from the free laboring population of this country, and put it into the pockets of the owners of the Southern machinery."[229]

By the 1840s, John Quincy Adams made it clear that the prospective added representation afforded the South an advantage over every aspect of governance:

> The principle is that the House of Representatives of the United States is a representation only of the persons and freedom of the North, and of the persons, property, and slavery of the South. Its practical operation has been to give the balance of power in the house, and every department of the government, into the hands of the minority of numbers.[230]

Although the South's representation in Congress did not have a majority, it consistently presented a solid voting bloc. The other voters in Congress rarely spoke with one voice or purpose. Adams's frustration when confronting the "solid South's" voting bloc is evident in the following remark: "Do you not see that the one hundred representatives of persons, property, and slavery, marching in solid phalanx upon every question of interest to their constituents, will always outnumber the one hundred and forty representatives only of persons and freedom, scattered as their votes will always be by conflicting interests, prejudices, and passions?"[231]

Adams argued further that representation of the Southern states with regard to the three-fifths clause gave "the entire control of the national policy, and, almost without exception, the possession of the highest executive office of the Union" to Southern states and their representatives. The ability of Southern states to elect presidents due to their added representation in the House refers to Article II, Section 2 of the Constitution, where it states the following:

> Each State shall appoint . . . a number of electors, equal to the number of Senators and Representatives.

Adams focused his ire on another protection afforded Southern institutions in the Constitution. This clause dealt with runaway slaves. Article IV, Section 2, Clause 3 of the Constitution, commonly referred to as the "Fugitive clause," read as follows:

"The citizens of each state shall be entitled to all privileges and immunities of citizens in the several states.

A person charged in any state with treason, felony, or other crime, who shall flee from justice, and be found in another state, shall on demand of the executive authority of the state from which he fled, be delivered up, to be removed to the state having jurisdiction of the crime.

No person held to service or labor in one state, under the laws thereof, escaping into another, shall, in consequence of any law or regulation therein, be discharged from such service or labor, but shall be delivered up on claim of the party to whom such service or labor may be due."

Adams decried this provision by saying it ran counter to all tenor of legislation in the free states. It was contrary to the thinking of Northerners to give up a person to a foreign authority.

Adams also railed against the ruse that the federal government afford protections against slave insurrection by means of federal troops on indefinite standby throughout the South. One example he cited were the lives and treasure spent fighting the ongoing Seminole Wars. His disdain concerning the cost in federal expenditures used for the control of slavery is evident in the following remark:

The constitution guaranteed to every state in the Union a republican form of government, protection against invasion, and, on the application of the legislature or executive of any state, furnished them protection against domestic violence. Now, everybody knew that where this machinery existed the state was more liable to domestic violence than elsewhere, because the machinery sometimes exerted a self-moving power.[232]

Southern representatives defended these protections of slavery as strongly as abolitionists proclaimed their disdain for it. The South firmly believed an attack on slavery was to be construed as a threat to the existence and continuation of the nation. John C. Calhoun wrote in 1840 the following passage:

With the failure of our principles the whole scheme of our admirable system of government must fail. It is utterly impossible for the superstructure to stand on any other foundation, except the old Republican State Rights.[233]

Adams countered that the concepts of democracy could never be compatible with the South's peculiar institution:

Democracy, pure democracy, has at least its foundation in a generous theory of human rights. It is founded on the natural equality of mankind. It is the corner-stone of Christian religion. It is the first element of all lawful government upon earth.[234]

When Adams was elected to the House in 1830, he and William Slade of Vermont were the lone voices that stood against the encroaching power of the Southern planter establishment and their attempts to have slavery recognized under federal jurisprudence. With the passage of the Gag Rule in 1836, a new sense of urgency became evident to many in the North. Joshua Leavitt, for one, recognized that the fate of the country over the issue of slavery was centered in the House of Representatives. He soon found himself in Washington as a correspondent for *The Emancipator*, where he began to recruit a handful of House members to mount an attack against slavery and the Gag Rule.

Often impatient, Leavitt's style of recruitment leaned at times to the point of abusive, threatening the very coalition he was attempting to build in Congress. One member of Congress he came into conflict with was Joshua Reed Giddings. In late November of 1838, Giddings was a freshman member of the United States House of Representatives. As a newly elected Congressman from the Sixteenth District of Ohio, Giddings was willing to compromise with proslavery Whigs to preserve party unity. It wasn't long, though, before he had a change of heart.

On a cold night in January of 1839, while walking the streets of Washington, Giddings encountered slaves being driven to market. The coffle included about sixty men, women, and children, chained together as the crack of the whip drove the unfortunate souls to their destination.

> A slavedealer . . . with some thirty men, marching past the Capitol in double files, each fastened by the wrist to a long chain . . . next came nearly as many woman . . . followed by a wagon . . . containing the small children. The merchant was on horseback, armed with pistols, bowie-knife, &c., and bearing in his hand the 'plantation whip.' The whole procession gave a vivid impression of the barbarism at that time practiced at the seat of Government, and upheld and encouraged by the democratic party and by the southern members of the Whig organization.[235]

Although he had been aware of slavery as an institution, he was not prepared for the impact of coming face-to-face with it. That evening he called on William Slade of Vermont, an anti-slavery Whig member of the House. They talked of the slave markets in Washington and the character of those who protected such an institution. Both agreed that Southern men displayed "self-important airs" and "overbearing manners," while representatives from the North acted "diffident, taciturn, and forbearing." Giddings concluded that "Southern bullies" had forced everyone else into silence. From that meeting on, Giddings dedicated his efforts to the pursuit of abolition.

Slade introduced Giddings to other members of the House who shared his outrage against slavery, in particular the one member whose entire career was now devoted to breaking the Gag Rule—John Quincy Adams. Giddings, like Adams, rejected the philosophy behind the South's denial of the constitutional right of petition. He realized that the South, led by John C. Calhoun, would defend slavery—to the point of jeopardizing the Union. Giddings wrote; "It had become evident to southern statesmen that freedom of debate and the right of petition must be put down, or slavery must fall before the tide of civilization."[236]

Adams became a mentor to the freshman member of the House—advising, cajoling, and instructing Giddings in the finer points of parliamentary procedure. Giddings shared with the elder statesman the belief that the greatest threat to the Constitution and the Union was slavery. Years later, when Lincoln asked Giddings if he should look to Senator Clay as a political model, Giddings replied, "John Quincy Adams, rather than Henry Clay, was the better example."

With Adams, Slade, Gates and other members of the House, the new Ohio congressman found the support and voice to speak out against slavery. On February 18, 1839, Giddings rose on the House floor and delivered his first abolition speech about the slave trade in the District of Columbia. As he sat down upon yielding the floor, he was met with a chorus of insults, calls for his censure, and glowers from Southern members. Adams, beaming with a smile not unlike a father at a son's graduation, walked to Giddings's seat, laughed heartily, and congratulated him.

In January of 1841, the other Joshua, Joshua Leavitt, returned to Washington to legally assist Adams in his upcoming presentation of the Amistad case before the Supreme Court. Leavitt secured lodging at one of many boarding houses that were fixtures near the Capitol.

In the years prior to the Civil War, where a representative and senator choose to lodge clearly reflected their allegiance and political proclivity with regard to the divisiveness that plagued the nation. Two of the more famous boarding houses, now long forgotten, were Mrs. Lindenberger's and Mrs. Sprigg's.[237]

Located between A and East Capital Streets, and a short walk from the Capitol building, Lindenberger's Southern boarders proclaimed for the supremacy of states' rights. By 1836, it was home to several of the South's leading legislators, including the conscience and voice of agrarian interests, Senator John C. Calhoun and Representative James Henry Hammond of South Carolina.

At the opposite end of the spectrum was Mrs. Sprigg's Boarding House. It catered to a Northern clientele who supported emancipation and a strong Union. It was the residence of so many radical Northern legislators that Mrs. Sprigg's became known as "abolition house."

> Twenty-four boarders now lived at the house, several of them abolitionists; the others, according to Weld, who arrived in late December for a five-week stay, were 'favorably inclined.' Weld and other boarders seemed protective of Mrs. Sprigg's interests, fearing that the house's reputation as the 'Abolition House' would hurt her business.[238] —Professor Hugh Davis

One of the more renowned residents of Mrs. Sprigg's was a freshman congressman from the *Seventh Congressional District* of *Illinois,* elected to the House of Representatives in 1846, who arrived with his new wife. His name was Abraham Lincoln.

Eventually, Mrs. Sprigg's Boarding House was torn down to make way for the present site of the Library of Congress, but in the late 1830s and throughout the '40s and '50s, it was a hotbed of abolition. The letters and diaries of legislators and guests who resided at each of these lodgings testify to the political leanings of the clientele. When Theodore Weld resided at Mrs. Sprigg's during the winter of 1841-42, he wrote to his wife the following description:

> I will now tell you how I am situated. Mrs. Sprigg's is directly in front of the

Capitol and about as far from it as from our home to Mrs. Holmes's or Mr. Spear's. The iron railing around the Capitol Park comes within fifty feet of our door. Our dining room overlooks the whole Capitol Park which is one mile around and filled with shade trees and shrubbery. I have a pleasant room the second floor with a good bed, plenty of covering, a bureau, table, chairs, closets and clothes press, a good fireplace, and plenty of dry wood to burn in it. We have about twenty boarders, mostly members of Congress, 8 of them from Pennsylvania and the rest from the free states. Only Gates and Giddings [are] abolitionists, but all the others are favorable. They treat brother Leavitt and myself exactly as though we were not fan[a]tics, and we talk over with them at the table and elsewhere abolition just as we should at home.[239]

The frequent communal mealtime "think tanks," at Lindenberger's and Mrs. Sprigg's fostered the basis for arguments that were debated on the House and Senate floors. The Gag Rule was conceived at these think-tanks when Senator Calhoun and Representative Hammond dined together at Lindenberger's, and it was at Sprigg's where Joshua Leavitt, along with Weld, Giddings, and other members of the House began to formulate a legal precedent to circumvent it.

Upon his arrival in Washington in January of 1841, Leavitt made the rounds of Congress, and recruited a devout group of Whigs in the House who were willing to make opposition to slavery their leading agenda. Chief among the group were Joshua R. Giddings, William Slade of Vermont, Seth M. Gates of New York, and Sherlock J. Andrews of Ohio. They came together to form their own select committee, a group unsanctioned by any congressional measure.

Prior to the formation of the select committee, there were moments of disagreement that threatened the evolving coalition of abolitionists. When the selection of a new speaker arose in the 26th Congress, after several weeks of debate that delayed matters before the House, the vote recorded by Gates, Slade, and Giddings (for R. M. T. Hunter, a Virginia slaveholder), came close to putting a permanent division in the anti-slavery members of the House. Leavitt wrote the following in *The Emancipator*: "When called upon to perform the first official act in the election of a Speaker, they every one gave openly and with their own voice, the name R. M. T. Hunter as their choice—a man who, twelve months ago, trampled at once upon liberty and the constitution, by voting for Atherton's Gag!"[240]

Leavitt gave no ground concerning his beliefs on slavery. Without a political constituency to answer to, Leavitt had little patience with Whig members who compromised on the issue. His relentless pressure to not buckle against the slavocracy of Southern representation came into conflict with the political realities of the Whig party line. For Leavitt, the goal was breaking the gag and allowing open debate on slavery. Giddings, on the other hand, suggested that Leavitt, ". . . deserves a strait jacket."[241]

As members of the Whig party, Giddings, Gates, and Slade defended their positions on party matters and their voting records in the House by arguing the economic principles they pursued were favorable to the free North and that of Whigs in general. Leavitt, as editor of *The Emancipator*, shot back with scathing editorials: "Those that feel and act on the ground that the paltry matters of revenue are more important than the great question of HUMAN FREEDOM can have but small interest in the anti-slavery cause."[242]

With unrelenting zeal, Leavitt attacked those he felt chose compromise on slavery. One was either "with Leavitt" or "against Leavitt." There was no middle ground.

At first, his efforts only resulted in further disharmony among Northern anti-slavery Whigs. Seth Gates wrote about Leavitt's crusade to reform Whig members of Congress by describing him "with his iron pen, invincible zeal, indomitable courage, untiring faith and indefatigable labors."[243] This was soon to change.

Prior to his untimely death, President Harrison had requested a special session of Congress. Convened in the summer of 1841, it addressed the economic plight of the nation and the ramifications of the divisiveness in Congress. Leavitt attended the session as the reporter for *The Emancipator*, and to pursue those in Congress he felt were "bowing of the knee to the dark spirit of slavery."

But now, with John Tyler sworn in as the new president and the Whigs in disarray, the agenda for the session took on a different dimension. In an attempt at party cohesion, the Whigs called a truce with regard to their attempts to breach the Gag Rule. Regardless, John Quincy Adams and a handful of radical anti-slavery Whigs refused to go along. Over the summer session a thaw in relations between Giddings and Leavitt became evident, and Giddings conceded as much when he told Leavitt, "While on my part it shall at all times be my greatest pleasure to aid you in the discharge of your high duties in every way in my power. If you suffer the cause in which we are both engaged suffers."[244]

Leavitt finally buried the hatchet when he confided that Giddings was, ". . . as sincerely opposed to the domination of the slave power."

This acclamation from Leavitt signaled an end to the divisiveness. With Giddings's appeal for unity and Leavitt's tactical retreat, the anti-slavery contingent in the House found its footing with the creation of the select committee. Giddings wrote the following to his wife on February 18, 1842 concerning the select committee:

> The select committee about which little is said will open the whole field [of slavery] for discussion in a shape in which the Gag or any Gag which it is possible for Congress to pass cannot touch them.[245]

As they met and discussed several approaches to breaking the gag, it became apparent what was needed was a precedent-establishing Federal jurisdiction over an issue that related to slavery. If established, such a precedent would allow the subject of slavery to be discussed on the House floor without being held hostage to the Gag Rule.

Leavitt's involvement with the Amistad case, coupled with his previous experiences at the helm of the American Seamen's Friend Society, presented a legal understanding of domestic and international law concerning the slave trade. A precedent, or what is referred to as *stare decisis* (the doctrine by which decisions of a higher court or appellate court are binding and must be followed by lower courts), began to merge into a convincing legal argument.

It had been established that the importation of slaves from Africa had been banned by treaty with Great Britain and other European powers. In fact, it was the very treaty that John Quincy Adams now presented as part of his argument in the Amistad Case before the Supreme Court.. The enforcement of these measures was, for the most part, undertaken by the British and had come into conflict with the United States on several occasions with regard to visit (boarding) and search. The Southern contingent in Congress was particularly concerned and outraged at any attempt by Her Majesty's Navy to interfere with commerce or the institution of slavery. The South, as well as many members of the House from the North, vigorously claimed that ships that flew the flag of the United States came under the laws and protections of the United States.

Then there was the legal precedent that related to incidents of mutiny on the high seas. Leavitt believed that mutiny could not be prosecuted if it was shown that those who took possession of a ship were being held against their will prior to seeking their freedom, based on Justice Story's opinion in the Amistad case:

> "We may lament the dreadful acts, by which they asserted their liberty, and took possession of the Amistad, and endeavoured [sic] to regain their native country; but they cannot be deemed pirates or robbers in the sense of the law of nations, or the treaty with Spain, or the laws of Spain itself; at least so far as those laws have been brought to our knowledge."[246]

Leavitt understood that if slaves who had commandeered a ship by a mutiny entered a port disarmed and gave themselves up to the local authority, they would not be considered pirates or robbers. The act of releasing the ship to authorities would prove those fugitives used the ship as a conveyance to seek their freedom, rather than for personal gain.

Further, if the incident occurred on a United States flagged ship, where men acted to secure their freedom while being transported on the high seas, such an act would fall under interstate commerce and would have all the authority and protections found under federal law.

The preamble of the Constitution states: "secure the blessings of liberty to ourselves and our posterity." In the Fifth Amendment of the Bill of Rights, it is written; "... nor be deprived of life, liberty, or property, without due process of law."

The coastal shipping of slaves from the Upper South to the markets of the Lower South sailed a route on the high seas, passing outside the jurisdictional territories and state boundaries that enforced slavery. As we have seen, it was *Forbes v. Cochrane* that stablished a legal precedent regarding the territorial jurisdiction of slavery. "The law of slavery is a law *in invitum* [against the will of the subject,] and when a party gets out of the territory where it prevails. . . the right of the master, which is founded on the municipal law of the particular place only, does not continue."[247]

Rather, once an intercoastal ship left the territorial waters of a state, it entered the jurisdiction of federal law. If a series of resolutions based on an incident that involved interstate transportation of slaves on the high seas were to be presented on the House floor, would these resolutions come under federal jurisdiction rather than state law or municipal code?

Although similar situations had occurred with American flagged ships such as the *Enterprise*, *Hermosa*, and *Comet*, all coastwise slave ships, these ships had been forced into a British port by force of nature, such as going aground, being blown off-course on stormy seas, or needing repairs. The persons on board these ships did not use force to seek their freedom. Rather, local authorities of the colony granted it to them. The difference in seeking freedom by force and then entering a foreign port as free people was that they could be prosecuted for mutiny, and if there was a loss of life—murder. Demands would then be made to return the individuals to the United States for trial.

Regarding the intercoastal slave trade, if a ship came to enter any port in the United States, slaves who had secured their freedom on the high seas would be remanded by extradition to the state of origin to be tried on charges of mutiny, and possibly piracy. However, if these slaves sought shelter in a foreign port that did not recognize slavery, they would have the legal designation of passenger, rather than the commodity of slave. Extradition, if it existed by treaty, would be difficult as one side referred to the individuals as passengers who were held against their will.

Further, if upon entering a port they did so unarmed, this act would negate any accusation of piracy based on Justice Story's opinion in the Amistad case: "If then these negroes are not slaves, but are kidnapped Africans . . . and kidnapped and illegally . . . detained and restrained on board of The Amistad, there is no pretense to say that they are pirates or robbers."[248]

In the Amistad case it was found that slaves held against their will were legally within their right to seek sanctuary, and need not be returned to the state of origin. Established by treaty and law, they were not recognized as slaves, but as free adults. Similarly, a slave on the high seas, under the jurisdiction of interstate commerce, came under the protections of the United States Constitution. They would legally be within their rights to seek freedom, and need not be returned to the state of origin for prosecution.

However, it was crucial that the newly freed seek sanctuary in a port that did not recognize slavery, and the ports of sanctuary along intercoastal slave routes that fulfilled that requirement were British. Leavitt, while a member of the American Seaman's Friend Society, had become familiar with the routes of intercoastal slave ships and knew these vessels passed within a day's sail of ports under the protection of English law. The port of Nassau, Bahamas, was easiest to access, due to location and opportunity.

One advantage of seeking refuge in a British port was that the American and Foreign Anti-Slavery Society had an established working relationship with the British and Foreign Anti-Slavery Society. The British society had been effective in the abolition of slavery in all English colonies in 1833, and had strong ties with colonial authorities and leading members of parliament. Leavitt could rely on the British society to render legal assistance to newly freed slaves, once they reached a British port. And, their assistance would be invaluable to presentation of fact to Her Majesty's government for the defense of the fugitive slaves.

Another factor that added a layer of support to such a scheme was Leavitt's involvement in the American Seamen's Friend Society, where he had been responsible for the placement of preachers into foreign ports. These preachers shared many beliefs Leavitt espoused, including abolition. Their assistance would prove invaluable as they might well be the first on the scene to give aid and advice to newly arrived freed slaves. As associates of Leavitt, most gladly assisted in any attempt to bring individuals to freedom and into the flock of local churches.

As to the question of extradition, it was common knowledge that England had no extradition treaty with the United States. However, Leavitt was under no false illusion regarding the hue and cry Southern members of Congress would raise, demanding return of the slaves for trial to the state of origin. This was where the situation would face its strongest test.

If such a situation occurred with the interstate transportation of slaves on the high seas, it would create an opportunity to test the stranglehold planters held over Congress. Presentation of a series of resolutions would rely on the legal interpretation of the resolutions. The resolutions would state that individuals could not be returned to the state of origin for trial based on the fact that they sought liberty under the protections and jurisdiction of the Constitution as found in the Commerce Clause, Article 1, Section 8, Clause 3: "Congress shall have power . . . To regulate commerce with foreign nations, and among the several States, and with Indian tribes."

If this proved the case, then such resolutions would not be tabled under the Gag Rule, because the subject pertaining to slavery was not protected by state law, nor a municipal ordinance, but instead, clearly came under federal jurisdiction.

If such an incident could be presented, debated, and read into the records of the House and Senate, based on the fact that the Gag Rule only applied to slavery as it was enforced by state law and municipal codes, then in fact and practice the Gag Rule would be broken. Federal jurisdiction was the key. Once precedence was established, the Gag Rule, for all practical purposes, would cease to exist.

In February of 1841 Leavitt rose early and prepared himself for opening arguments before the Supreme Court in the Amistad case. Adams wrote in his diary on February 24, 1841, "snow powdered the face of the earth."

On such a snowy morn, one can easily imagine Joshua Leavitt gazing out of the front window of Mrs. Sprigg's Boarding House as he prepared for his attendance as Adams's legal assistant. He might have gazed across the street at the Capitol, and mulled over arguments Adams was to present on behalf of the *Amistad* Africans.

Leavitt had judiciously researched the Amistad case and recognized possible legal similarities to the intercoastal slave trade. After his careful consideration of the details in the Amistad case, Leavitt may have said to himself in a soft, calm voice that disguised his excitement, "This would, in fact, break the Gag Rule."

The Creole Incident

THE BEGINNING OF THE END OF SLAVERY

BOOK VI: THE VISIT

19

The Plot

One of the facts alleged by the New Orleans papers, which adds to the excitement occasioned by this mutiny and murder, is "That Mr. Bourne, a Baptist preacher in Richmond, instructed them as to the mode of procedure before they left, as was learned from an examination of the slaves at Nassau."
—London Times, Friday, January 14, 1842

On August 25, 1841, Joshua Leavitt convened a meeting with a few of the top members of the American and Foreign Anti-Slavery Society in Troy, New York. In attendance were Henry Highland Garnet, Theodore Weld, Theodore Wright, and George Bourne. If the subject of a slave insurrection was discussed at this meeting, it is unlikely that any evidence existed, due to the repercussions, if such a plot were discovered.

Although there were other slave revolts during the two hundred and forty-nine years slavery legally existed in the United States, the proposition that slaves were instructed by abolitionists while in Richmond slave pens to create a slave revolt on board an intercoastal slave ship needs further substantiation.

To venture into the bowels of slavery to surreptitiously instruct slaves how to accomplish a slave rebellion on a slave ship must have seemed preposterous. The difficulty in recruiting closely watched men who were enslaved, and poorly educated with restrictions on their movement made the endeavor all the more improbable. If discovered, there would be little sympathy in a town like Richmond, and the punishment would be swift and severe. This alone would have dissuaded most from making such an attempt.

At the same time, the hectic process of buying and selling slaves at Richmond's Shockoe Bottom could have facilitated such an endeavor. In October of 1841, Richmond would have been a beehive of activity of buyers and speculators and newly-arrived slaves, along with the support personnel and cottage industries of the slave trade. Practitioners, from slave jailers to tailors and clothiers who supplied slave uniforms, to blacksmiths and foundries that manufactured the chains and locks used to control slaves, were respected civic leaders of the community.

The morning ritual of grooming and exercise went on with a callous efficiency as buyers looked over slaves who would go on the block that day. Many slaves would be shipped south on the next available slaver, as evidenced by the vessels *Long Island, Orleans,* and the *Creole,* all moored at the docks of Shockoe Bottom in late October, 1841.

The increase of out-of-towners representing planters, shippers, and auction houses from the Lower South were welcomed with an accommodating cordiality. During peak selling season, it was not uncommon to become anonymous in the crowd. For example, Otis Bigelow from New York visited the Richmond slave markets and had the following recollection of Lumpkin's slave pen:

> I went far enough in the rear not to be noticed until he turned into an entrance, over which was the sign 'LUMPKIN'S JAIL.' I entered a large open court. Against one of the posts sat a good-natured fat man, with his chair tipped back. It was Mr. Lumpkin. I duly introduced myself as from New York, remarking that I had read what the Abolitionists had to say, and that I had come to Richmond to see for myself. Mr. Lumpkin received me courteously and showed me over his jail. On one side of the open court was a large tank for washing, or lavatory. Opposite was a long, two-story brick house, the lower court fitted up for men and the second story for women. The place, in fact, was a kind of hotel or boardinghouse for negro-traders and their slaves.[249]

However, the mere attempt to recruit slaves for a rebellion was not enough to ensure success. It was important that the slaves, if they gained their freedom, follow a series of careful instructions. For example, the revolt had to occur on the high seas, outside state territorial waters. One ideal location would be Abaco Island in the Bahamas. It was here that the intercoastal slave ships frequently "hove to" to replenish the ship's fresh water supply. The advantage for the conspirators was that the ship would be only a day's sail from a British port. It was also important to avoid as much bloodshed as possible. A death would be construed as murder, unless it could be proved to be an act of self-defense. Furthermore, once the ship was secured, there was the matter of the newly freed slaves entering a port unarmed and surrendering themselves, along with the ship, to local authorities. It was believed that these precautions would negate charges of piracy and help avoid extradition back to the port of origin for trial.

One advantage of a British port was that England and the United States had let lapse an extradition agreement, although it was certain that the upcoming treaty conference in the spring of 1842 would rectify this oversight. This fact added to the immediacy of the attempt.

If instructions were not carefully followed, the incident was doomed. The possibility that the whole affair would be discovered not only jeopardized freedom for slaves, but also threatened abolitionists and members of Congress. More important, if the plot was discovered, it would strengthen the South's hold on the House and Senate.

Failure was not an option. It would require a steely resolve with no qualms about creating a slave revolt. The man, or men, sent to instruct the slaves would have had knowledge of Richmond's Shockoe Bottom, be able to assume the identity of a buyer, and have a clear understanding about the timing, manner, and execution of a revolt. The one person Leavitt knew who could facilitate such an attempt was Reverend George Bourne.

> Since my visit to Richmond, the horrors of bondage, to me always a source of bitter anguish, have been exhibited to my view on a more extended scale than I had ever previously witnessed them. Here almost every morning the crimson auction flag, fit emblem of the purpose it proclaims, announces on its conspicuous label, that the blood and bones of American citizens are publicly to be vended! Here, half covered with rags, and loaded with chains, human beings are driven together in crowds, and by beings calling themselves human, are sold and brought. Within a few days past, I have beheld in Richmond hundreds of men, women, and children, thus exposed in the open streets, and bartered off like brute animals.[250] —George Bourne

As a member of the radical American and Foreign Anti-Slavery Society, Bourne had the support and means to carry out such a daring operation. Once in Richmond, Bourne would appear as just another businessman on a buying trip, one of many strangers in Richmond for the selling season.

There was still the crucial question of who to recruit. One factor that would have marked a person as a possible recruit were scars of resistance: telltale signs from whippings, beatings, and disfigurements. While such signs would have been a "caveat emptor" to perspective buyers, they would also have been a clear indicator to someone looking to recruit individuals for an attempt to mutiny a vessel at sea.

Regarding a plot to revolt, such an adventure would partially rely on recruiting slaves already known to those in the abolitionist movement. This would greatly increase the chance of success. A person (or persons) of reasonable intelligence, if not some basic form of education, and some knowledge of sailing and navigation who could be trusted, would be ideal for a revolt. It is documented that certain men who participated in the revolt on the *Creole* had such knowledge. George Portlock and Doc Ruffin could read a compass, and Pompey Garrison had sailed the route to New Orleans on previous voyages. Another consideration involved those who had prior contact with abolitionists and were considered capable. It was known that Madison Washington returned to Virginia to secure his wife's freedom. The possibility that he would be captured and sold South was likely, since he had been warned by many of this eventuality. The fact that Madison would be taken to Richmond, auctioned, and sold would have made him a prime candidate to recruit.

Although it would seem foolhardy to visit the slave markets without a specific list of slaves to contact, the actual process to instruct the slaves is only conjecture. But, a slave could have been approached and cautiously relayed instructions, possibly in one of the private showings, where for a few brief moments the provocateur was alone with the individual. The one incentive offered was the simple possibility of freedom.

What is definitely known is that Madison Washington was purchased by a broker from New Orleans named Thomas McCargo. McCargo's nephew, Theophilus J. D. McCargo, and a slave driver by the name of John R. Hewell, were present in Richmond and escorted Madison and forty-nine other slaves to New Orleans, on board the brig *Creole*.

Another factor that strongly supports the theory of a plot concerns involvement of intercoastal slave ships other than the *Creole*. It stands to reason that if abolitionists were recruiting slaves for an insurrection on board slave ships, it was pertinent to recruit several different slaves who were being shipped on different ships—to ensure the plot had a reasonable expectation for success.

From *Niles National Register*, dated December 18, 1841, the following seems to indicate that this may have been the case.

> We have some interesting particulars in relation to the conduct of the British authorities in Nassau. That the entire scheme was resolved upon before the brig left Richmond, is evident from the fact, that the negroes boasted at Nassau that they expected to encounter the brig *Long Island* and *Orleans*, which sailed from Richmond in company with the *Creole*, with cargoes of slaves. . . [251]

In the spring of 1841, the brig *Orleans* was reported to have been in a previous failed plot that was to be carried out by slaves being shipped to New Orleans. In Solomon Northup's book, *Twelve Years a Slave*, he relates how he and two others planned to take over the *Orleans* and gain their freedom. But due to the unforeseen death from smallpox of the leader of the revolt, the *Orleans* arrived safely in New Orleans without incident.

Had the *Orleans* returned to Richmond at the same time as the *Creole*, now ready to sail with a new cargo of slaves? To reasonably back up the report that the *Orleans* and the *Long Island* may have been involved in a slave revolt at sea, it would be necessary to show that both ships sailed with the *Creole*. If it can be shown that the *Creole*, *Orleans* and the *Long Island* sailed together, this would add weight to the report in *Niles National Register* wherein it states, ". . . the negroes boasted at Nassau that they expected to encounter the brig *Long Island* and *Orleans*, which sailed from Richmond in company with the *Creole*, with cargoes of slaves . . ."

Following is an excerpt from the *Creole* log, dated Saturday, October 30, 1841:

> Saturday, Oct. 30th, 1841—All this day, light, variable winds. At eleven A.M. got under way, and worked down the bay. At eight p. m. came to anchor in Lynnhaven Bay, in company with brigs *Orleans* and *Long Island*, and several other sail. So ends this day.

> Sunday—Nothing of importance. Got under way and proceeded to sea. Winds S. E. etc.

Suffice to say, the brig *Creole* was, in fact, the company of the slavers *Orleans* and *Long Island*, as all three ships awaited favorable tide and weather in Lynnhaven Bay before putting to sea.

The idea of a conspiracy planned by a handful of radical abolitionists may seem farfetched, a scheme drawn from random events. However, there are others who acknowledge the impact that Madison Washington was about to have on his times.

The abolitionist faithful on both sides of the Atlantic, however, were more prescient than later historians and quickly grasped the full impact of Madison Washington's actions in their battle to destroy the South's peculiar institution.[252]

The existence of clandestine activities during this period of American history is not that unusual. For example, a certain "O.J." Smith was directed by President Tyler to pay off the press in Maine and Massachusetts to garner public support for upcoming negotiations between the United States and Her Majesty's government. The negotiations, which culminated with the Webster-Ashburton Treaty, sought to rectify a series of disputes between England and the United States. One of the disputes concerned the intercoastal slave trade and the recent Creole Incident, which threatened the outcome of the negotiations. The money was derived from a slush fund maintained by the president and contributions from certain parties in Her Majesty's government.

Then there were Albert Fitz's espionage missions, employed by Secretary of State Daniel Webster. England's objections over the recent arrest of a British citizen named Alexander McLeod, coupled with the border dispute between Maine and Canada, was enough of a concern that the United States sent spies to investigate whether England was using its colony of Bermuda for war preparations. Interestingly, Albert Fitz was recommended to Webster as an effective secret agent by fellow New Englander, John Quincy Adams. Others, such as Duff Green and John B. Hogan, also carried out espionage for Secretary Webster at the time of the Creole Incident. However, further substantiation was required to establish any credibility to the claim that slaves were instructed on the means to carry out a revolt prior to their departure from Richmond.

The following newspaper reports may add some credence to such a claim.

The New Orleans Bulletin of December 3, 1841:
Mutiny and Murder on board the Brig Creole.
Slaves set free by British Authorities.
The brig Creole, Capt. Ensor, with a cargo of tobacco, five passengers, and 135 slaves as steerage passengers, from Richmond, bound for New Orleans, sailed from Hampton Roads on the 27th of October. On the evening of the 7th of November, the slaves rose in mutiny, murdered Mr. Hewell, a passenger, and owner of most of the slaves, desperately wounded the captain and several others, and compelled the second mate and crew to navigate the vessel into a British port. That this horrid affair was not the effect of a sudden outburst of passion, appears clear, from what was acknowledged

by some of the culprits on their examination at Nassau, that Mr. Bourne, a Baptist preacher in Richmond, had instructed them as to the mode of procedure, before they left. The further particulars will be found in the following letter, which, being open, we were permitted to copy on board the Creole.[253]

And from the Boston Liberator, December 24, 1841:

"After the arrival of the *Creole* at Nassau, the slaves acknowledged that a Baptist minister at Norfolk, named Bourne, had advised them with regard to their course, and given them directions how to proceed. Mr. Goddard learned at Nassau that Bourne had formerly resided there, and had absconded, leaving his family. He is an Englishman, and about forty years of age."[254]

And from the Times of London, Friday, January 14, 1842:

"That Mr. Bourne, a Baptist preacher in Richmond, instructed them as to the mode of procedure before they left, as was learned from an examination of the slaves at Nassau . . ."[255]

Times, Friday, January 14, 1842
The Creole Affair.
The New Orleans Picayune published a few additional particulars in relation to this affair. Bourne, the Baptist Minister, who is said to have been the adviser of the outbreak (but statements of this kind should be received with great caution,) is represented to be an Englishman 40 years of age, and who some time since ran away from his family at Nassau. N. P. The Picayune adds: "Forty of the slaves on the Creole were owned by Thomas McCargo, of Richmond; the balance belonged to Johnson and Eperson. Mr. Howell was the agent of McCargo, and was well known in the city. Three of the slaves were killed in the affray, and another died of his wounds after his arrival at Nassau. Five more-four females and a boy-refused to accept of their freedom, and came to the port in the Creole. It is worthy of remark that a dog, belonging to the captain, fought furiously against the negroes, and bit several of them seriously. He was finally killed.[256]

20

The Brig Creole

A few more beatings of the wind and rain,
Ere the winter will be over-
Glory, Hallelujah!
Some friends have gone before me,-
I must try to go and meet them-
Glory, Hallelujah!
A few more rising and settings of the sun,
Ere winter will be over-
Glory, Hallelujah!
There's a better day a coming-
There's a better day a coming-
Oh, Glory, Hallelujah![257]

The *Creole* was built in Richmond, Virginia, in the year 1840. Classified as a brig, the ship had a square stern; one deck and two masts; a length of ninety-five feet; the breadth, twenty-five feet, six inches; her depth was eight feet, nine inches. The *Creole* weighed in at one hundred-eighty-seven and 25/95 tons and on her bow was a lady's figurehead. The *Creole* was built for the purpose she now was employed in, as a coastal slaver.[258]

An enrollment—a certification or registry of her as a commercial ship—was issued each year she had been in service. The enrollments for the *Creole* were numbered 126 and 137. The one issued in 1841 read as follows:

In conformity to An Act of the Congress of the United States of America, entitled 'An Act for Enrolling and Licensing Ships or vessels to be employed in the Coasting Trade and Fisheries, and for regulating the same,' Isaac Davenport Jr. of the City of Richmond-State of Virginia, having taken or subscribed the oath required by the said Act, and having sworn that David Curry of the said city and himself are citizens of the United States, and sole owners of the ship or vessel, called the Brig Creole of Richmond, whereof Robert Ensor is at present Master, and as he hath sworn is a citizen of the United States, and that the ship or vessel was built at Richmond in the year one thousand and eight hundred and forty and (unreadable) having certified that the said ship or vessel has one deck and two masts and that her length is ninety five feet; her breadth twenty-five feet, six inches; her depth eight feet nine inches; and that she measures one hundred & eighty seven and 25/95 tons; and a ladies figure head: And the said Isaac Davenport Jr. having agreed to the description and measurement above specific, and sufficient security having been given according to the said Act, the said Brig Creole has been duly enrolled at the Port of Richmond. Given under my hand and seal at the Port of Richmond, this nineteenth day of October, in the year one thousand eight hundred and forty-one.[259]

It was signed on the nineteenth of October, 1841 by the court collector, H Weston. Johnson and Eperson of Richmond owned the vessel and had it insured for $16,000, while the cargo of tobacco and slaves were insured for $50,000 by the Louisiana Insurance Company.[260] The insurance was common business practice and had in the past protected owners from the loss of cargo. One recent example concerned Robert Lumpkin, who owned slaves shipped on the ship *Hermosa* the previous year. The *Hermosa* had shipwrecked at Abaco and the colonial wreckers, who had come to rescue the crew, also took the slaves to Nassau and set them free.

The slaves on the *Creole* were owned by a variety of people; Thomas McCargo, Johnson & Eperson, Henry Hewell, and Robert Lumpkin—who owned ninety of the slaves. The majority of slaves were brought aboard the *Creole* on the twentieth of October, 1841, while in Richmond. As the *Creole* was being readied for its voyage, the slaves were allowed some freedom of movement on the ship but were closely watched. Madison Washington was reported to have been assigned as the cook for the slaves, which gave him a daily opportunity to communicate with most of the male bondsmen on board. Each night, all slaves were chained below decks.

The manner in which the slaves were to be shipped was a practiced routine, calculated down to the last detail. The slaves were chained, two together, and were packed into the hold of the *Creole* much the same way as was the practice during the Middle Passage, when slavers plied their trade from western Africa to the New World. A typical male was allocated a space six feet long by sixteen inches wide; every woman a space of five feet ten inches by sixteen inches wide; every boy, five feet by fourteen inches; and every girl, four feet, six inches by twelve inches wide. Between the male and female slaves on the *Creole* was the cargo of the brig—boxes of tobacco, some hemp, and several cases of wine.

It has been written that this was the *Creole's* maiden voyage. However, recent research has shown that this was not the case. Records show the *Creole* had delivered a shipment of slaves to New Orleans as recently as August 1841. On its return voyage to Richmond, the ship's manifest shows the vessel had sailed from New Orleans on August 13, 1841. It further reveals that a twenty-eight-year-old slave, classified as "yellow" and named R. Freeman, was being shipped aboard the *Creole* by Captain Ensor on the return voyage to Richmond.

The fact that both the *Orleans* and the *Creole* made earlier voyages from Richmond to New Orleans in 1841 suggests the shipment of slaves from

Richmond to the Lower South was carried on throughout the year. The implication is that the intercoastal slave trade was far more extensive and the numbers of slaves shipped south from the Chesapeake ports to New Orleans was far greater than presently reported.

The policy of those who plied this trade was to separate male and female slaves. On the *Creole*, male slaves were placed in the forward hold, all except old Lewis, a servant of Theophilus J.D. McCargo, and Elijah Morris, a servant to William Merritt. Elijah Morris was one of the slaves Madison Washington had recruited in the slave pens, and Elijah found himself in the fortunate position of being kept above decks during the voyage, where he became familiar with the ship's routine, the preparation and sailing of the *Creole*, and the performance of the crew.

Female slaves were put in the aft hold—except four female servants, who were taken into the cabins as "fancy girls." These girls were sequestered in the stateroom of John Hewell, and had the privileges of concubines—better food, drink, and the comfort of a warm bed. To ensure a more pleasurable relationship, and to avoid having to force compliance, the white overseer often attempted to mollify his charges with gifts and favors. Not all girls purchased for the purpose of pleasure participated as concubines. Some refused the demands of their captors. No matter. Either through gifts or force, white overseers usually got what they wanted, despite protests. The one inducement that was a constant was flogging. Tales of fancy girls misused on the intercoastal ships were not uncommon.

> There was lately found, in the hold of a vessel engaged in the southern trade, by a person who was clearing it out, an iron collar, with three horns projecting from it. It seems that a young female slave, on whose slender neck was riveted this fiendish instrument of torture, ran away from her tyrant, and begged the captain to bring her off with him. This the captain refused to do; but unriveted the collar from her neck and threw it away in the hold of the vessel. The collar is now at the anti-slavery office, Providence. To the truth of these facts Mr. William H Reed, a gentleman of the highest moral character, is ready to vouch.[261] —Theodore Weld

Between the male and female slaves was stored the cargo.[262] As groups of slaves were brought aboard the *Creole*, it was all but impossible for those already stored in the holds to know who was now onboard. If by chance a wife, mother, daughter, sister, father, son, or brother were on board, with men and women separated, there was little way of knowing the other's fate. From his days with the American Seaman's Society, Leavitt was well-aware of the manner in which the slaves were shipped and separated. The knowledge that men were in the forward hold, away from the crew's quarters, while women were kept in the aft hold was crucial intelligence that Bourne would have passed along to those he recruited.

Those slaves who were boarded onto the *Creole* on October 20, 1841 who participated in the revolt were the following: Madison Washington, Elijah Morris, Ben Blaire, Andrew Bunkind, and Willy Glover. Each of these men had been purchased by Thomas MacCargo, and both Madison and Elijah played a significant role in the revolt. Eventually over twenty men would take a role in the revolt, with nineteen being implicated and held on charges of mutiny and murder.

The *Creole*, heavily laden with cargo and supplies, departed Richmond, Virginia, at midnight on twenty-fifth of October with one hundred two slaves on board. It made its way down the James River in tow by the steam vessel *Ben Sheppard*. At City Point the *Creole* was released to sail on its own. Between the twenty-sixth and the thirty-first of October, the *Creole* made its way down the James River toward the open sea. During this time, several slaves a day were boarded, bringing the total number to one hundred thirty-five. The following entries are from the ship's log:

Remarks—Monday, Oct. 25, 1841—All this day clear and cold, at midnight left Richmond in tow with steamer Ben Sheppard. Ends this day.

Remarks—Tuesday. Oct. 26, 1841—All this day fresh gales from S. W. and clear wr. At night A.M. cast off from the steamboat, and made sail at ten A.M. Came to anchor at Minse's at one P. M..   Got under way and worked down the river. At nine came to anchor at Hog Island. So ends this day.

Remarks—Wednesday, 27th Oct. 1841—All this day light breezes from S. E. and clear. At six A.M. got under way and worked down the river. At six P. M. came to anchor at Day's Point. Put Captain Ensor on board the steamboat for Norfolk, and took three negroes on board. So ends this day.

Thursday, 28th Oct. 1841—All this day fresh breezes from S. E. At noon got under way. At five P. M.   came to anchor at Newport News. Capt. Ensor came on board with thirty-three negroes. So ends this day.

Friday, Oct. 29, 1841—All this day fresh breezes from east, and some rain. At one got under way. At four came to anchor at Sewel's Point. So ends this day.

Saturday, Oct. 30th, 1841—All this day, light, variable winds. At eleven A.M. got under way, and worked down the bay. At eight P. M.   came to anchor in Lynnhaven Bay, in company with brigs *Orleans* and *Long Island*, and several other sail. So ends this day.

Sunday—Nothing of importance. Got under way and proceeded to sea. Winds S. E. etc.

Another source that conforms to the log were the affidavits taken of the crew and passengers from the *Creole*.

The brig *Creole* sailed from Richmond, Virginia on 25 October, 1841, with 102 slaves on board . . . That about 90 of said slaves were shipped on board the 20th of said month, of which 41 were shipped by Robert Lumpkin, about 39 by John R Hewell, 9 by Nathaniel Matthews, and 1 by William Robinson;

that from that time about one or two a day were put on board by John R. Hewell, until about the said 25th day of October, so as to make the whole number 135 slaves.[263]

The *Creole* finally proceeded to sea on Sunday, October 31, 1841. Laden with tobacco, hemp, wine and one hundred thirty-five human beings, the vessel was severely cramped. By the time the *Creole* set sail for New Orleans, many of those held in bondage had been on board for over a week. It was late in the season and the weather was turning bad.

During clear weather, the slaves were brought up on deck twice a day for feeding and exercise. The men remained secured by the ankle to a long chain that ran along the bulwarks on either side of the deck. The woman and young children, when brought up on deck, were allowed some freedom of movement. The first meal was usually served about nine in the morning and consisted of horse beans with some pork mixed in and rice. Water was rationed to a half pint at each feeding. After the morning meal, the slaves were forced to dance about, usually accompanied by a fiddle or banjo. It was considered a therapeutic measure to ensure against scurvy and suicidal depression. The other form of inducement to dancing was the always persuasive "cat-o'-nine-tails."

During rough weather or squalls, the slaves were confined below decks and were fed in the hold where the air became thick and noxious to breathe. There were a series of air portals on each side of the ship that allowed fresh air to circulate below decks. But when the seas became too rough, it became necessary to cover these openings to keep from shipping water. Along with this precaution, the hatches were battened down, portholes sealed, and gratings covered.

On Tuesday, November 2, the ship began to encounter rough seas. In the *Creole's* log, it was noted at the noon entry, ". . . middle part flyin [sic] clouds and heavy seas, S.E."

By the evening of November 3, the weather had turned increasing severe. Again, from the ship's log: "latter part lite [sic] winds and cloudy heavy sea from S.E. vessel labouring [sic] heavy Latt. By obs, 35 degrees 48."

The situation took on a more ominous aspect by Thursday, November 4. ". . . heavy sea vessel labouring heavy making considerable water kept one man at the pump So ends this day" [264]

From the fourth on, the slaves were confined below decks due to the weather. On Saturday, November 4, a barrel of beef was opened to feed the slaves, and the fifth cask of water was tapped.

There were two separate groups of slaves, those under the charge of William Henry Merritt, listed as a passenger but in fact hired by the captain as an overseer and could almost be considered part of the crew. The other group was overseen by John Hewell, an experienced slave driver who had the particular charge of those slaves owned by Thomas McCargo. Although McCargo's nephew Theophilus was a passenger on the vessel, he was considered too young and inexperienced to handle the slaves.

It was thought that the crew was sufficient enough to quell any disorder that might break out. Zephaniah C. Gifford, the first mate of the *Creole*, in a sworn statement made in the city of New Orleans on December 18, 1841, stated: "The slaves were all carefully watched, were perfectly obedient and quiet, and showed no signs of mutiny and disturbance, and all things went well, and nothing material occurred, excepting of making and taking in sail." [265]

21

Prelude to a Showdown

I cannot but be much gratified that my course in reference to the important subjects of the currency and Abolition should receive your approbation, and [that of] those whom you represent on this occasion. They are, indeed, questions of the first magnitude, full of difficulty and danger . . . We have now, for the first time since the Government went into operation, an opportunity to apply an effectual corrective, quietly and peaceably, but which, if permitted to pass without being embraced, will, it is to be feared, be lost forever . . .[266] —John C. Calhoun 1840

For a democracy to fulfill its requirement of participation by the governed; free, fair, and open debates on issues must be employed. Nothing was more ominous to this form of democracy than the imposition of the Gag Rule. Since 1836, representatives of the slave-holding states were unimpeded in their goal to legally incorporate Southern institutions into federal jurisprudence. Their march toward a reformation of the Constitution was led by the one person who personified Southern ideals and was the leading voice for the reformation of the Constitution: Senator John Cadwell Calhoun of South Carolina.

Born March 18, 1782, in what was referred to as District Ninety-Six, Abbeville, South Carolina, Calhoun was filled with the Southern philosophy of agricultural pursuits and the use of slave labor as the machinery of the South. Although he attended Yale and Tapping Reeve's law school in Litchfield, Connecticut, he returned home uninfluenced by Northern ideas of free labor. He married Florida Bonneau on January 8, 1811, at Bonneau Ferry, South Carolina, and set out on his illustrious career in politics. He was elected to the South Carolina state legislature and then went on to the United States House of Representatives. He served as President Monroe's Secretary of War in 1817, was elected to the United States Senate, was vice president for both John Q. Adams (1825-1829) and Andrew Jackson (1829-1832) and became secretary of state in John Tyler's administration.

The death of both parents and an only sister while Calhoun was an adolescent left a lasting scar that many thought contributed to his aloof posture. He is described as a lonely man, obsessed over his position as protectorate of Southern institutions. John Niven, one of Calhoun's biographers, wrote the following:

> ... Calhoun was a driven man and a tragic figure. His ambition, his personal desire to achieve leadership, was often thwarted by lesser men than he. The life he made for himself, the security he felt on his plantation with his dependent retainers, and the agriculture pursuits that represented to him and to his neighbor's stability in a rapidly changing environment were beyond price. Any menace to the Southern institutions he valued was to be resisted with all the force of his character and his intellect.[267]

Calhoun was a disciple of the Jeffersonian school of government, a concept that democratic government and the virtues of republicanism have their foundation in agriculture. Calhoun modeled his South Carolina Exposition and Protest of Nullification on the Virginia-Kentucky Resolutions, written by Jefferson and Madison in 1799. The Virginia-Kentucky Resolutions asserted that, ". . . the several states who formed [the Constitution] [are] sovereign and independent."

Jefferson expressed the view that the federal government was a compact that could be superseded by the states through a process of nullification, ignoring a federal directive if it was felt to be in any way an infringement on state sovereignty. Jefferson believed the Virginia-Kentucky Resolutions presented a rightful remedy should the federal government usurp power. However, Jefferson later found such concepts incompatible with the meaning of constitutional government when he became president. The realities of governing such diverse states under one government, coupled with the threat of European intervention in the affairs of America, caused Jefferson to reevaluate his earlier concepts on states' rights.

This, though, did not deter Calhoun from his belief in state sovereignty. He considered the United States a union of states as communities, and not a union of individuals. In fact, he took the argument to the point where it threatened the very concept of union. Calhoun believed that the people of each state were sovereign at the time of ratification of the Constitution; that in the process of ratifying the constitution each acted as a sovereign and separate unit. The constitution, according to Calhoun, is a compact between separate and sovereign states; that each separate and sovereign state has a right to judge the terms of the compact and take actions as appeared necessary to maintain the rights of the individuals of the states, maintaining each state's sovereignty.

In opposition of Calhoun's defense of Southern institutions was John Quincy Adams. Adams's interpretation of governance can be traced back to the previous generation of the Founding Fathers. Adams's father, the second president of the young republic, diametrically opposed those ideals of government attributed to Jefferson. Adams's opposition to the Jeffersonian school of government became the source of competition between the two Founding Fathers that lasted until their deaths. Ironically, both Jefferson and Adams died on the same day: July 4, 1826, mere hours apart.

Adams's son, John Quincy, continued the harsh assessment of Jeffersonian government. He also had certain misgivings of Jefferson the man, as reflected in his assessment of Jefferson:

> His love of liberty was sincere and ardent, but confined to himself, like that of most of his fellow-slaveholders. He was above that execrable sophistry of the South Carolina nullifiers, which would make slavery the corner-stone of the temple of liberty. He saw the gross inconsistency between the principles of the Declaration of Independence and the fact of Negro slavery; and he could not, or would not, prostitute the faculties of his mind to the vindication of that slavery, which, from his soul, he abhorred. But Jefferson had not the spirit of martyrdom.[268]

The nullification crisis, formulated by Calhoun, brought the nation to the brink of civil war as several sovereign states threatened to leave the Union. Adams shot back against Calhoun's ideas of nullification: "It is the odious nature of [this] question that it can be settled only at the cannon's mouth."[269]

The flashpoint was never reached due to strong actions taken by President Jackson and Congress, which defused the crisis, but only temporarily. The issue of states's rights and slavery would not be so easily swept under the rug. By Calhoun's own admission, the nullification crisis only brought to the surface the true source of contention that threatened the Union: "I consider the Tariff but as the occasion rather than the real cause of the present unhappy state of things."[270]

Calhoun argued the right of secession existed when he stated in the Nullification Resolutions "that each state of the union has the right whenever it may deem such a course necessary for the preservation of its liberties or vital interests, to secede peaceably from the Union, and that there is no constitutional power in the general government, much less in the executive department, of the government, to retain by force such State in the Union."

Herein lies the dilemma. Calhoun was not wrong in his interpretation. Legal secession could be legislated if those who desired to leave the Union had enough representation to secure its passage in the House and Senate. This interpretation goes back to the inception of the Constitution.

The Constitution developed from a number of compromises and is not accidentally ambiguous in its nature. To satisfy objections of individual states and their sovereignty so as to obtain ratification, no word in the Constitution prohibited a state from withdrawing from the Union, and every power not expressly given to the national government belonged to the states and the people.

> The usual argument for State rights was based on the contention that the Constitution was the creation of the several states acting as separate and sovereign political entities. On this basis the confederate nature of the union and the legal right of secession were deemed to follow logically." —Charles Grove Hanes[271]

But secession was not the only course of action available to Calhoun and the South. Calhoun actively sought to strengthen the protections in the Constitution pertaining to states' rights. He planned to reform the Constitution to what he believed were its original designs based on a Jeffersonian agrarian society.

The first step toward Southern domination of the government had been accomplished with the imposition of the Gag Rule. By denying debate on the subject of slavery, the Gag Rule all but insured the majority of new representation in Congress would be amenable to agrarian interests.

On the other hand, without the Gag Rule the Southern way of life would cease to exist. By 1840 Calhoun astutely recognized this fact, expressed in a letter to A. T. Moore.

"Our geographical position, our industry, pursuits, and institutions, are all peculiar. Our safety and prosperity depend on maintaining, in their full vigor, the restrictions imposed on the powers granted by the Constitution."[272]

Although confident he could lead the South in reordering the government, Calhoun was opposed by those who saw the Gag Rule as a mechanism that not only restricted debate in Congress by curtailing abolitionist petitions, but, more important, allowed the unimpeded growth of Southern representation. By 1841, this competition between North and South began to focus on the annexation of Texas.

Rarely has there been a more astute politician than Calhoun. It was evident to him that the second session of the 27th Congress in December of 1841 would be the make-or-break point in Southern ascendancy. In a letter written in October of 1841, to Representative Dixon H. Lewis of Alabama, Calhoun recognized the critical junction afforded the South.

> Never before was there so fair an opportunity of reforming the Government and restoring the Constitution; and if permitted to pass, never, I fear, will there be such another.[273]

In October of 1841, Calhoun conveyed his perceptions when he wrote the following: "The coming session of the Legislatures of the States will all become centers of movements this fall, in the false if not the true direction. We have great advantages . . . Let me add, we of the South have by far the deepest stake in events taking at this time the proper direction. To all it involves liberty and prosperity, but to us it is existence.[274]

By November of 1841, Calhoun was certain the opportunity to take control was at hand. "[A] thorough reformation of the Government and restoration of the Constitution may be effected . . . Many of my friends think the time has arrived when my name ought to be presented for the next presidency . . . I can best restore the Constitution & reform the government."[275]

Calhoun began to enlist support from his constituents and his party for a presidential run in 1844. Calhoun was convinced his election, combined with control of Congress by Southern representation, would provide the means to dictate the direction of government. The following letter, dated October 1841, to Dixon H Lewis, a representative from Alabama's Fourth District and an early supporter of Calhoun, implies Calhoun's willingness to be drafted as a candidate for the president of the United States.

> As to myself I can say to you who knows [sic] me, without having sincerity

impeached, that I would not accept the office, even of chief magistrate, if voluntarily offered by the people, except on the principle of duty. It is at all times and under all circumstances, a toilsome task to perform its duties as they ought to be; but to discharge the duties of a reform administration, as the next must be, if the country is to be saved-to correct the abuses of the Departments . . . and to put down Federalism effectually, and restore the Constitution to the simplicity & purity, intended by its framers, would be a Herculean task & would consume the rest of my days, which I am anxious to devote to other purposes. But, if I am thought to be the one, that ought to be selected for the great work, I would not shun it, or shrink from the duties & responsibilities attached to it.[276]

Although the designs of Senator Calhoun seemed within his grasp, there existed a flaw. Herman Melville's depiction of Bannadonna in "The Bell Tower,"[277] written in 1855, eerily resembles Calhoun and his preparations for the upcoming Congress. Little did he realize there was a plan already in place to breach the wall of censorship the South had erected in the form of the Gag Rule. The flaw was built into the very institution he so strongly defended. It lay hidden and dormant in the intercoastal slave trade that plied its human cargo between the old tobacco plantations of the Upper South and the sugarcane fields of Louisiana.

As October turned to November of that fateful year of 1841, Senator Calhoun would have been preparing to leave Fort Hill, South Carolina, for his return to the Senate. The ironic twist was that at that same moment, passing off the coast of South Carolina, the intercoastal slave brig, the *Creole*, was on its voyage south. Upon its storm-washed decks rode the fate of its crew and cargo, and most important to Senator John Caldwell Calhoun, the fate of the South and the future of the United States of America.

22

Mutiny and Murder

Nine days out the Creole encountered rough weather. Most of the slaves were sea-sick and were therefore not watched as closely. On Sunday evening of November seventh, 1841, the Creole was ordered by the captain to be 'hove to', to prepare for a stop at the Abaco Island. The following morning; latitude 28 degrees, 30', longitude 76 degrees at 12 o'clock noon. At half past nine of the same evening, Madison Washington was discovered in the section of the ship where the women were kept by Mr. Gifford.
—Affidavit of Lucius Stevens, sailor, 10 November, 1841

In early November, 1841, the *Creole* tacked east and then south along the eastern seaboard of the United States. For several days the ship encountered severe weather and the holds of the ship where the slaves were kept were not as closely watched. The *Creole* was presently headed for Hole-in-the-Wall, a series of islands in the Bahamas. Once through Hole-in-the-Wall, the *Creole* would sail toward the tip of Florida and then across the Gulf of Mexico to the mouth of the Mississippi. It usually took twenty to twenty-five days to complete the trip from the Chesapeake ports to New Orleans, longer if the weather was bad.

On the night of November 7, 1841, at eight P. M., Captain Ensor believed the *Creole* was near Abaco Island. In fact, the ship was at latitude 27 degrees 46' north, and 75 degrees 2' west. Ensor ordered the ship to "lay to," meaning, to bring (a ship) into the wind and hold stationary.[278] The *Creole* stopped for the night to await first light before it proceeded on to Abaco Island and Hole-in-the-Wall.

The order to have the ship "lay to" would have been noticed by the slaves confined below decks. The sound of the crew moving about on deck as orders were shouted and the change in the way the ship laid in the water informed those below that the *Creole* was in the vicinity of Abaco Island. This alerted Madison Washington and his fellow conspirators that they were within a day's sail of a British port and freedom.

The following events are based on depositions of the crew and passengers on board the *Creole*. They were given at three different times: the first taken at Nassau before the American consul, John F Bacon, between November 9 and 17, 1841, followed by depositions taken by Robert Duncome, police magistrate, and J. J. Burnside, justice of the peace of Nassau, between November 9 and 12, 1841. A protest was made by the crew and passengers before W. Y. Lewis, a notary public, in New Orleans on December 2, 1841. Although there are no known surviving records of interviews, affidavits or depositions taken of the slaves on board the *Creole*, there are references made with regard to such interviews, affidavits, and depositions.

> There are two versions of the Creole affair, one derived from the protest of certain persons who formed part of the crew of that vessel . . . and the other, founded on private information from Bahama . . . From the latter account, it appears, that the negros having discovered their proximity to a British island, demanded to be landed there; that this was resisted by the captain, passengers and crew; that thereupon a struggle for the mastery commenced which terminated in the triumph of the negros, and the loss of two lives, one a passenger on board the Creole, who had the care of a portion of the slaves, and one of the negros who died of injuries he received on his arrival in Nassau.[279]

The affidavits of the crew and passengers are the main source of information for what occurred onboard the *Creole* the night of the uprising and all follow a similar sequence of events. After battling heavy seas since leaving the shelter of Chesapeake Bay, the crew was finally given a night of respite from the arduous task of sailing the vessel the past seven days on stormy seas.

This strongly suggests the crew of the Creole was exhausted, and the opportunity to have a restful night in calm waters may have been a factor in the crew's readiness. Affidavits of the crew and passengers portray a ship unaware of any threat on the night of November 7, 1841. However, there is the matter of insurance claims that were made for indemnity for loss of cargo. In those proceedings the court found that members of the crew were not forthcoming in regard to the precautions taken to secure the slaves the night of the insurrection.

The following is taken from the protest of the crew and passengers at New Orleans: "Sunday the seventh day of November, eighteen hundred and forty-one, at about nine o'clock, p. m. . . . that Mr. Gifford was then on watch, and was told by Elijah Morris, one of the slaves of Thomas McCargo, that one of the men had gone down aft among the woman."

Gifford went to retrieve Merritt, who was in charge of the slaves.

> Personally appeared before me, John F Bacon, consul of the United States of America at Nassau, Bahamas, William H Merritt, who being sworn, deposeth and saith: . . . That he was a passenger [William Merritt] on board the brig Creole . . . that he had no interest in the vessel or cargo, but in consideration of his attending to the slaves during the passage, he was to be charged nothing for his passage.[280]

Merritt further stated the following in his deposition given before Robert Duncome, police magistrate of Nassau, Bahamas: "On Sunday, Nov. 7, 1841 at about nine p. m., deponent was called at his cabin door by the first mate, Mr. Gifford, who informed him there was a man in main-hold with the female slaves."[281]

Merritt proceeded up on deck to the hatch over the aft hold and waited while Gifford retrieved a match and lamp. Upon his return, Gifford bent down and keyed the lock that secured the hatch.

Gifford asked Merritt to hand him the lamp and struck the match, lighting the wick. The lamp went out just as quickly in the brisk breeze, since they were in an unprotected area. Gifford turned to Merritt, and handed him the lamp and match. Neither man was eager to go into the hold, considering the condition the hold would be in due to the rough weather.

Merritt carefully stepped down the ladder. At the base of the ladder Merritt stopped and tried to see into the darkness. He struck the match and was about to apply it to the wick when he felt someone at his back.

Then had the grate taken off, entered the hold, and struck the light, and discovered that the person was Madison Washington.[282] —William H. Merritt

Merritt was jolted and took a step back. The match burned out and darkness enveloped both men with only the dim light of the night coming from the hatch above. Merritt's words came out in a quick, excited manner. "Doctor, you are the last person I should expect to find here and that you would disobey the orders of the ship."[283] Merritt tried to regain his composure and reestablish his authority, but in the dark confined space, it was difficult not to feel apprehensive.

Madison stared hard at Merritt and answered in a cold, monotone, "Yes sir, it is me."

Both men stood there for a heartbeat, neither knowing what to do. Finally, Madison made for the hatch. "I am going up. I cannot stay here!"

Madison knocked Merritt back against the wall and quickly made his way up the hatch. From above, Gifford tried to stop Madison from reaching the deck, but Madison's adrenalin was rushing. He struggled with Gifford, threw him back, and ran up on deck.

Madison raced across the deck toward the forward hatch. Gifford regained his feet and quickly grabbed a pike, a round slender wood staff tipped with an iron end, as he came up behind Madison to strike him. Just then a shot rang out.

A pistol had been fired by some person unknown, with the ball having struck deponent on the back of the head; immediately deponent ran to the cabin and called out he was shot.[284] Zephaniah C. Gifford, 1st mate of the brig *Creole*

Madison turned and shouted, "Come on, my boys, we have commenced; we must go through with it. Rush boys, rush aft. We've got them now!" Shouting to the slaves below, who were alarmed from the sound of the pistol and the yelling, Madison commanded, "Come up every damn one of you. If you don't and lend a hand, I will kill you all and throw you overboard."

Quickly, the deck was overrun with slaves. Gifford ran to the cabin and roused the captain and the others, exclaiming: "I've been shot! There is a mutiny by the slaves!"

The alarm was given and the crew and passengers awoke to a confusion of sounds. The captain, who had been sprawled out asleep on the cabin floor, quickly came to his senses and shouted out orders that "all turn out." Lucius Stevens, the second mate, rushed up the companionway just as John Hewell came out of his cabin.

Meanwhile, Merritt had gotten the lamp lit. When he heard the pistol shot, he blew it out and stood motionless, listening to the ruckus above. He then went on deck where he was immediately grabbed, and a struggle ensued.

One of the slaves cried out, "Kill him, God damn it. He is one of them!"

Another slave grabbed a handspike and swung it at Merritt's head. Merritt ducked as the pike whistled by and struck the slave who was holding Merritt. They all went down in a heap. As they struggled in the dark, rolling deck, Merritt broke free and made his way to the cabin.

Hewell, awakened by Gifford, jumped down from his berth and grabbed a musket. He rushed to the companionway where he was met by Captain Ensor and some of the crew coming up. By then, Ben Blacksmith and three other insurgent slaves were rushing forward from the deck. Hewell advanced with the cocked musket, and reached the top step of the companionway. After a brief struggle, Hewell got off a shot, which scattered the mutineers. The musket had only been primed with powder and held no shot.

The four slaves regrouped, charged, and grabbed for the gun, wrenching it away, after which Hewell grabbed a handspike. At first, in the dark and confusion of the narrow companionway, the four slaves believed Hewell had grabbed another gun. The four retreated while Hewell advanced against them, hoping to gain the deck. When they realized he was armed with only a handspike they fell on him with clubs and knives and stabbed him not less than twenty times. Hewell staggered back into the stateroom of the young McCargo who, having gotten dressed on hearing the alarm, stood wide eyed as Hewell exclaimed, "I am dead—the Negroes have killed me."

Hewell then crawled into a berth and died.

Meanwhile, Gifford made his escape after rousing the crew. He had run back on deck and up the main rigging to the main-top, while Merritt had become trapped in the cabin. Merritt tried to escape through the skylight without being discovered, but to no avail. He heard the fighting above, and from the sounds of the struggle, it appeared the slaves were gaining the upper hand. In short order, the mutineers began to pound on the cabin door. It would only be a matter of minutes before they gained entry. Merritt hid himself in Hewell's berth, and three of the female concubines covered him with blankets and sat on the edge of the bed, crying and praying.

Lucius Stevens, having seen Hewell pass him by, bleeding, looked up the companionway and saw the slaves cautiously making their way down. He heard them yell out, as they made clear their intentions regarding the second mate, Stevens. Stevens escaped to his own room and locked the door behind him. He later stated in a deposition given before the American Consul, John F. Bacon, on November 10, 1841:

> The blacks were all on deck, and heard them exclaim, 'The captain, mate, and Mr. Hewell are dead, and now we will have that long, tall son of a bitch, the second mate.' Immediately there rushed down the cabin, one with a musket, one with a club and one a knife; the cabin door at the same time was crowded with blacks, armed with clubs; heard several of the crew crying for mercy. The three blacks were then searching for this deponent, (Stevens) and examined the starboard state-rooms, one of which was occupied by the captain's wife and children, without finding deponent; when they exclaimed; 'Let these alone for the last. We want the second mate, and the ship will be ours.' At this moment another black rushed into the cabin, and pointed to deponent's state-room, saying; 'This is his room; immediately one pointed a gun at the door, and other came around it armed with clubs, as he opened the door the gun was fired: in consequence of deponent's turning away the muzzle, one of the slaves was wounded; deponent then ran on deck, when one of the blacks struck him, with a piece of a flag-staff, and another stabbed at him with a knife.[285]

Neither thrust did much damage. In the dark and confusion, Stevens ran to the fore royal yard, where he stayed until morning.

The search for Merritt continued, as the slaves quickly gained control of the ship. The captain, badly wounded and bleeding, along with several of the crew, had made their way up the rigging, and in the dark, clung to their precarious perches, watching and listening to the incident unfolding below. Merritt was soon discovered and dragged on deck with others of the crew. They were lined up, terrified, and threatened with instant death. With death imminent, they experienced great relief when Madison Washington stepped forward and offered to spare their lives if they helped navigate the ship to Nassau.

By one A.M. the ship was in the control of the newly freed slaves, with Madison Washington as captain.

There were occurrences when the newly freed focused their harassment on Lucius Stevens, the second mate and acting chief of the brig, especially after finding him hiding in the rigging. Stevens stated in his deposition before Robert Duncome, Police Magistrate at Nassau;

> About half-past four in the morning he was discovered, when Elijah Morris and four others which deponent can designate, said, 'Come down, you damn son of a bitch, and receive your message.' Deponent came down rather slow, and when he was in the fore-top, he asked them what they wanted to kill him for? Elijah Morris replied, 'Damn you, the best thing for you is to come down and receive your message.' Deponent then came on deck, and asked for five minutes, and told them if they spared his life, he would take them to an English island in three days . . .[286]

Stevens was placed in the hold, where Ben Blacksmith told him, "you will be thrown overboard, as there are a number of bad negroes on board."

Later, Elijah Morris took him aside and said, "Stevens, I do not want to see you hurt, but they talk strong of having you overboard tonight."

Stevens begged to see Madison Washington, who released him from the hold and assigned him to go about his usual duties. At eleven A.M., Stevens was allowed on deck to take observations of the sun, then ordered below again.

At eight p. m. that evening (Monday, November 8), Stevens was walking the quarter-deck when a shot was fired and he heard a ball whistle past. Gifford immediately came up from the cabin and ordered Stevens to go up the masthead and look for the Abaco light.

> While deponent was going up the rigging, he saw one of the party loading a gun, and heard one of the party say, "make haste, be quick;" he got out of reach of them, in consequence of his going up too quick; they did not fire, only laughed.[287]

Although these actions suggest that several of the newly freed had a vendetta against Stevens and focused on him for either amusement or revenge—or both—their actions did not go to outright revenge or murder. In fact, once the slaves had secured the ship, the crew and passengers were protected. The depositions made clear a surprisingly benevolent attitude of the slaves toward the crew and passengers of the *Creole*, as stated by first mate Gifford; "The wounds of the sailors were dressed by the negroes, and the sailors were left to do as they please."[288]

Elijah Morris, when asked after the fight if they intended to kill the sailors, said, "No, I expect we shall rise again among ourselves, but the white people will not be hurt."[289]

In depositions taken by the colonial authorities at Nassau and the protests taken by W.Y. Lewis, a notary public in New Orleans, on December 2, 1841, William Devereux, Henry Speck, John Silvy, Jacques Lacombe, Francis Foxwell, and Blinn Curtis all concur that the slaves stated their intention was freedom: "The nineteen said, all they had done was for their freedom."[290]

In the early hours of November 8, Gifford and Merritt were told to take in the sail because it was too early. Gifford, realizing that the order conflicted with one given earlier to make sail, asked whom he was to obey. Madison Washington then ordered Gifford and Merritt to make sail and told Stevens to go about his regular duty.

Gifford told Stevens to take a bottle of water up to the captain in the maintop. Stevens started up but was called down by Madison and Elijah Morris. "Come down here, you son of a bitch."

Merritt consulted with Madison, and the captain was lowered to the deck and placed in the fore-hold with Stevens. Shortly thereafter, the captain's wife was allowed to go to him. At eight A.M., the captain and his wife were released from the hold and put in the aft cabin under guard.

It is somewhat possible that the revolt was a chance to take advantage of a spontaneous opportunity. Several slaves were aware of their location in relation to Abaco Island, and knew of earlier events where ships had been forced by the stress of weather to seek shelter in a British port, or were wrecked on Abaco. This knowledge lends a possibility to the idea that the slaves took advantage of the moment. The *Comet* (1830), *Encomium* (1834), and *Enterprise* (1835) were all slave ships that came under British jurisdiction in the Bahamas due to weather. The *Hermosa*, a coastal slave ship that shipwrecked at Abaco a year before, was known to some of the slaves on board the *Creole*. English wreckers had taken those slaves to Nassau and set them free. But, the possibility is not a strong one.

In the deposition taken of the *Creole* crew in New Orleans, it was stated that, "Ben Blacksmith, D. Ruffin, and several other slaves said they wanted to go to the British islands. They did not want to go anywhere else but where Mr. Lumpkin's Negroes went last year (alluding to the shipwreck of the schooner *Hermosa* on Abaco).

These earlier situations proved that once a slave entered a port under Her Majesty's jurisdiction, slavery was no longer recognized or enforced. More important, the newly freed slaves were not returned to the States, but instead, were protected in their new-found freedom by English law.

However, there were profound differences between those previous incidents and the actions that occurred on board the *Creole*. The previous cases were not premeditated acts to seek freedom, but rather, opportunities that allowed slaves being shipped south to gain their freedom. Each of these incidents gave the slaves a chance to remain in English colonies at the behest of the colonial authorities.

The slaves on board the *Creole* would now find out if protection under British jurisdiction would be afforded to them, too. The Creole Incident was a situation where the slaves demanded their freedom and secured it by force, rather than by an offer from the English colonial authorities. Although the previous cases were of opportunity and happenstance, the *Creole* Incident was a revolt implemented by nineteen slaves who sought their freedom. How they conducted themselves going forward would be the basis for either prosecution on charges of piracy, mutiny, and murder; or vindication under the laws of England. Further, would it establish that there was justification in seeking their freedom under the protections and provisions found in the Constitution of the United States?

To complicate matters, several newspaper articles claimed the slaves were instructed, which suggests there was premeditation. It begs the question: Were the slaves instructed, or did they have the personal fortitude to enter a British port on their own with as little bloodshed as possible so as to avoid any possible capital charges?

"That Mr. Bourne, a Baptist preacher in Richmond, instructed them as to the mode of procedure before they left, as was learned from an examination of the slaves at Nassau."[291]

The actual "mode of procedure" Madison Washington and the slaves followed during and after the revolt adds weight to the claim that they may have received instruction. Without a doubt, Washington commanded his fellow conspirators to carefully follow his instructions so as to avoid charges of mutiny, murder, and piracy.

As the *Creole* sailed toward Nassau, Bahamas, under the command of Madison Washington, the consequences of actions taken by the nineteen would soon be scrutinized by the British authorities at Nassau. Whether they had received prior instruction or not, Madison and the eighteen others who had led the revolt now placed their fate under what was hopefully the auspices and protections of British colonial law.

23
Nassau, Bahamas

The wounds of the sailors were dressed by the negroes, and the sailors were left to do as they pleased. That during the affray two of the negroes were severely wounded by handspikes . . . On Monday afternoon, Madison got the pistol from one of the nineteen, and said he did not want them to have any arms when they reached Nassau.[292]

The success of the mutiny on Sunday had settled into a tense reality by the early morning hours of Monday. The seas had calmed and day broke with clearing skies and a bright sun. The *Creole* rode easily on swells that no longer fell into whitecaps as a steady, gentle breeze out of the south-southeast buffeted the sails. All of the crew had been accounted for and the wounded attended to. Of the crew of five sailors, only Henry Speck and Blain Curtis were wounded, though not severely. The captain was the most seriously wounded, but would recover.

Earlier that morning, William Merritt was brought to the ship's stateroom to face Madison Washington and the other leaders of the revolt. With a musket pointed at his chest, Merritt was instructed to inform the crew that the *Creole* would now sail to Nassau, New Providence, Bahamas. A chart was produced and Merritt explained the route and read to Madison and the others the *Coast Pilot*.[293] It was agreed that if Merritt oversaw the navigation, his life would be spared. It was also known that ". . . Pompey Garrison had been to New Orleans and knew the route. D Ruffin and George Portlock knew the letters of the compass . . ."[294]

Madison had made sure there would be no secret communications among the crew, and that the course set for Nassau was a true course. He recalled Purvis telling him of the false course set by the crew on board *La Amistad* that had resulted in the capture of the Africans. Every effort was made to ensure it would not be repeated on the *Creole*. Madison, Elijah Morris, Doc Ruffin and Ben Blacksmith took turns watching the compass to be sure the course set for Nassau was complied with. When Merritt was observed writing altitude readings on a slate, he was ordered to rub out the words in writing and directed to write only figures and symbols. On one occasion, Gifford was threatened with death if he spoke to Merritt or communicated in any way with any member of the crew without the approval of one of the nineteen.

The nineteen were the new masters of the ship, with Madison in the role of captain. When not on watch, Madison and the others confined themselves to the cabin at the aft of the ship. Although they had succeeded, Madison would not feel at ease until he was in an English port and off the *Creole*. As instructed, he planned to enter the port unarmed and allow the *Creole* to be returned to authorities in Nassau. In the meantime, he made sure there would be no further bloodshed or harm to crew and passengers.

Interestingly, it was reported that Madison's wife, Susan, had been sold and placed on board the *Creole*, unbeknownst to her husband. However, there is no mention in the depositions from the crew or passengers that substantiate this. The only acknowledgement of the nineteen and of the female slaves being together was made by Gifford in his deposition in New Orleans:

"Madison gave the orders for the cooking for all but the nineteen should be as it was before, and appointed the same cook for them . . . some of the nineteen were hugging the female servants in the cabin; and one of them said he had picked out one of them for his wife . . ." [295]

Although it may have been a device used to enhance Madison's heroic story, the possibility of Susan being on board is not unlikely. Susan would have been considered a problem slave, since she was known to have had correspondence with her husband while he was in Canada. William Wells Brown, a fugitive slave and active abolitionist who resided in Buffalo, New York, wrote the following of Susan and Madison.

> After the arrest of her husband, and his confinement in Richmond jail, it was suspected that Susan had long been in possession of the knowledge of his whereabouts when in Canada, and knew of his being in the neighbor-hood; and for this crime it was resolved that she should be sold and sent off to a southern plantation, where all hope of escape would be at an end.[296]

It is possible that she was brought on board the *Creole* during one of its numerous stops as the brig made its way down the James River after departing Richmond. It is also feasible that she remained on the ship without Madison's knowledge. The *Creole's* log makes mention of slaves brought on board the *Creole* at six p. m. on the twenty-seventh and again on the twenty-eighth:

> Remarks—Wednesday, 27th Oct. 1841.—All this day light breezes from S. E. and clear. At six A.M. got under way and worked down the river. At six p. m. came to anchor at Day's Point. Put Captain Ensor on board the steam-boat for Norfolk, and took three negroes on board. So ends this day.

> Thursday, 28th Oct. 1841. —All this day fresh breezes from S. E. At noon got under way. At five p. m. came to anchor at Newport News. Capt. Ensor came on board with thirty-three negroes. So ends this day.

At five p. m., being close to dark, the male slaves would have been below decks and out of sight, thus unaware of the new slaves being put on board.

Further, it is known that the thirty-three slaves put on board on October 28 at Newport News were owned and shipped by a Mr. Johnson.

> The men and women slaves were divided. The men were all placed in the forward hold of the brig, except old Lewis and a servant of Mr. Thomas McCargo, who stayed in the cabin as assistant servant; and the woman in the hold aft, except six female servants, who were taken in the cabin. Between them was the cargo of the brig, consisting of boxes of tobacco.[297]

As for what might have occurred on board between Susan and Madison, it may never be known. However, there is the possibility of a reunion. The affidavit of Gifford, who stated "some of the nineteen [who revolted] were hugging the female servants in the cabin; and one of them said he had picked out one of them for his wife . . ." alludes to this possibility. It is also conceivable the crew may have misinterpreted this observation. Based on statements attributed to Her Majesty's government and the insurance companies that insured the ship and its cargo, it was insinuated that the crew greatly misrepresented events on board the *Creole*.

Sources from contemporaries of Madison Washington support a claim of a reunion. William Wells Brown wrote the following:

> The next morning "Captain Washington" (for such was the name he now bore) ordered the cook to provide the best breakfast that the store room could furnish, intending to surprise his fellow-slaves, and especially the females, whom he had not yet seen. But little did he think that the woman for whom he had risked his liberty and life would meet him at the breakfast table. The meeting of the hero and his beautiful and accomplished wife, the tears of joy shed, and the hurrahs that followed from the men, can better be imagined than described. Madison's cup of joy was filled to the brim. He had not only gained his own liberty and that of one hundred and thirty-four others, but his dear Susan was safe.[298]

This account is from a later article by R. Edward Lee:

> From that point the slaves took command of the Creole (and guns) with Madison Washington as captain. He demanded that the ship be steered into British waters. Reluctantly, the helmsmen did as they were told with loaded muskets pointed at their heads. On the tenth day "Captain" Washington ordered the cook to "provide the best breakfast that the storeroom could furnish." When the women slaves entered to eat, Susan appeared with them. She did not know that Madison was aboard the *Creole*. A tearful and noisy scene took place with Madison and Susan embracing and weeping. Slaves cheered and whooped.[299]

A contemporary account is from the abolitionist, L Maria Child:

> The next morning Captain Washington ordered the cook to prepare the best breakfast the store-room could furnish, for it was his intention to give all the freed slaves a good meal. The women, who had been greatly frightened by the tumult the night before, were glad enough to come out of their close

cabin into the fresh air. And who do you think was among them? Susan, the beautiful young wife of Madison was there! She had been accused of communicating with her husband in Canada, and being therefore considered a dangerous person, she had been sold to the slave trader to be carried to the market of New Orleans. Neither of them knew that the other was on board. With a cry of surprise and joy they rushed into each other's arms. The freed slaves threw up their caps and hurrahed again and again till the sea gulls wondered at the noise. O, it was a joyful, joyful time. Captain Washington was repaid for all he had suffered. He had gained his own liberty after having struggled for it in vain for years, he had freed a hundred and thirty-four of his oppressed brethren and sisters and he had his beloved Susan in his arms, carrying her to a land where the laws would protect their domestic happiness. He felt richer at that moment than any king with a golden crown upon his head.[300]

And finally, this rendition, a quote from an article written by Col. T. W. Higginson, for the Atlantic Monthly, June 1861, captures a moment:

She was locked to his breast, she clung to him convulsively. Unnerved at last by the revulsion to more than relief and ecstasy, she broke into wild sobs, while the astonished company closed around them with loud hurrahs.[301]

Although each of the renditions displays a consistency, there is no historical evidence that Madison and Susan were reunited the next morning while breakfast was being served, or that there was a great celebration of the fact.[302]

Monday passed without incident. The crew, being closely watched, wanted no further trouble and went about their business. It was critical that the nineteen who led the revolt enter Nassau harbor unarmed, so as to avoid any charges of piracy – a hanging offense. From the depositions of William Devereux, the cook on brig Creole, Henry Speck, John Silvy, Jaques Lacombe, Francis Foxwell and Blinn Curtis, all seamen on brig Creole, taken before W Y Lewis, a Notary Public at New Orleans, on December 14, 1841, we learn the following.

On Monday afternoon Madison got the pistol from one of the mutineers, and said he did not wish them to have any arms when they reached Nassau . . . The nineteen Negroes had thrown overboard and burnt all their weapons before they arrived at Nassau.[303]

The following morning at eight A.M., the Creole was spotted from Nassau's harbor tower and a pilot boat was dispatched to meet it. Mr. Hamilton, a black pilot, and his men came on board to guide the ship into Nassau Harbor on New Providence Island. The control of the ship was given up to the pilot, who was acting under the legal authorities of the island. The fate of the one hundred thirty-five people once held in slavery was now in the hands of the British colonial authorities. When the pilot and his men came aboard the Creole, they mingled with the slaves, telling them they were now free and could go ashore and could never be carried away from here.

The crew, on the other hand, became alarmed at the possibility of losing its cargo. When the regular quarantine officer came alongside the *Creole*, Gifford asked to be taken ashore. Once ashore, Gifford was directed to the American consul, the state department representative of the United States government in Nassau, John F. Bacon. Upon hearing of the mutiny and murder that took place on board the *Creole*, Bacon and Gifford proceeded to the colonial governor's residence.

In November of 1841, the governor of New Providence and all other Bahamas islands was His Excellency Colonel Sir Francis Cockburn, knight, commander-in-chief, et al. Other officials were C.R. Nesbitt, colonial secretary; G. C. Anderson, attorney general; and Mr. Barnside, inspector general of the police.

Upon Gifford's arrival at Government House, he recounted his interpretation of the events that had transpired. On behalf of the *Creole* and all interested, Bacon then requested that the governor put a guard on board to protect the vessel and its cargo. There were five hundred regular British soldiers on the island, divided into four equal companies, each commanded by a captain. Bacon specifically stressed keeping the slaves on board until such time . . . as they should know what to do."

The governor complied and sent a guard of twenty-four Negro soldiers commanded by a white officer, to the *Creole*.

Nassau, November 9, 1841

Sir: The Governor has instructed me to acknowledge the receipt of your letter of this date, relative to alleged mutiny and murders on board of the American brig *Creole*, and to acquaint you that, for the fulfillment of the object of your letter, his Excellency has ordered a military party on board of said brig. There will be, however, no impediment to any of the white persons on board landing here.

I have the honor to be, sir, your most obedient servant.

C.R. NESBITT, Colonial Secretary.

Meanwhile, the *Creole* had dropped anchor about a mile from the American consulate. The captain and the two wounded sailors were taken ashore. Shortly thereafter, a contingent of British soldiers commanded by a Lieutenant Hill and a Captain Fitzgerald arrived and took possession of the vessel. The soldiers mingled with those on board, telling them they were free once they were in a British port. Captain Fitzgerald was overheard telling Mary, one of the slaves owned by McCargo, that it was foolish that they, (meaning the slaves on board the *Creole*) had not killed all the white people on board and run the vessel aground. He said if that was the case, they would have been free by now and there would have been no more trouble.

While the *Creole* lay at anchor, colonial authorities maintained a punctual schedule until matters could be sorted out. The British officers and soldiers on board were changed each morning at nine. At sunset, the male slave passengers were ordered below deck and released to go on deck at sunrise. The females slave passengers were given free rein of the ship but were not allowed to go ashore. A sentry was stationed each night over the hatchways of the holds below deck.

On Wednesday the tenth, the inspector general of the police, Mr. Barnside, and two civil magistrates came aboard to investigate the accusations made by Gifford. Over the next two days, they interviewed the white people on board. After conducting the interviews, it was ascertained that Ben Blacksmith, Madison Washington, Doc Ruffin, and Elijah Morris were the ringleaders of the revolt and that others were involved. These individuals were separated and put in a longboat tied alongside the *Creole* with a guard posted over them.

From the onset, when the British authorities were apprised of the situation, their attitude toward the ship and its contents took a different interpretation than that held by the Americans. The British kept referring to those on board as "passengers," while the Americans called them "slaves." It was becoming clear that the British authorities had little interest in allowing the passengers to be returned to the States, especially those accused of mutiny and murder.

American consul Bacon and the crew of the *Creole* quickly realized that their authority over the *Creole* was slipping away. On the day the *Creole* arrived at Nassau, the governor and his council replied to Bacon's request: "not to suffer any of the slaves on board to land until further investigations can be made."

The reply from the colonial authorities was telling. Cockburn issued the following statement through his colonial secretary.

Council Chambers

Bahamas, November 9, 1841

We wish to state to you, as the representative of the American Government, that the circumstances detailed to the Governor this morning in your presence, respecting the events which took place on board the American brig Creole on the night and subsequently to the seventh of November, have been given all possible consideration to by the Governor and Council, by whom the following decisions have been come to:

1st. That the courts of law here have no jurisdiction over the alleged offenses.

2d. But that as an information had been lodged before his Excellency the Governor, charging the crime of murder to have been committed on board of the said vessel while on the high seas, it was expedient that the parties implicated in so grave a charge not be allowed to go at large, and that an investigation ought therefore to be made into the charges . . . that all parties implicated in such crime . . . should be detained here until reference could be made to the Secretary of State to ascertain whether the parties detained should be delivered over to the American Government or not, and if not, how otherwise to be disposed of.

3d. That as soon as such examinations should be taken, all the persons on board of the Creole, not implicated in any of the offenses alleged to have been committed on board of that vessel, must be released from further restraint.

4th. That a detailed account of what has taken place should be transmitted to the British minister at Washington.

A true copy:

C. R. NESBITT, Colonial Secretary.[304]

The position of the colonial authorities concerning the *Creole* was clear. The "passengers" would be free to go as soon as the investigation was completed. This was in direct opposition to the views held by the American representatives and the crew of the *Creole*. The statements made by the governor and his council alarmed Bacon. He sent out messages to all the Americans in port to come to his aid. Within hours of the arrival of the *Creole* in Nassau, Bacon met with several American seamen from other ships anchored in port. As interviews of those on board the *Creole* were being conducted, Bacon began to put into action his own proposal.

Bacon and Captain Woodside from the bark *Louisia*, anchored in Nassau at the time, began to discuss a plan to board the *Creole*, commandeer it, and sail it to Indian Key where a United States vessel of war was stationed. Indian Key was only four hundred miles from Nassau and could be reached before the British could manage a response. The attempt was to be made in the early hours of the twelfth. A crew made up of seamen from the brig *Congress* and the *Louisia* would row surreptitiously up to the side of the *Creole* and board her, hoping to catch the British guard on board sleeping, or unprepared. Once in control of the ship, the Americans would sail her out of the harbor, releasing the guards outside the break, as the *Creole* made for the open sea.

Over the following days, Woodside and the American Consul met and planned the boarding and takeover of the *Creole*. Muskets and cutlasses were obtained from the *Congress* and efforts were made to obtain others from dealers in Nassau. All refused to sell to the Americans. No matter, for it was known that those slaves who had taken over the *Creole* had destroyed and thrown overboard all their weapons before entering Nassau. There would be no armed response from the slaves.

At the time of the *Creole* Incident, the population of Nassau and vicinity was thirteen thousand freed slaves, and about four thousand whites. The majority of the population's sympathies were definitely with the ex-slaves on board the *Creole*. Any attempt to interfere with their disposition—especially by foreigners who still maintained the institution of slavery in their home country—was not looked upon favorably by the majority population of Nassau. With the Americans in port trying to procure weapons from local dealers, it became obvious that an attempt to retake the *Creole* and sail her to Florida might be underway. Word spread quickly.

In small dinghies and launches near the *Creole*, and along the shore area where the *Creole* was anchored, a twenty-four-hour watch by the locals was instituted. Any suspicious movements of people or boats approaching the *Creole* would be reported to local authorities.

In the early morning hours of November 12th, John Bacon, the American consul, and Captain Woodside, along with several American seamen, met at the water's edge, a mile from the *Creole*. In the bottom of one of their boats, they placed the arms they had been able to collect, wrapped in an American flag. Woodside and the other seamen then pushed off quietly and rowed out to the middle of the harbor toward the *Creole*, as Bacon watched from shore. In the darkness, they made their way in two rowboats, carefully concealing their movements.

A local Negro in a nearby boat observed the loading of the arms. As the American seamen rowed off, he skillfully followed them, undetected. Then he went toward the *Creole*, rowed to the opposite side of the ship, and signaled to the British officer on board of the imminent visit by the American party. On receiving the intelligence, the officer readied his men and awaited the arrival of the Americans.

As the Americans rowed alongside the *Creole*, the officer of the watch came to the rail and looked down at the two approaching rowboats. He hailed them in a calm, purposeful English manner. "I say there," he said, "what purpose do you have in approaching this vessel?"

The Americans, now close enough to grab hold of the side of the *Creole*, looked up at the lone officer.

Woodside addressed the lieutenant. "Stand back. We're coming aboard," he said. "This is an American vessel and we're taking her back."

The lieutenant, in an even, polite tone, looked down at the American contingent and said, "My good sir, I think that would be inappropriate."

Woodside sternly answered, "Stand back, I say!"

The officer replied, "Very well," and stepped back.

The Americans were just about to begin ascending the side of the *Creole*. As they busied themselves with unfurling the flag that hid their weapons, there appeared quietly above them, along the rail of the ship, twenty-four black British soldiers holding muskets with fixed bayonets, hammers cocked, muzzles pointed, and aimed at the Americans.

The lieutenant calmly strode to the rail with his hands tucked behind his back and addressed the Americans in his best upper-crust accent, as they stared up with open mouths.

> "Keep off, or I will fire into you:" his company of twenty-four men were then all standing on deck, and drawn up in line, fronting Captain Woodside's boat, and were ready with loaded muskets and fixed bayonets, for an engagement.[305]

In the face of overpowering force, the Americans had no recourse but to abandon their plan. With clenched teeth and a curse under his breath, Woodside was forced to withdraw.

The failure of the plan was squarely placed on the interference of the British authorities. It was this interference, the Americans later protested, that "prevented aid from being rendered by the American sailors in Nassau, and caused the loss of the slaves to their owners."

Later, when the sun came up, Bacon again approached the governor and requested that time be given for the purpose of writing to Indian Key on the Florida shore, to have a "... vessel of war of the United States to come and protect the brig and her cargo on her voyage from Nassau to New Orleans." The British had seen and heard enough. The request was denied.

At ten o'clock on the morning of the twelfth, two persons came aboard the *Creole*: a Rev. Mr. Poole and the Rev. Mr. Aldrich (spelled in depositions as "Aldridge"), both Episcopal clergymen. This information was obtained from the disposition of William Woodside, the shipmaster of the bark *Louisa*, given to the consul of the United States of America, John F Bacon, on November 13, 1841, in Nassau, Bahamas:

> That he went [Woodside] on board [Creole] about ten o'clock, A.M., [12, Nov.] and soon after two white persons came on board, who he has since ascertained to be the Rev. Mr. Poole and the Rev. Mr. Aldridge [sic], Episcopal clergymen, who were for some time in familiar conversation with the slaves, and appeared to be giving them directions and instructions . . . Deponent heard Mr. Poole say he was going to England, and it was requisite he should know all about this business, so that he could represent the thing.[306]

In 2010, Patrice M. Williams, Assistant Director of Archives, Nassau Bahamas, wrote: "Please be advised that Rev. Pelham Stanhope Aldrich was a missionary from Canada. He arrived in the Bahamas in March 1841."[307]

The Rev Thomas Eyre Poole, MA. was the garrison chaplain at Nassau, New Providence, Bahamas.

Throughout the morning and on into the afternoon, the number of small boats around the *Creole* increased. This small flotilla that surrounded the *Creole* was in the command of the harbor pilot, Mr. Hamilton. The crewmembers on board the *Creole* became increasingly alarmed at the growing flotilla and the perceived threat it posed to the safety of the ship and crew. At one in the afternoon, Gifford went on shore and reported to Bacon the developments on and around the *Creole*. Bacon was waiting for a reply from the governor's council that he believed was in session discussing what to do regarding the *Creole*.

In reality, unbeknownst to Bacon, the decision by the council had been reached shortly before noon. The attorney general of the Bahamas, G. C. Anderson, and several magistrates had already been dispatched to the *Creole*. Upon their arrival, Anderson became aware of the flotilla and ordered that he be rowed out to speak to Harbor Master Hamilton and the others. In his report to the governor, he states the following:

> I visited each of the boats, and addressing the persons in them, informed them of the report which had been made by the consul, explained to them the liability which would attach to them if they acted in the way in which it was alleged they intended to act, and strenuously urged them to abstain . . . In answer, they one and all assured me . . . that they had merely assembled for the purpose of peaceably conveying to shore such persons on board of

the *Creole* that might be permitted to quit her . . .[308]

Attorney General Anderson then made his way to the *Creole* and boarded. Already on board were the magistrates, the crew of the *Creole*, the military guard, and the one hundred thirty-five passengers. The magistrates had ordered the captain of the guards to take the nineteen accused of murder and mutiny to the quarterdeck. Madison and the others, chained at hands and feet, were placed under guard and kept on the quarterdeck as the attorney general conferred with Gifford. He informed Gifford of the council's decision to free all the passengers, and allow them to go ashore or wherever they wanted to go. Gifford at first strongly protested this action until the attorney general replied that he had better, "make no further objections, but let them go quietly on shore, for if he continued in his objections there might be bloodshed."

The attorney general then addressed the nineteen being held:

> Men, there are nineteen of you who have been identified as having engaged in the murder of Mr. Hewell, and in an attempt to kill the captain and others; you will be detained and lodged in prison for a time, in order that we may communicate to the English Government, and ascertain whether your trial shall take place here or elsewhere.[309]

He then went to the rail on the quarterdeck and looked across the deck of the *Creole*, which was filled with passengers and crew. The afternoon was bright with a few clouds drifting in a deep blue sky. An occasional seagull flew overhead, at times motionless as it glided on the currents of warm air. A tropical breeze wafted over the harbor, gently swaying the ships at anchor, small waves slapping against the sides of the boats. It became very quiet as those aboard the *Creole* and the small flotilla waited. The attorney general cleared his throat, gave a quick glance at Gifford, and then turned his attention to those assembled before him.

"My friends, you have been detained a short time on board the *Creole*, for the purpose of ascertaining the individuals who were concerned in this mutiny and murder; they have been identified, and will be retained."[310]

He paused, and allowed a small smile to appear on his face. The wind picked up for a brief second, slapped at loose canvas and whistled through the rigging. Just as suddenly, it ceased, and everything became very still. Anderson announced in a clear voice, "The rest of you are free, and are at liberty to go on shore, and wherever you please."

Those on deck stood in disbelief for a frozen second. Had they heard what they heard? Then just as suddenly a great cheer went up from those on the boasts surrounding the *Creole*. A signal was given, the boats moved in and passengers began to disembark.

They were free.

> When the proceedings were over and all the slaves except the nineteen landed, a barge was sent from the barracks to the Creole, to take on shore the 19 prisoners and the guard that had been left over them. They were taken on shore to the barracks, and the 19 thence carried to prison. One of them died the day after he had been sent to prison, in consequence of

the wounds received in the affray.[311] —G. C. Anderson, Attorney-General, Nassau, Bahamas.

If Susan had been aboard the *Creole,* then once again she and Madison were to be separated. She would have watched as the prisoners were loaded onto the launch and taken to the barracks, and she may have walked along the shore in silence, keeping pace with the skiff. Madison would have turned his head to stare at her, as the only sound in the late afternoon was the dipping of oars and the straining of rowers as the launch and its passengers glided along the inner harbor.

Finally, she would have reached a point where she could no longer keep even with the launch. One prisoner strained at his chains as he looked back at her receding figure on shore. The memory of her; a beautiful, proud woman looking directly at him until neither could see each other.

Those who had taken part in the revolt and were imprisoned at Nassau were the following:

Horace Beverley
Walter Brown
George Burden (Basden)*
Richard Butler
Adam Carnay (died while imprisoned of "natural causes")
Pompey Garrison (a slave belonging to Thomas McCargo)*
William Jenkins
Benjamin Johnston, the blacksmith. a.k.a. Benjamin or Ben Blacksmith
Phillip Jones [a.k.a. Jordan Phillips]
Robert Lumpkins, or Lumpley
Elijah Morris (a slave belonging to Thomas McCargo.)**
George Portlock*
Doc Ruffin**
Peter Smallwood**
Warner Smith
Addison Tyler**
America [Woodis] Woodhouse
Madison Washington (a slave belonging to Thomas McCargo.)**

George Grundy died on board the *Creole,* by a wound to the head received during the revolt.

*Named by Captain Robert Ensor as persons who killed Mr. Hewell

**Named by Lucius D. Stevens as persons being accessories to the death of Mr. Hewell

24

The English

To all Mr. Everett's reasoning and argument, to his illustrations, always ingenious, but frequently inapposite, the Undersigned has only to reply that the demands of Mr. Everett are utterly at variance with the law of England. On the arrival of the 'Creole' in the port of Nassau, the negroes on board at once became free; and Her Majesty's Government possessed no legal power or authority to restore them to a state of slavery. —The Earl of Aberdeen[312]

The Creole Incident quickly became a point of contention between Her Majesty's government and the United States. From the moment Governor Cockburn of the Bahamas was informed of the arrival of the *Creole* and that a "mutiny and murder" had occurred on the vessel, the characterization of those events varied substantially between the English and the Americans. This was evident in a letter written by the American consul in Nassau, and printed in the *London Times* on January 13, 1842:

> By Her Majesty's subjects, and the authorities of the colony, the slaves of the *Creole* were considered and treated as passengers, they being allowed to go on shore in boats tendered to them from shore. The American Consul remonstrated against this, inasmuch as the slaves were American property, and had no more right to be removed from the vessel than the cargo of tobacco.

The tone of the articles that appeared in the English press became increasingly sympathetic toward the plight of the slaves, both those who were freed and those held in custody by the local authorities. Further, the press postulated, the incident had been at the least a moment of opportunity and at the most a premeditated action planned well in advance.

The *Anti-Slavery Reporter*, the newspaper for the British and Foreign Anti-Slavery Society, first reported the incident on December 29, 1841. In the January 26 issue, the *Reporter* suggested the Creole Incident might have been inspired by previous incidents involving intercoastal slave ships.

The slaves knew that a party wrecked on the Bahamas had previously acquired liberty; and this alone is enough to account for their attempt. If, however, they had learned also the particulars of the *Amistad*, it can hardly be doubted that their resolution was strengthened by the success of Cinque and his companions . . . Altogether the occurrence is evidently destined to produce a very powerful effect, both on the slave-holders and slaves.

The *London Times* considered the idea that the mutiny and murder were more than a serendipitous opportunity taken by the slaves on board the *Creole*.

"One of the facts alleged by the New Orleans papers, which adds to the excitement occasioned by this mutiny and murder, is 'That Mr. Bourne, a Baptist preacher in Richmond, instructed them as to the mode of procedure before they left, as was learned from an examination of the slaves at Nassau."[313]

The following Friday, the *London Times* printed the entire Protest of the crew and officers of the *Creole*, but more telling of the character of the paper and its readers was a letter to the editor following the depositions of the crew. It ran under the heading "To the editor of the *Times*."

Sir . . . I maintain that the slaves who seized the *Creole*, and put to death some of the crew, were as completely justified in their acts as prisoners of war would have been who, after having been captured by an enemy and confined below, rose upon the prize crew, and by force of arms repossessed themselves upon the vessel, and brought her into a friendly port. What right had the Americans over these slaves in the *Creole*! Was it by the consent of these slaves that they were made prisoners, and stowed away in the hold of the *Creole*! If not, the slaves clearly had a right to liberate themselves in any way they could, and if in the course of their efforts to liberate themselves they had killed every one of the crew, they would have been completely justified. This cannot be considered into a case of piracy.[314]

The charge of piracy, a hanging offense, held out the possibility of the nineteen being returned to the States for trial. Those in England who were concerned over the fate of Madison Washington and his companions argued the charge of piracy could not, and should not, be applied based on the actions the nineteen took. To presume the press influenced the government in this matter would be conjecture. However, the court of public opinion arguably favored the nineteen.

The *Times of London* also published excerpts from the debate that was beginning to rage in the United States Senate. On January 17, 1842, the *Times* published comments by Senator Calhoun:

(Calhoun) had the particulars of the *Creole* before him. It was the most flagrant case: nay, he considered it a case of naked piracy; and Government, as soon as the official report was revised, should demand the pirates for punishment.

Calhoun and the Southern contingent in Congress made it clear that, in their view, those responsible for the "affray" on board the *Creole* should be charged with piracy and returned to the state of origin for trial. Calhoun and the

Southern representatives based their findings on the legal interpretation that the slaves were considered cargo and property, and that "the cargo," acted in defiance of the legal standing established by state and municipal codes of Virginia.

This was evidently a concern to Henry Stephen Fox, the British Ambassador in Washington. In a letter to the British foreign minister in London, dated December 28, 1841, Ambassador Fox argued that the case should be heard in Nassau, based on previous cases and a "further consideration."

> Her Majesty's government will no doubt have received from the Governor of the Bahamas Islands a full report of the proceedings which took place in the case of the American ship "Creole," brought into the port of Nassau by a number of Virginia negroes who had mutinied and taken possession of the vessel from their masters.
>
> An impression prevails that the 19 negroes detained at Nassau, charged with the murder on board the "Creole," of one of the American slave-owners, will be delivered up for trial in the United States. I conclude that this will not be the case. The Americans have not the right, under any circumstances whatever, to claim from Great Britain the surrender of the fugitive criminals. The Supreme Court in the United States decided two years ago that Holmes, the Canadian murderer, should not be delivered up to the British authorities. In the case of the two Brambers, guilty of murder in Ireland, the United States authorities interfered in 1838, to prevent those offenders being surrendered to Great Britain by the State authorities of New York. And in the present case a further consideration arises. The Virginia negroes accused of the murder are now free men, and not slaves. But, if surrendered for trial in America, the Federal Government would possess no power by law, even if it should so desire, to prevent the negroes from being replaced in slavery in the event of their being acquitted of the murder. They would, immediately upon setting foot in this country, fall back as slaves into the power of their former owners in Virginia.[315]

The phrase, "they would, immediately upon setting foot in this country, fall back as slaves in the powers of their former owners in Virginia," establishes the legal dilemma that dictated the outcome of the Creole Incident. If the slaves were returned to the state of origin, any attempt to present a petition or resolution on their behalf in the House or Senate would be tabled under the standing Gag Rule, based on the fact that the accused were being tried as slaves in a state, rather than a federal, court. To those in the House of Representatives who were preparing the resolutions concerning the *Creole*, returning the slaves would all but end their plans to break the Gag Rule.

If the prisoners were tried in the Bahamas, an advantage was that they would be tried as free men, not slaves. As to the charge of piracy, mutiny, or murder, that the incident occurred on the high seas would force their prosecution to come under the jurisdiction of either the federal government or the nation's courts where they were being held. The main concern was to keep the nineteen from being returned to the States for trial and to avoid any trial and conviction. Those in Washington who awaited the fate of the accused nineteen knew Her Majesty's government had to be convinced to be of like mind in this regard.

In Nassau, American Consul John Bacon had the opportunity to bring charges against the accused in colonial courts. However, he demurred. In a letter from Bacon to Governor Cockburn, dated November 14, 1841, Bacon gave his reasons for not pursuing a trial in Nassau: "If they are to be tried here, it would, therefore, be almost impossible to obtain the attendance of all the witnesses, without which the persons implicated could not be convicted, though guilty."[316]

Although Bacon did not proceed to trial in Nassau, he requested that the accused be "[f]orwarded to the United States by this same vessel (the brig *Creole*)."

Governor Cockburn's answer was firm and unequivocal:

> With respect to your request, that the nineteen slaves who appear to have been implicated in the murder and other violences committed on board the "Creole" when at sea, should be delivered over to you for the purpose of being secured and sent to America for trial, I can only refer you to the document already furnished to you by my order in council, and by which it was already determined that the parties referred to should be detained here until instructions should be received on the subject from Her Majesty's government; and under your apparent acquiescence in which, and your agreeing to attend the investigation, the same was proceeded with.

(Signed) I have, &c. Francis Cockburn, Governor.

From the outset, Her Majesty's government contested the American assumption that the fugitives held in Nassau should be returned to the States for trial. British jurists stated that, "the rights of an American master over his slave rests simply on American law. The English law now in force in the harbour [sic] of Nassau distinctly announces that within its sphere it will recognize no act in support of them. To claim that English authorities shall detain (or suffer for not detaining) a slave as a slave, is therefore to claim that American law shall override most positive and distinct English enactments in English territory."[317]

The argument by the English also explored the question of international piracy law and under whose jurisdiction the nineteen came.

"These slaves are considered to have committed what is certainly by the municipal law of America and England an act of piracy-a murder on the high seas. But is it, with the attendant seizure of their vessel, within the definition of piracy, as given by the law of nations?"

It could be argued that under English law they were being held against their will as slaves, and in the process of seeking their freedom, a death occurred. This would hardly stand as an act of murder or mutiny. As to the charge of piracy, by not retaining control of the ship but instead returning the vessel, in the words of Justice Story, delivered as part of his decision in the Amistad case, "[t]o the custody of the officers of that port, in order to be taken care of and restored entire to the true proprietor . . ." negated any charge of piracy.

Governor Cockburn referred the matter to the Home Office in London, where the incident would be considered before the highest officials in Her Majesty's government.

There were individuals in England who became actively involved with the disposition of the accused nineteen. Once word of the incident reached London, members of the British and Foreign Anti-Slavery Society began to formulate a memorial for the defense of the accused with the intention of presenting it to Lord Aberdeen, the Foreign Secretary of Her Majesty's government.

Since its inception, the American and Foreign Anti-Slavery Society had established strong ties with its counterpart, the British and Foreign Anti-Slavery Society. Through correspondence and reciprocal visits, each anti-slavery society met and worked with abolitionists on both sides of the Atlantic. As recently as the 1840 Anti-Slavery Convention held in London, the issue of the slave trade between the several states, upon the high seas in international waters was seen as a violation of international law and treaty. To contest this practice would not only allow stricter enforcement of the ban on the commerce of slavery on the high seas, it could further extend the ban to the intercoastal slave trade between the states. More important, both societies believed the intercoastal slave trade was the Achilles heel that provided a viable means to break the Gag Rule. It was evident that the Creole Incident presented such an opportunity to test its validity. But for this to occur, the nineteen could not be returned to the States.

The members of each society acted to facilitate a coordinated effort on behalf of the defense of Madison Washington and his fellow compatriots. Those in the British and Foreign Anti-Slavery Society, Messrs. William Allen, Joseph Sturge, John Scoble, Rev. J. H. Hinton, and Messrs. John Beaumont, Henry Tuckett, Benjamin Wiffen, and John Dunlop of Edinburgh, played an active role in the preparation of a memorial for the defense of the nineteen that would be presented to Her Majesty's foreign secretary.

The fact was that several members of the British and Foreign Anti-Slavery Society had recent and extensive experiences in American politics and had visited the United States, Canada, and the Bahamas to research slavery and freed slaves.

John Scoble, a British clergyman and antislavery leader, was a member of Joseph Sturge's West Indies expedition of 1836-1837. Familiar with abolitionists in both America and the Bahamas, Scoble had corresponded with Joshua Leavitt.

John Howard Hinton, an English Baptist minister, was a member of the governing committee of the British and Foreign Anti-Slavery Society. Hinton served on the committee that aided in the defense of the *Creole* mutineers before Parliament in 1842.

Joseph Sturge, a Quaker corn merchant from Birmingham, England, was the leader of the British and Foreign Anti-Slavery Society. He had traveled extensively in the West Indies with Rev. John Scoble to report on the conditions of newly freed slaves after the Emancipation Act of 1834. In 1839, Sturge began a correspondence with Lewis Tappan and, through Tappan, became familiar with Leavitt and his work.

The other member of the British and Foreign Anti-Slavery Society who was involved with the defense of the accused nineteen was Joseph John Gurney. It has been reported that Gurney actually met Madison Washington while on a visit to Hiram Wilson's home in Canada and had tried to dissuade Madison from returning to Virginia to save his wife. Fredrick Douglass, an acquaintance of Gurney's, spoke to this fact when he stated; "He went to Virginia, [Madison Washington] against the entreaties of friends, against the advice of my friend Gurney."[318]

On investigation of timelines and places each individual was considered to have been between 1839 and 1841, it is not impossible that Gurney may have met Madison. It was reported that in August of 1839 Gurney was in Canada, visiting Hiram Wilson.

> August 26, 1839. At Toronto I was glad to form the acquaintance with Hiram Wilson, the excellent agent of the American Anti-Slavery Society, who was watching over the interests of the negroes in Canada. About 100 slaves per month were at that time making their escape into this land of freedom. It gave me pleasure to aid him in promoting the formation of schools for the Christian education of their children.[319] —Joseph John Gurney

As to the memorial being prepared by the British and Foreign Anti-Slavery society, it not only relied on the official depositions of the crew and passengers taken in New Orleans, but also on other sources they had obtained from third parties in Nassau.

> There are two versions of the *Creole* affair, one derived from the protest of certain persons who formed part of the crew of that vessel, made before a notary at New Orleans; and the other founded on private information from Bahamas.[320]

This suggests that Reverend Poole, upon returning to England from the Bahamas, may have presented affidavits he took from slaves on the *Creole*.

> That he went [Woodside] on board [Creole] about ten o'clock, A.M., [12, Nov.] and soon after two white persons came on board, who he has since ascertained to be the Rev. Mr. Poole and the Rev. Mr. Aldridge, Episcopal clergymen, who were for some time in familiar conversation with the slaves, and appeared to be giving them directions and instructions . . . Deponent heard Mr. Poole say he was going to England, and it was requisite he should know all about this business, so that he could represent the thing.[321]

On February 2, 1842, the memorial was presented to Lord Aberdeen, the foreign secretary to Her Majesty's government:

No. XIX.
CASE OF THE CREOLE
To the Right Honorable the Earl of Aberdeen,
Her Majesty's principal
Secretary of State for Foreign Affairs.

My Lord, . . . However much the Committee of the British and Foreign Anti-slavery Society may regret the existence of any causes of irritation between the governments of Great Britain and the United States, arising out of the existence of slavery in the latter country, and of the slave-trade on the coast of Africa, they cannot but rejoice that in the eyes of enlightened humanity and of Christian philanthropy, the cause of human freedom, civilization, and happiness, is earnestly sought to be promoted by the former; and that a large body of the citizens of the United States, in common with the people of England, are uniting their best efforts for the removal of those causes of irritation, by the universal extinction of the evils to which, unhappily, they owe their birth.

The case of the *Creole*, like that of the *Amistad*, is exciting not only the profound attention of public men, but stirring the deep sympathies of the public mind on both sides the Atlantic. In common with the friends of humanity at large, the Committee feel the deepest solicitude as to the ultimate fate of the negroes now in the custody of Her Majesty's authorities at the Bahamas, for the part they are reported to have taken in the affair of the *Creole*. That solicitude induces them to lay before your lordship conclusions to which they have arrived after a careful review of this deeply interesting and important case, and which they venture respectfully to submit to the consideration of Her Majesty's government.

There are two versions of the *Creole* affair, one derived from the protest of certain persons who formed part of the crew of that vessel, made before a notary at New Orleans; and the other founded on private information from Bahamas. From the first it appears that the *Creole* left Hampton Roads, in the state of Virginia, on the 30th of October last, 'laden with manufactured tobacco in boxes and slaves,' for New Orleans; that whilst on the voyage a part of them, nineteen in number, 'rose on the officers, crew, and passengers, killed one passenger, severely wounded the captain and a part of the crew, and compelled the first mate to navigate the said vessel to Nassau, New Providence.'

It appears also from the same protest, that after they had accomplished their object, they were guilty of no excesses, but treated all the whites on board with great humanity, dressing the wounds of those that were injured, supplying them with their usual food, and only keeping them apart and under such restraints as were necessary to secure their safe arrival at a British port;

and to use their own simple but emphatic language, 'all that they had done was for their freedom.' On their arrival at Nassau, they were charged with mutiny and murder, and placed under the custody of the authorities of the island until the government shall decide whether they shall be tried there, or elsewhere, for the alleged crimes.

From the latter account, it appears that the negroes having discovered their proximity to a British island, demanded to be landed there; that this was resisted by the captain, passengers, and crew; that thereupon a struggle for the mastery commenced, which terminated in the triumph of the negroes, and the loss of two lives, one a passenger on board the *Creole*, who had the care of a portion of the slaves, and one of the negroes, who died of the injuries he received on his arrival at Nassau, where those implicated in the rising were given into custody, and the remainder of the slaves allowed to go free.

Whichever of these accounts be the true one, or whatever may have been the means by which the negroes achieved their liberty, the Committee presume it cannot alter the decision of her Majesty's government in the case. They are persuaded that under the circumstances which took place, neither the charge of mutiny or murder can be sustained in a British courts of justice. If these offences have been committed, they have been committed against American citizens, on board an American vessel, and can only be dealt with in American courts. The negroes of the *Creole* were forcibly placed on board that vessel as slaves—they were detained for the New Orleans market. This they knew; and to avoid the horrors and degradation of the condition that awaited them, as well as to relieve themselves from the bondage in which they were held, they rose upon those to whose custody they had been committed, asserted their natural rights, and after a short but severe struggle, secured their freedom. That homicide was committed during the affray is justly to be deplored and deprecated; but that homicide is to be traced to the resistance made by those who endeavored by force of arms to retain them in slavery, not to a spirit of vengeance on the part of the negroes. They sought not life but liberty; and that obtained, their subsequent conduct must be regarded as an admirable specimen of forbearance, self-government, and humanity. In confirmation of the views of the Committee, they refer to the decisions of the United States courts in the case of the Mendians [the name of the tribe that the majority of the *La Amistad* captives were from] found on board the *Amistad*, in which it was held that the alleged offence of murder, with which they stood charged, having been committed on board a *foreign* ship, was without their jurisdiction, and such they have full confidence will be the decision of the British courts also.

The only question, which remains to be noticed is, whether the United States have a right to claim these negroes, either as slaves or as felons. The Committee conceive the first point as finally settled by the British government: they cannot and will not be delivered up as slaves; and with respect to the other point, they conceive it is equally clear that these negroes cannot be delivered up, merely because they have been charged with a capital crime by some American citizens. They are not felons by the laws of England, nor by the laws of nations; but even if they were so, the United States have no authority, under treaty with Great Britain, to require them to be delivered over to the vengeance of their laws; and the uniform custom of that country runs counter to such a demand. They will not deliver up criminals to the demands of this country, whatever the offence may be with which they stand charged.

The Committee feel themselves, therefore, at liberty to consider the negroes, recently taken from on board the *Creole*, and now in the custody of her Majesty's officers in Bahamas, to be safe; and they have respectfully, yet earnestly, to request, in their behalf, that her Majesty's government will be pleased to afford them such protection as their circumstances may require.

On behalf of the Committee,
Joseph Sturge, Chairman"

Sturge, Scoble and Hinton avoided any suggestion of collusion, aid, or instruction relative to the nineteen and the revolt. If it were implied the nineteen had been instructed in a plot to seize the vessel, such premeditation could have criminalized the act and jeopardized the status of the accused.

Instead, the main emphasis was directed on the idea that the nineteen should "not be returned" to the states for trial. Further, it was the goal of the memorial to suggest that those being held in Nassau be released and that all charges against them be dropped.

At the time of the Creole Incident, there were several disagreements and concerns between the United States and England that dealt with slavery. One was a particularly offensive practice enforced by municipal law in the South. When a ship, regardless of flag of origin, entered a Southern port in the United States, any sailor on board who was of African descent was ordered to be detained in the local jail until the ship departed. The captain of the ship was also ordered to compensate the jailers for the room and board provided. If the ship's officers failed to pay the required cost of the incarcerated sailor, then the sailor would be sold into slavery. This particular practice was a major affront to the English government, who considered an English ship to be sovereign territory and its sailors, British subjects. Although protests were frequently made to the United States government, the indifferent reply to such complaints stated only that, the jurisdiction was a state matter, not a federal one.

Other matters also contributed to strained relations between England and the United States. One was the Aroostook War, a border dispute between the British colony of New Brunswick [Canada] and Maine that verged on becoming a shooting war. Maine had called up ten thousand militiamen for action against New Brunswick, which deployed a similar number of troops on its border.

Both sides of the conflict quickly escalated. Finally, after the president authorized further deployment of fifty thousand men, and Congress appropriated $10 million dollars for the campaign, a truce was arranged between Maine and New Brunswick, pending a diplomatic settlement.

The British ministry found it imperative to seek a settlement before the situation deteriorated further. A special mission to the United States headed by Alexander Baring, 1st Baron Ashburton, was scheduled for the upcoming spring of 1842. The intention was not only to establish a new treaty to settle the boundary dispute between Canada and the United States, but to address issues of extradition, foreign slave trade, the right to search on the high seas, and other matters that threatened goodwill.

The Creole Incident seriously threatened the success of these negotiations, while at the same time emphasized the need for dialogue between the two countries. President Tyler needed a resolution of the Creole Incident and passage of the Webster-Ashburton treaty to maintain control over his presidency. The fact that Tyler complained about the *Creole* and publicly demanded that England return the slaves and mutineers was only a public demonstration to retain Southern support for the treaty. In fact, Tyler was more than happy to resolve the *Creole* problem so as not to impede the Treaty's progress. Both England and the United States realized an equitable settlement would benefit each nation's future.

England was enjoying the rise of Empire. With the defeat of Napoleon and the establishment of the Royal Navy as the tip of the spear of England's power, Great Britain's role as the preeminent world power was secured. This was further reflected in the boom of commerce and production associated with the industrial revolution, along with the expansion of colonization. Queen Victoria sat on the throne and became one of the longest-reigning monarchs in history. Pax Britannica[322] was in full bloom; the sun never set on the Union Jack.

The United States was on the verge of its own great expansion. The term "manifest destiny" was only a few short years away and the claim to vast territories to the west of the original colonies beckoned like sirens. Texas was the next logical step in this westward push, and both the United States and England had designs on this newly independent republic. Once again, slavery played a significant role. England viewed Texas as a necessary impediment to America's westward expansion. With Canada to the north and an independent Texas republic to the south, England righteously felt that the American dream of a continental nation stretching from the Atlantic to the Pacific would be contained.[323]

Economically, England viewed Texas as a low-tariff, or free trade, area that provided Britain with a flourishing market for English goods in exchange for cotton. Britain believed Texas would act as a counterbalance to the United States on the North American continent, if it was backed with strong treaties with England.

The British and Foreign Anti-Slavery Society had its own interest regarding the Republic of Texas, and hoped to influence Texas as a republic that "would discourage further American expansion and would, like Canada, constitute an asylum for people of colour [sic]."[324]

England's interests in Texas did not go unnoticed in Washington. The United States viewed the Republic of Texas as part of a logical progression of its westward expansion, and the danger of allowing a European foothold on the western edge of the United States was a constant source of anxiety. The pressure in Congress to admit Texas as a territory, with designs to later divide it into several states, was becoming a main topic of discussion. Texas, meanwhile, played a crafty game of courtship between England and the United States, negotiating the best possible deal in terms of territory and sovereignty.

Ironically, due to internal problems with the Seminole Wars in Florida, an economic depression in the United States in 1836, and the sectional and political strife that accompanied the addition of Texas into the Union, the United States Congress rejected a proposal to annex Texas in 1837. However, by 1841, with the Gag Rule in place and the threat of England's intervention in the Republic of Texas, Congress began to reconsider the Texas question.

Concern over Texas coming into the Union as a slave state was compounded by the possible further seizures of Mexican territory that consisted of present-day New Mexico, Arizona, Nevada, and California. The influx of new states would add voting power to either the slave South or free North, and undermine the fragile balance that existed in Congress.

Abolitionists on both sides of the Atlantic were not only concerned about Texas, but the threat of further expansion of slavery into Mexico. Correspondence between the two anti-slavery societies in England and America spoke to this apprehension:

> We perceive at present but one obstacle to our ultimate and entire triumph, and that is the possible annexation of Texas to the United States. Should this renegade republic be received into the union, not only would the permanency of slavery be secured in this country, but the curse would probably be spread over Mexico, and perhaps far beyond it. The annexation is the last hope of the slave-holders, and to effect, their agents at Washington will endeavor to involve this country in a war with Mexico—a measure which they justly believe would result in a union with Texas.[325]

Lord Aberdeen, England's foreign secretary, was fully appraised of the situations that existed in 1842. With upcoming negotiations in Washington headed by Lord Ashburton, Aberdeen felt the Creole Incident was both an inconvenience and an asset. Although a resolution would lower the rhetoric between the two nations, a strong showing by England regarding the disposition of the nineteen being held in Nassau would act to strengthen England's hand in the negotiations. To further complicate negotiations over the Creole Incident was the fact that the American secretary of state, Daniel Webster, and Lord Ashburton, had previous dealings with Barings Bank, a financial institution run by the Ashburton family. To avoid complicating the up-coming negations further, the United States sought a face saving remedy.

The United States government began to realize that if the slaves were not returned for trial, there was the possibility of reparations. The Department of

State was instructed to apply pressure to seek reparations from the English government concerning the *Creole* and its cargo. Secretary of State Daniel Webster informed the American representative in London, Mr. Edward Everett,[326] as to the official position of the United States. Everett was instructed to present a protest to the British Foreign Office.

On 29 January 1842, Webster wrote to Everett, "I regret to be obliged to acquaint you with a very serious occurrence, which recently took place in a port of the Bahama islands"[327]

Webster then briefly explained details of the incident, based on affidavits of the *Creole's* crew, and laid out the position of the United States:

[T]his case, as presented in these papers, is one calling loudly for redress . . . Under these circumstances, it would have seem to have been the plain and obvious duty of the authorities at Nassau . . . to assist the American consul in putting an end to the captivity of the masters and crew, restoring to them the control of the vessel, and enabling them to resume their voyage, and to take the mutineers and murderers to their own country to answer for their crimes before the proper tribunal.

Webster also realized that any expectation of bringing the accused to trial—in Nassau or the United States—was futile. He confessed to Everett his misgivings on pursuing extradition:

What is to be done with them? How are they to be punished? The English Government will probably not undertake their trial or punishment; and of what use would it be to send them to the United States, separated from their ship, and at a period so late as that if they should be sent, before proceedings could be instituted against them the witnesses might be scattered over half the globe.[328]

The best that could be achieved was to gain a stronger bargaining position in the upcoming Ashburton negotiations. Secretary Webster instructed Everett to "avail yourself of an early opportunity of communicating to Lord Aberdeen . . . the subject of this dispatch . . . you will seek to impress it with a full conviction of the dangerous importance to the peace of the two countries of occurrences of this kind, and the delicate nature of the questions to which they give rise."[329]

Everett made his protests to the English foreign secretary, the Earl of Aberdeen, to establish the facts, based on depositions of the crew and passengers of the *Creole*. He demanded that the English government redress the wrong committed in Nassau to American property, and urged at great length the various grounds upon which he regarded it as a violation of the comity and usages of nations, and petitioned for a claim of indemnification.

Recognizing that Everett was posturing for the upcoming treaty negotiations, the English government would not be bullied. Aberdeen replied in a blistering letter that underscored England's stand on slavery:

To all of Mr. Everett's reasoning and argument, to his illustrations always ingenious, but frequently inapposite, the undersigned has only to reply, that the demands of Mr. Everett are utterly at variance with the Law of England . . . Such of them as had been accused of crime and were detained in custody it was found could not be tried in the colonial Courts for an offense committed out of British jurisdiction, and if not cognizable by these Courts it was equally impossible to transfer the accused persons to the Courts of any other Nation . . . It is true however, that although there was no jurisdiction to try these persons for mutiny or murder they might have been prosecuted in the Courts of the Colony for Piracy. Her Majesty's Government took the necessary measures to institute such a prosecution, but the information received and the opinion of Her Majesty's Law Advisors convinced them that there was no grounds by which it could be effectually supported. No Evidence of any practical intent appeared in the conduct of the accused, and Her Majesty's Government felt that it would be a mockery to submit persons to an Indictment which they were convinced could not be sustained.[330]

Aberdeen goes on, making pointed references of England's attitude toward America's "peculiar institution." The lack of Aberdeen's subtlety underscored the animosity Her Majesty's government felt toward the practice of slavery. Aberdeen took particular aim when Everett based part of his argument on a supposition that if slavery existed in England, and an American ship was forced into a British port that had "persons of that colour . . . would it be reasonable that British Authority should act upon their condition and sell them for slaves?"

Everett argued further: Did the British authorities have any more right with regard to the *Creole* to take slaves off an American ship and make them free?

Aberdeen answered with a firm reproach:

Now, it appears somewhat strange that Mr. Everett should suppose an imaginary case of this description, when he recollects, what is the Nature of the Law actually existing in some of the States of the Union, and in which the principle at least of the hypothesis he depicts is nearly realized. For the last twenty years a law has been enacted and is rigorously enforced in those States by which every free Negro or person of colour employed on board a Merchant Ship entering the port, is arrested and thrown into jail, where he is detained in close confinement until the departure of the vessel. The Captain is compelled by Law to defray the Expense of the maintenance of the free Negroes in prison which the accounts furnished by the Sheriff of the District appears to be sufficiently onerous. A description is also taken of the person; and according to the provisions of the Act, they are liable to the infliction of corporal punishment in the event of their return. It is only within the last few weeks that the Undersigned has received Intelligence of five British Subjects having been thus incarcerated . . . Such being the Law of the State, the Undersigned has not demanded Indemnification and redress. Neither has he demonstrated against the absent of Comity and Hospitality.[331]

The final slap in the face came when Aberdeen reminded Everett of a document the Americans had delivered to the English some years earlier:

The Undersigned . . . would respect the concurrence of Mr. Everett, as a citizen of the United States, if he were to hold as self evident truth in the memorable language of the declaration of American Independence 'that all men are created equal, that they are endowed by their creator with certain inalienable rights; that among these are life, liberty and the pursuit of happiness."[332]

The matter was settled. The nineteen accused would not be returned to the United States for trial. However, what should be done about the charges of mutiny and murder?

On Monday, the fourteenth of February, 1842, in the House of Lords, Lord Brougham made a motion to inquire for "the production of any correspondence which might have taken place between his noble friend (The Earl of Aberdeen) opposite and the American Government as to the ship *Creole*."

Lord Aberdeen rose and made the following announcement:

Communication had taken place between her majesty's Government and the Governor of the Bahamas on the subject to which his motion was referred; and perhaps his noble and learned friend would not press this motion at the present stage of the transaction, when he informed the house what had been the course pursued by the Government on the subject. As their Lordships might well imagine, the Government had given to the case its most serious consideration, and had availed itself of all the legal assistance which was desirable respecting it, and they came to the conclusion, that by the laws of this country there was no machinery, or authority, for bringing those persons to trial for mutiny or murder, and still less for delivering them up. Accordingly, orders were sent out by the Secretary for the Colonies for releasing those persons who had hitherto been detained.

The Creole Incident

THE BEGINNING OF THE END OF SLAVERY

BOOK VII: CHESS

25

The Opening Gambit

We have now, for the first time since the Government went into operation, an opportunity to apply an effectual corrective, quietly and peaceably, but which, if permitted to pass without being embraced, will, it is to be feared, be lost forever. —Senator John C. Calhoun[333]

On November 19, 1841, the *Creole* left Nassau for New Orleans. On the first of December at eleven o'clock in the evening, the *Creole* made the Southwest Pass bearing north by west, distance about twelve miles. The next morning the *Creole* took on a pilot and crossed the bar in tow of the steamboat *Shark*, discharged the pilot, and proceeded up the Mississippi River for the Port of New Orleans.

The *Creole* arrived at New Orleans on December 2, 1841, when the necessary surveys were called and the crew discharged what was left of the cargo (which included Lydia Gordon, listed on the ships manifest as "brown, age 17, stood 5-feet 5-inches," along with four others). The *New Orleans Picayune* ran the following article on December 3, 1841:

> Our community was thrown into considerable excitement yesterday, by the arrival of the Brig *Creole*, with the intelligence that 135 slaves on board had risen, in the vicinity of Abaco, murdered a passenger, severely wounded the Captain, and forced the vessel into Nassau, New Providence, where most of the slaves were set at liberty by the British authorities . . . After the arrival of the Creole at Nassau, the slaves acknowledged that a Baptist minister at Norfolk, named Bourne, has advised them with regard to their course, and given them directions how to proceed.[334]

Word of the revolt quickly spread on both sides of the Atlantic. The news had reached Washington as early as December 11, and in England the facts were reported on January 13, 1842 as "Mutiny and Murder at Sea." Interestingly, by Friday the fourteenth the incident was being referred to in English papers as only a mutiny.

In Boston's abolitionist paper, *The Liberator*, the Creole Incident was treated as a blow to Southern institutions, while the *New York Journal of Commerce* ran the heading "The Creoles-Strike for Liberty!"

As expected, many Southern papers ran up the red flag of protest at the actions of Great Britain. Some went as far as to suggest that war was the appropriate answer to their meddling. The *Richmond Enquirer* stated the following:

> What American can read it [protest of the crew and officers of the *Creole*] without feeling his throat swell with indignation at the atrocious conduct of Her Majesty's Governor . . . What is then the first duty of our Government? To demand peremptorily of Great Britain redress for the wrongs thus committed against our citizens, and reparation for the great destruction of American property on board the *Creole*.

Senator Henry Clay of Kentucky mentioned the possible loss of his wine shipment on board the *Creole* in a letter to James B. Clay on December 12; "I shall be very sorry to lose that Wine that was sent by the Creole. As that vessel is again in the port of N. Orleans, can you not ascertain what was done with it?"[335]

The Creole Incident soon found its way onto the floor of the House and Senate. The reaction of Southern interests was visceral, with little regard for decency or common sense. The mere death of an American citizen seemed of little import to the Southern members. Their response was to protect and defend Southern institutions, and to attack any interlopers that might threaten their system. In the Senate, on December 22, Senator Calhoun brought up the Creole Incident:

> He denounced the principles maintained by Great Britain in this case, [the Formosa, a coastal slaver forced into Nassau by stress of weather a year earlier, where the authorities freed the slaves] and more especially in the case of the *Creole*, as the most dangerous innovation on national rights and national honor ever claimed by one independent power of another . . . Is it now time that this question was settled, and that it should be known whether this Government will extend its protection to the property of its own citizens?

Senator Barrow of Louisiana went further:

> The South would be compelled to fit out armaments and destroy Nassau, and also the towns which trampled underfoot the laws of nations and the rights of American citizens. This seizure of domestic property was not more high handed than if the British placed cruisers at the mouth of the Chesapeake, or at the mouth of any other harbor, and seized on slaves for the purpose of taking them to Jamaica or to the Bahamas.

The serious nature of loss of property in the form of slaves was not only a cause for saber rattling, but added fuel to the regional competition for control of the government.

The 27th Congress would prove to be one of the most contentious assemblages to date concerning the direction and control of the United States. All was set for the ultimate showdown. Southern representatives felt confident that their views would come out victorious, and with the Gag Rule firmly in place, stood prepared to take control of the government. Even before the convening of the House and Senate, John C. Calhoun, ever the astute politician, displayed an appreciation of the coming session of Congress. In a letter to Ephraim R. Calhoun from Fort Hill, South Carolina, dated September 11, 1840, Calhoun sums up his interpretation of events that faced the South and its institutions:

> Never before had the government so fair an opportunity of returning to the old and primitive principles and policy of the republican party; and let me add, if it should be lost, never again, in all human probability, will it have so fair a one . . . the way is completely prepared. The whole fabric of Federal policy has been brought to the ground: the funding system, the national banks, the protective Tariff, and the miscalled American system, in all its ramifications lie prostrate. What remains is to persist in the course that has already accomplished so much; to place the Tariff on a fair and equal footing; introduce a rigid system of accountability and economy in the public expenditures, and to put down the fell spirit of abolition, with its abettors, in order to lay a solid foundation for the prosperity and liberty of the country, and let me add, for the safety of the South and its institution . . . Be not deceived. The object of the party, now making such mighty efforts to seize the reins of government, is a national bank of vast capital and power, sufficient to control the State institutions. . . that a National bank, under existing circumstances . . . is utterly incompatible with our political institutions and liberty.

By 1841, the Whigs had lost much of their political base, in large part due to the death of President Harrison and the divisiveness of the bank issue, and the Southern Democratic Party (Republican) became the controlling majority in Congress. Yet, Calhoun warned of complacency in a letter to Orestes A. Brownson; "Whiggery itself is overthrown, never to rise again, under its present name & form. But experience has taught me, that it is far easier to gain a victory in politics, than to reap its fruits . . ." (Fort Hill, 31st October 1841).

By November of 1841, Calhoun clearly realized that the Whigs were no longer a political threat and that a power vacuum now existed in Washington. To John R. Mathews, (Clarkesville, Georgia), Calhoun wrote the following as he was preparing to leave for Washington for the opening session of Congress:

> Our victory is complete (referring to the defeat of Whigs in Ala., Ind., Tenn.) . . . a thorough reformation of the Government and restoration of the Constitution may be effected." (Fort Hill, November 1841)

If there was any doubt as to Calhoun's intentions, he left little when he wrote the following letter:

> Many of my friends think the time has arrived when my name ought to be presented for the next presidency . . . I can best restore the Constitution & reform the government.[336]

As he prepared to leave for Washington in late November 1841, Calhoun wrote Armistead Burt, a relative by marriage and an influential member of the South Carolina legislature, "If my friends should think my services ever will be of importance at the head of the Executive, now is the time."

In the House, representatives for a stronger Union and the abolition of slavery gathered forces to prepare for the coming showdown. Adams, along with Joshua Reed Giddings of Ohio, William Slade of Vermont, Seth Gates of New York, John Mattocks of Vermont, Sherlock Andrews of Ohio, Nathaniel Borden of Massachusetts, and Francis James of Pennsylvania came together in December of 1841 and began to work closely with Joshua Leavitt, editor of *The Emancipator*. These men constituted what Giddings liked to call "a select committee about which little is said . . . but which in the future history of our government will fill a larger space than that of any other select committee of this or any former Congress."

Adams and his select committee were painfully aware of the formidable interests arrayed against them. It had been just a year earlier that the severest Gag Rule to date was voted a standing rule of the House.[337] Adams wrote in his diary on November 20, 1841 the following excerpt:

> I walked out before dinner and called at the office of Mr. Ellis Gray Loring, with whom I had about an hour's conversation. He is under no small concern from apprehensions upon two points at the approaching session of Congress; one, the rule excluding the reception of all petitions, resolutions, and papers relating to slavery; and the other, upon the revived project of annexing Texas to the United States . . . I look forward to both these designs with alarm and anguish, not from the power of the South, which can effect nothing by itself, but from the experience of the treachery of the Northern representation, both to Northern interests and principles.

Adams and his allies feared the Constitution would become a rigidly interpreted code subject to the whims of individual states. In 1824 Chief Justice Marshall warned against this in his opinion of *Gibbons v. Ogden*:

> Powerful and ingenious minds, taking as postulates that the power expressly granted to the government of the Union, are to be contracted by construction into the narrowest possible compass, and that the original powers of the States are retained, if any possible construction will retain them, may, by a course of well-digested but refined and metaphysical reasoning sounded on these premises, explain away the Constitution of our country, and leave it a magnificent structure, indeed, to look at, but totally unfit for use.[338]

In an excerpt from his diary, Adams revealed his apprehensions and his willingness to confront Southern institutions in the upcoming session of Congress:

> I find impulses of duty upon my own conscience which I cannot resist, while on the other hand are the magnitude, the danger, the insurmountable burden of labor to be encountered in the undertaking to touch upon the slave-trade. No one else will undertake it; no one but a spirit unconquerable by man, women or fiend can undertake it but with the heart of martyr-

dom. The world, the flesh and all the devils in hell are arrayed against any man who now in this North American Union shall dare join the standard of Almighty God to put down the African slave-trade; and what can I, upon the verge of my seventy-fourth birthday, with a shaking hand, a darkening eye, a drowsy brain, and with all my faculties dropping from me one by one, as the teeth are dropping from my head—what can I do for the cause of God and man, for the progress of emancipation, for the suppression of the African slave-trade? Yet my conscience presses me on; let me but die upon the breach.[339]

26

Sprigg's Boarding House, Washington, D.C.

My dearest Love. I arrived here Thursday evening at six o'clock.
Well, came at once to Mrs. Sprigg's, found Leavitt, Giddings and
Gates expecting me, and received from them a hearty welcome ...
I will now tell you how I am situated. Mrs. Spriggs is directly in
front of the Capitol and about as far from it as from our home to
Mrs. Holmes' or Mr. Spear's.[340] —Theodore Dwight Weld

As senators and representatives convened on Washington in the early winter of 1841-42, the members of the select committee found lodging at Sprigg's Boarding House. Ironically, Mrs. Sprigg, a Virginian, hired slaves to work in her boardinghouse, but seemed to be essentially apolitical. Though most of the boarders had abolitionist leanings, when they were confronted with a slave, they seemed to be disconcerted. James Brewer Stewart relates this in his book, *Joshua R. Giddings and the Tactics of Radical Politics,* wherein he states:

> In fact, Leavitt thought it might be considered indiscreet to talk to the slaves too much, [those that worked at Sprigg's] though he did wonder what effect the talk of fugitive slaves and other matters at the dinner table had on the slaves.[341]

Not all lodgers at Sprigg's were members of Congress. Representative Giddings had obtained a room there for Joshua Leavitt upon his arrival in December for the opening session of Congress. At that session, Leavitt witnessed Adams's motion to repeal the Gag Rule lose by only three votes. This close vote bolstered the select committee's resolve to break the Gag Rule. Now, with the Creole Incident a fact, the select committee began to prepare for the inevitable showdown with the planters.

To aid in the preparations and research needed for a as series of resolutions that would be based on the Creole Incident, Leavitt and Giddings decided to enlist the aid of Theodore Weld and made arrangements to bring him to Washington.

Soon after Giddings, Gates, Slade, and Leavitt settled themselves at Mrs. Sprigg's boarding house, Adams moved that the House repeal the Gag Rule, and his attempt failed by a mere three votes. The sign augured well for the developing group of insurgents, but they needed help in researching anti-slavery issues, for the congressmen were constantly plagued with committee duties, and Leavitt, as Washington reporter for the Emancipator, had his readers to attend to. Giddings and Leavitt decided that Theodore Weld, now in semi-retirement, should come to Washington to assist in the work.[342] — James Brewer Stewart

Giddings, Gates, and Andrews were Theodore Weld's personal converts to abolition and were well acquainted with his legal expertise on the subject. Weld chastised those who turned a blind eye to slavery, and strongly believed they were as guilty as those who kept slaves.

Our government stands first chargeable for allowing slavery to exist, under its own jurisdiction. Second, the states for enacting laws to secure their victim. Third, the slaveholder for carrying out such enactments, in horrid form enough to chill the blood. Fourth, every person who knows what slavery is, and does not raise his voice against this crying sin, but by silence gives consent to its continuance, is chargeable with guilt in the sight of God."[343] —Theodore Dwight Weld

Weld arrived in Washington in late December for a five-week stay. The committee secured a room at Sprigg's for Weld, and on his first night in Washington, along with Leavitt, he called on Mr. and Mrs. Adams. The discussion went straight to the Gag Rule and the recent Creole Incident. Adams was adamant about the intercoastal slave trade and recognized its blatant disregard of international law.

If the African slave-trade was piracy, the coasting American slave-trade could not be innocent, nor could its aggravated turpitude be denied . . .[344] —John Quincy Adams

Weld was impressed with "Old Man Eloquent" and the furor he was eliciting over a series of petitions; one from the citizens Georgia that accused Mr. Adams of being a monomaniac and a few days later, a petition from the citizens of Haverhill, Massachusetts, praying for a peaceful dissolution of the Union. Weld wrote to his wife Angelina and her mother, Sarah Grimkè, to describe Adams on the House floor:

Old Nestor lifted up his voice like a trumpet, till slaveholding, slavetrading, and breeding absolutely quailed and howled under his dissecting knife . . . Lord Morpeth, the English abolitionist of whom you have read, was present, and sat within a few feet of Mr. A.[345]

At one point, Weld, Gates, and Leavitt took time away from their research to attend an open house hosted by President Tyler. Weld reported to his wife with a hint of smugness, they "took care not to shake hands with him." In fact, the three stayed only fifteen minutes and then went to visit Adams.

A week later, Adams called a meeting of the select committee in a room of the House chambers to coordinate a plan of action. The committee agreed that Weld's attention should center on Adams's campaign to break the Gag Rule, with the main focus on preparing resolutions regarding the Creole Incident. Giddings found a niche at the Library of Congress where Weld began searching the "ancient records" for fertile subject matter with which to agitate. Until the committee learned of the disposition of the nineteen in Nassau, it was decided to present a series of petitions on the House floor that were guaranteed to inflame Southern passions.

Specifically, petitions prayed ". . . colored men be recognized as citizens of the United States and permitted to hold lands in the territories . . . Another prayed to be relieved from taking up arms in defense of a government which sustained slavery. Another prayed relief from all support of slavery and of the slave trade."[346]

The select committee then tested the traditions of the House when Giddings secured a desk for Leavitt on the House floor, which was unheard of then—as well as now.

> In the meantime, the author [Joshua R Giddings] had obtained a seat inside the bar for the Rev. Dr. Leavitt, a very competent reporter, who thought he could report Mr. Adams with tolerable accuracy. But Mr. Andrews, of Kentucky, seeing this, called on the Speaker to enforce the rule prohibiting all persons, except members and their officers, from sitting within the bar. This was done with the undisguised intention to suppress whatever Mr. Adams might say on that occasion. But Mr. Leavitt obtained a seat outside the bar, where he could hear Mr. Adams, took notes, and wrote out the remarks at night, and they appeared in one of the Boston papers.[347] —Joshua R. Giddings

The editor of the leading abolitionist newspaper, *The Emancipator*, now sat just outside the bar, directly behind the leading voice for abolition, John Quincy Adams. Adams led the attack, and the South strongly defended its position against the growing assault on slavery. One of Adams's petitions concerned "citizens of Georgia, setting forth that while Mr. Adams possessed all the qualities of a statesman . . . they regarded him a monomaniac," and prayed that he be removed as chairman of the committee on Foreign Affairs. Leavitt was almost beside himself with glee as he observed the Southerner's fury: "A hen with her head cut off is but a faint picture of their gyrations at this moment."[348]

This was certainly not the only time Old Man Eloquent baited the Southern members. In 1837, Adams, in his high-strung New England voice, presented a petition: "[H]e held in his hand a paper, on which, before presenting it, he desired to have the decision of the Speaker. It purported to come from slaves; and wished to know if such a paper came within the order of the House respecting petitions."

This threw the House into chaos and after several days of debate, members from the South demanded Adams be tried and censured. Mr. Adams rose and spoke; "In regard to the resolutions now before the house, as they all concur in naming me, and charging me with high crimes and misdemeanors, and in calling me to the bar of the house to answer for my crimes, I have thought it my duty to remain silent until it should be the pleasure of the house to act on one or the other of these resolutions . . . I asked the Speaker whether he considered such a paper as included within the general order of the House, that all petitions, memorials, resolutions, and papers, relating in anyway to the subject of slavery, should be laid upon the table . . . I should not send the paper to the table until the question was decided whether a paper from persons declaring themselves slaves was included within the order of the House. This is the fact."[349]

Adams's deliberate provocation of Southern slaveholders is further detailed when he revealed one other fact concerning the petition "purporting to be from slaves." A Southern representative from Alabama, who demanded the censure of Adams, believed the petition was for the abolition of slavery. Mr. Adams objected to the gentleman moving it: "[The gentlemen] must amend his resolution; for, if the house should choose to read this petition, I can state to them they would find it something very much the reverse of that which the resolution states it to be; and that if the gentleman from Alabama still shall choose to bring me to the bar of the house, he must amend his resolution in a very important particular, for he probably will have to put into it that my crime has been for attempting to introduce the petition of slaves that slavery should not be abolished; and that the object of these slaves, who have sent this paper to me, is precisely that which he desires to accomplish, and that they are his auxiliaries, instead of being his opponents."[350]

These same stalling tactics were now being employed by Adams and the select committee to distract Southern representatives until a series of resolutions being researched by Weld, that would break the Gag Rule, were completed and the disposition of the nineteen was known. Further, for the Creole Resolutions to be successful it was imperative that Southern representatives enter into the House record their support of the Constitution and the Supremacy Clause.

Not an easy task.

On January 24, 1842, Adams presented a petition that sought to accomplish just such an outcome:

I have in my hand the memorial of Benjamin Emerson and forty-five other citizens of Haverhill, in the State of Massachusetts, praying Congress to adopt immediate measures for the peaceful dissolution of the Union of these States . . . because no Union can be agreeable which does not present prospects of reciprocal benefits. Because a vast proportion of the resources of one section of the Union is annually drained to sustain the views and course of another section, without any adequate return. Because, judging from the history of past nations, that Union, if persisted in, in the present course of things, will certainly overwhelm the whole nation in utter destruction.[351]

How better to draw the South into proclaiming for a strong Union than to present a petition for the dissolution of the Union.

The firestorm that ensued engulfed the House for several weeks as the members called for, once again, the censure of ex-president John Quincy Adams. The Southern members of the House had been longing for just such a situation, where they would finally check Adams's attempts to break the Gag Rule. The Southern delegation was to be headed by young Thomas Marshall of Kentucky, nephew of the late chief justice of the Supreme Court, John Marshall. Marshall, along with Representative Gilmer of Virginia, presented a series of resolutions outlining the charges against Adams:

> Resolved, therefore. That the Hon JOHN QUINCY ADAMS . . . has offered the deepest indignity to the House of which he is a member, an insult to the people of the United States of which that House is the legislative organ, and will, if this outrage be permitted to pass unrebuked and unpunished, have disgraced his country...the House deem it an act of grace and mercy when they only inflict upon him their severest censure for conduct so utterly unworthy of his past relations to the State and his present position[352]

When a vote was taken to either proceed with the censure of Adams or lay it on the table, all the lodgers at Sprigg's, several Northern members of Congress, and even some members of the South voted to lay the motion on the table, and avoid a trial in Congress. However, Adams himself voted not to lay the motion on the table, daring the House to censure him. The final vote was 112-94 for the House to try Adams.

This extraordinary exchange lasted from January 25 to February 7, 1842. Adams's defense is etched into the annals of House lore and stands as a testament to his strength, courage, and ability. In the end, Adams prevailed, since the two-thirds vote needed for expulsion was not there. During the trial Adams destroyed the South's arguments, as well as the young Marshall. Marshall was overheard stating, "I would rather die a thousand deaths than again to encounter that old man."[353]

The South did present a resolution, but produced the opposite of what they intended. The South admitted on the House floor that the Union was inviolate.

> [T]he Federal Constitution is a permanent form of government . . . and that anyone purporting to dissolve the Union was committing a crime of high treason.[354]

The very Constitution the Southern gentlemen just swore to support contained Article 1, Section 8, paragraph 3, wherein it states without equivocation: "The Congress shall have power . . . to regulate commerce with foreign nations, and among the several States, and with Indian tribes."

Although Southern members may not have been aware of the significance of their action, they were soon to find out how truly significant it was.

As the storm clouds gathered, and the inevitable clash drew near, Madison Washington and the others awaited their fate in a prison barrack in Nassau. Their one desire was to be with the ones they loved. Far from the political turmoil of Washington, they questioned if they would ever be free, or would they be returned to slavery—or worse, receive death by hanging.

27

Check

I can find no language to express my feelings at the consummation of this act. —John Quincy Adams

In the second session of the 27th Congress there was no solid opposition against the South and its peculiar institution, save for a few annoying, radical abolitionist representatives and their harassing petitions. The Gag Rule, functioning as a stopgap against abolitionist prayers in opposition to slavery, allowed Southern representatives and their Northern lackeys the ability to turn a deaf ear toward such entreaties.

Yet, those who persisted in attacking the bulwark of Southern solidarity refused to back down. By late February and early March of 1842, these assaults on the Gag Rule had intensified to a point where decorum in Congress was replaced with enmity.

> The contest upon the right of petition and the freedom of debate evidently increased; slaveholding members became irritable, and Northern members who sympathized with them appeared vexed and discontented. Personal feelings began to take the place of political sympathy; the social relations of members were broken up, and the common civilities of life were no longer observed by a portion of southern members.[355] —Joshua R. Giddings

In the Senate, Calhoun frequently held forth on the attacks on Southern institutions by the abolitionists:

> The peculiar institution of the South—that on the maintenance of which the very existence of the slaveholding States depends, is pronounced to be sinful and odious, in the eyes of God and man; and this with a systematic design of rendering as hateful in the eyes of the world—with a view to a general crusade against us and our institutions. This too, in the legislative halls of the Union. . . The subject is beyond the jurisdiction of Congress; they have no right to touch it in any shape or form, or to make it the subject of deliberation or discussion.[356]

While the South was poised to render the scattered remnants of the Whig abolitionist to the dustbin of history, those who opposed the South knew that to protect the Constitution, the right of petition had to be reestablished. The Gag Rule must fall.

To this end, John Quincy Adams and his allies went about preparing their arguments. Weld discovered a series of resolutions Senator Calhoun had presented in the Senate that were based on the *Amistad* revolt. He believed the resolutions fixed the South in a legal position regarding jurisdiction on the high seas. Calhoun's resolutions, adopted by the Senate, April 15, 1840, were as follows:

> *Resolved*—That a ship or vessel on the high seas, in time of peace, engaged in a lawful voyage, is according to the laws of nations under the exclusive jurisdiction of the state to which her flag belongs as much so as if constituting a part of its own domain.
>
> *Resolved*—That if such ship or vessel should be forced, by stress of weather, or other unavoidable cause into a port, and under the jurisdiction of a friendly power, she and her cargo, and persons on board, with their property, and all the rights belonging to their personal relations, as established by the laws of the state to which they belong, would be placed under the protection which the laws of nations extend to the unfortunate under such circumstances.[357]

Another aspect was the upcoming summit between the United States and England. Lord Ashburton was expected in Washington in the spring of 1842 to negotiate a treaty. Of note was an article that provided for the extradition of criminals. It was conceivable, if not probable, that this provision would be used to return fugitive slaves. This made it crucial that the Creole Resolutions be presented prior to the Ashburton negotiations. If a settled extradition agreement between England and the United States were established by treaty prior to the introduction of the Creole Resolutions, it would predestine them to being tabled under the Gag Rule.

A turning point was reached in late winter of 1842, when word reached Washington concerning the fate of the nineteen held on charges of mutiny and murder:

> Madison Washington and his companions are safe. The Earl of Aberdeen made the gratifying announcement in the House of Lords on the 14th instant, [February, 1842] that orders had been sent by the colonial secretary for their release.[358]

Hearing this momentous news, the select committee prepared to act. It was the intention of the committee to have John Quincy Adams present the Creole Resolutions on the House floor. His careful attention to legal details, along with his position and history, would add a certain gravitas to the resolutions. Yet, as is often the case of best made plans, there were matters at hand that needed to be resolved concerning the actual resolutions.

Adams's recent battle against Southern slaveholders in Congress over the Haverhill petition had not only exhausted the elderly statesman, but made him vulnerable to further Southern attacks. Like a hungry pack of wolves, Southern members lay in wait, licking their wounds, eager to fall on a vulnerable member who dared to attack their peculiar institution. This time they would not fail.

Upon perusing the resolutions, Adams took issue over a legal point. In the resolutions it stated, "That by adopting the Constitution, no part of the aforesaid powers were delegated to the Federal Government, but were reserved by, and still pertain to each of the several States."

This referred to the institution of slavery being a state municipal code, and, as such, implied that individual states had legal authority to establish—or abolish—the institution under the Tenth Amendment of the Constitution. Giddings, in his book, *History of the Rebellion* explains Adams's protest over the wording of certain passages in the resolution.

> He [Adams] was perfectly frank in saying that he could not support the one which denied the right of the Federal Government to abolish slavery in the States, while he believed and held the principle that in case of an insurrection or war, the Federal Government might under the *war power* abolish it.[359]

Giddings argued that the resolutions were being presented in time of peace and were not applicable to a state of war. He reasoned that during a war, certain laws would be suspended in a national emergency in order to save the country.

Adams replied, "The friends of slavery in future years and *during time of war*, would quote these resolutions as denying the right of the Federal power to interfere with slavery even amidst domestic insurrection or foreign invasion; but he added, '*I will cheerfully sustain all but that which denies the right to the Federal government.*'"[360]

So it was decided, with Adams's careful and cautious blessing, that the choice of who would actually present the Creole Resolutions would now be assigned to the representative from Ohio's Sixteenth Congressional District, the honorable Joshua Reed Giddings.

In the House of Representatives, certain days were set aside for the presentation of petitions, organized on the sequence of states by alphabetical order. Professor William Lee Miller, in his book, *Arguing About Slavery*, explains the process in 1842 with the following passage.

"According to House rules, the first thirty days of a congressional session were all petition days . . . Thereafter, as the House got down to business, only every other Monday was a petition day."[361]

From the records of the *Congressional Globe*, dated Monday, March 21, 1842, the House began the early part of the day's business with matters of the district court in West Tennessee, petitions on the manufacture of cotton and duties relating to the protection of; a request to the president to supply to the House a list of all appointments to office by the executive and state departments, a variety of resolutions dealing with expenditures, committees, and a resolution by Mr. Medill declaring, ". . . a disrespect to the House for any member thereof to present a resolution for the dissolution of the Union."[362]

The Speaker then recognized Mr. Giddings. Giddings rose in his seat and said he had a series of resolutions he wished to present, ". . . upon a subject which had called forth some interest in the other end of the Capitol, and in the nation. I desire to lay them before the country, and would call them up for action at the next opportunity."[363]

The chamber became quiet as heads turned toward Giddings. Adams leaned back in his chair and clasped his hands behind his head, waiting for the fuse to burn down to the powder. Leavitt, seated behind Adams, scribbled furiously, barely looking up as he quickly wrote out, word for word, the utterances of the House.

Weld was in the visitor's balcony, leaning his chin on the railing as he looked down on the House floor, while other members of the select committee all crowded close to watch Giddings.

Giddings took a deep breath and gave a copy of the resolutions to the House clerk. The clerk solemnly walked to his desk near the Speaker's dais with Giddings's resolutions in hand as several members carefully followed his progress to the podium. When the clerk arrived at the dais, he shuffled and straightened the papers, cleared his throat, and then began to read in a clear voice that could be heard in the farthest reaches of the House:

> Resolved, That, prior to the adoption of our Federal Constitution, each of the several States comprising this Union exercised full and exclusive jurisdiction over the subject of slavery within its own Territory, and possessed full power to continue or abolish it at pleasure.

The clerk paused, took a sip of water from a glass on his desk. He looked at the Southern representatives, cleared his throat, and continued:

> Resolved, That by adopting the Constitution, no part of the aforesaid powers were delegated to the Federal Government, but were reserved by, and still pertain to, each of the several States.

The Southern members now began to listen with rapt attention. They stood about with folded arms waiting to see what Giddings and his friends were up to. Giddings motioned for the clerk to continue.

> Resolved, That by the 8th section of the first article of the Constitution, each of the several States surrendered to the Federal Government all jurisdiction over the subjects of commerce and navigation upon the high seas.

There was a noticeable stirring on the House floor, as the direction of Giddings resolutions were, at the least, suspect. All of the Southern delegation, and many of the other members present, had stopped and turned to watch Representative Giddings as his resolutions were read. The clerk increased the volume in his voice, ignoring as best he could the obvious attention he was now drawing to himself:

> Resolved, That slavery being an abridgment of the natural rights of man, can exist only by force of positive municipal law, and is necessarily confined to the territorial jurisdiction of the power creating it.

As the resolutions began to delve into the issue of slavery, a perceptible buzz went up from the planters. Without missing a beat, the clerk read on, becoming louder and more assertive in his delivery.

Resolved, That when a ship belonging to the citizens of any State of this Union leaves the waters and territory of such State and enters upon the high seas, the persons on board cease to be subject to the slave laws of such State, and thenceforth are governed in their relations to each other by, and are amenable to the laws of the United States.

Cries of "foul" went up, and jeers to "sit down" began. Giddings stood firm as the clerk raised his voice and continued on.

Resolved, That when the brig *Creole*, on her late passage to New Orleans, left the territorial jurisdiction of Virginia, [*louder*] THE SLAVE LAWS OF THAT STATE CEASED TO HAVE JURISDICTION over the persons on board said brig, and such persons became amenable only to the laws of the United States.

The Southern representatives were now on their feet, calling upon the Speaker to yield the floor, while the Speaker hammered his gavel and shouted for order. Members of the select committee were also on their feet, along with several Northern representatives. They applauded, as smiles creased their face. Giddings had the clerk press on.

Resolved, That the persons on board the said ship, in resuming their natural rights of personal liberty, violated no law of the United States, incurred no legal penalty, and are justly liable to no punishment.

Resolved, That all attempts to regain possession of, or to re-enslave, said persons, are unauthorized by the Constitution or laws of the United States, and are incompatible with our national honor.

Resolved, That all attempts to exert our national influence in favor of the coastwise slave trade, or to place this nation in the attitude of maintaining a 'commerce in human beings,' are subversive of the rights and injurious to the feelings and the interests of the free States; are unauthorized by the Constitution and prejudicial to our national character.[364]

Giddings stood erect, defiant in the face of the mayhem and cries to table the resolutions. Mr. Smith of Virginia asked if this didn't come under the Gag Rule. Mr. Triplett of Kentucky inquired if the question of reception would not take precedence of the motion to lay on the table. The Speaker replied that the question of reception could not be raised. The resolutions were on their way to being "laid on the table," or in layman's terms, "killed." A vote was called, and the stunning outcome was that the resolutions were *not* to be laid on the table.

The House fell into a shouting match between those who supported Giddings and those who were out for his head. Mr. Holmes of South Carolina remarked, "There are certain topics like certain places, of which it might be said, 'Fools rush in, where angels fear to tread.'"[365]

Mr. Fessenden, a Whig of Maine, "thought the resolutions were too import-ant to be voted on without greater deliberation."

Mr. Floyd of New York stated, "[H]ere are eight or ten resolutions settling important questions between Federal and State government, which the members had only heard orally, but had not seen."

Mr. Cushing of Massachusetts went to the clerk's table and read Giddings's resolutions. He then proclaimed: "They appeared to be a British argument on a great question between the British and American Government's, and constituted an APPROXIMATION TO TREASON, on which he intended to vote no."[366]

Adams attempted to call for a division in the vote, as he wished to vote for parts of the resolutions, but not all of the resolutions, and Mr. Fillmore inquired if it was in order to ask the author of the resolutions to withdraw them.

Giddings replied that he, ". . . was unwilling to see members, acting under the excitement of the moment, commit themselves against doctrines which he was conscious would meet the approval of their judgments in moments of cool reflection; and he withdrew the resolutions, saying he had intended only, on that occasion, to call attention to the subject, and ask a vote at some future day, and as they would now be published, he would withdraw them, and present them for action at the next day when the resolutions would be in order."[367]

However, Southerners had the scent of blood and would not let reason or proper parliamentary procedure impede their quest to deliver a blow to the radical abolitionists. The Speaker came down on the side of the planters and ruled that Giddings's motion to withdraw the Creole Resolutions would not be in order. The Southern contingent in the House now attacked with a vengeance. Mr. Botts of Virginia, a wealthy slave owner, presented a series of resolutions demanding the censure of Joshua R. Giddings.

> Resolved, this House holds the conduct of the said [Giddings] member as altogether unwarranted, and unwarrantable, and deserving the severe con-demnation of the people of the country, and of this body in particular . . .[368]

With calls for censure, Giddings pleaded that he would need two weeks to prepare his defense. After some debate, he was given only until the next day. The House then adjourned.

All that night, Giddings prepared his defense. After a sleepless night, he rode early to Adams's home to seek his advice. Adams was blunt: ". . . that the House would not permit any defense to be made: that the vote would be taken without debate, and that appearances indicated the passage of the resolution of censure."[369]

Giddings asserted that the members of the House, after a night of reflection, would not condemn him without allowing him to present a defense. Adams reply was chilling. "You are not as familiar with the slaveholding character as I am. *Slaveholders act from impulse*, NOT FROM REFLECTION; they act together from interest, and have no dread of the displeasure of their constituents when they act for *slavery*."[370]

On Tuesday, March 22, 1842, the House met and began with the usual presentations of petitions on various subjects—the building of a canal in Illinois, an extra allowance for carrying the mail and the construction of post roads, a new mail route in Indiana, raising the tariff to protect the iron interests, matters relating to naval affairs, and a series of other minor requests for government funding. The House then turned its attention to the events of the previous day.

Joshua R. Giddings rose and began his defense. "I stand before the House in a peculiar situation . . ."[371]

Immediately, Mr. Cooper of Georgia stood and objected. Adams's warning from that morning was being actuated: Giddings would not be allowed a defense. Although not permitted to defend himself, Giddings did manage to present his thwarted speech to the reporter of the *Intelligencer*, so as to have it published.

When I rose so often during the confusion of business in the House this day, and was so often called to order, the last time by Hon. Mark A. Cooper, of Georgia, I *had written out*, and desired to have stated to the House, what follows: 'Mr. Speaker, I stand before the House in a peculiar position. It has proposed to pass a vote of censure on me, substantially for the reason that I differ in opinion from the majority of the members. The vote is about to be taken without giving me time to be heard. It would be idle of me to say that I am ignorant of the disposition of a majority to pass the resolution. I have been violently assailed in a personal manner, but have had no opportunity of being heard in reply. I do not now stand here to ask for any favor or to crave any mercy at the hands of the members. But in the name of an insulted constituency—in behalf of one of the sovereign States of the Union—in behalf of the people of these States and the Federal Constitution—I demand a hearing, agreeably to the rights guaranteed to me, and in the ordinary mode of proceeding. I accept no other privilege—I will receive no other courtesy.[372]

The first resolution against Giddings, "That this House holds the conduct . . . as unwarranted and unwarrantable and deserving the severe condemnation" passed with little to no debate. The Speaker then brought to a vote the censure resolution based on the premise that Giddings's resolutions on the *Creole* interfered with the negotiations that were to be conducted between Great Britain and the United States, ". . . of the most delicate nature, the result of which may involve those nations and the whole civilized world in war. . . and whereas mutiny and murder are therein justified and approved in terms shocking to all senses of law, order and humanity; therefore."[373]

Although a substantial majority adopted the resolution of censure, Giddings was shocked at the swiftness of his trial. While the business of the House droned on, he gathered his belongings from his desk.

Adams wrote in his diary the following observations:

March 22, 1842.

I can find no language to express my feelings at the consummation of this act. Immediately after the second vote, Giddings rose from his seat, came over to mine, shook cordially my hand, and took leave. I had voice only to say, 'I hope we shall soon have you back again.' He made no reply, but passed to the seats of the members, his friends, and took leave of them as he had done of me. I saw him shake hands with Arnold, who had voted against him. He then left the House, and this evening the city.[374]

Giddings wrote of his departure from the House.

When the Speaker announced the resolutions 'carried,' the author rose, and taking formal leave of the Speaker and officers of the House, of his colleagues, of Mr. Adams, and a few other personal friends, passed out of the hall. As he reached the front door, he found Senators Clay and Crittenden of Kentucky, who had been spectators of the scene just described. As Mr. Clay extended to him his hand, he thanked him for the firmness with which he had met the outrage perpetrated upon him, declaring that no man would ever doubt his perfect right to state his own views against the slave trade, particularly while the Executive and the Senate were expressing theirs in favor of it.[375]

Giddings at once sent his resignation to the Speaker of the House, with a copy to the Governor of Ohio, and left the city for his residence.

28

Mate

Blessed, forever blessed, be the name of God!
—Diary of John Quincy Adams, December 3, 1844

The censure of Giddings left the select committee in disarray. As for the Southern representatives, they gloated over their victory of their precious, but now, somewhat precarious, Gag Rule. But vindication was fleeting. Almost overnight, the mood in Congress took on a discernable realization that the censure was a Pyrrhic victory that clearly overstepped certain bounds of decorum. Over the coming weeks, a feeling of regret and guilt descended upon certain members who had voted for censure. More telling was the upwelling of dissatisfaction over the actions of the House. The source of this outcry? The voice of the people.

But this public censure of a member of Congress for uttering his sincere convictions did much to awaken the people to a consciousness that their liberties were in danger.[376] —John Quincy Adams

The public outrage found voice in several members of House. On April 22, Mr. Arnold of Ohio held forth on the changing perception of an increasing number of the members of the House:

The attempt was made to make Mr. Giddings a martyr. It was one of the most barefaced attempts to defraud the people that he had seen in the whole country.[377]

The voice of Southern institutions, Senator John C. Calhoun, grasped the significance of what had taken place. The Creole Resolutions now hung like the sword of Damocles over the heart of the South's peculiar institution.

Even Mr. Calhoun, the leading advocate of slavery, while frankly declaring the author [Giddings] to have been *wrong in presenting his resolutions*, was never known to deny their doctrines.[378] —Joshua R. Giddings

Southern members of both the House and Senate tried to ignore the Creole Incident and Giddings's resolutions. Earlier, the Committee on Foreign Affairs in the Senate demanded reparations from Her Majesty's government for loss of property. Now, the leadership of the committee was unwilling to pursue any further actions, and made no further demands concerning the revolt on board the brig *Creole*.

> Mr. Calhoun ceased to call attention of the country to these claims for slaves: indeed, so far as the author could learn, Mr. Calhoun never subsequently mentioned the subject even in private conversation.[379] —Joshua R. Giddings

They just wanted it to go away.

As for Joshua R. Giddings, he was met with a hero's welcome upon his return to Ohio's 16th Congressional District. Giddings's Creole Resolutions were considered by a majority of the district's constituents as "sincere convictions" by a lawfully elected representative of Congress. Even the Democratic and Southern-leaning *New York Evening Post*, edited by William C. Bryant, came out in support of Giddings's right to present the resolutions.

"[T]he editor declared that were he a resident of Mr. Giddings's district, he would use every honorable effort for that gentleman's reelection."[380]

In Ashtabula County, Ohio, a convention was held in support of Giddings. A series of counter resolutions were adopted in support of his claim. The fourth resolution struck at the very heart of the Gag Rule. It strongly stated, ". . . that every attempt to abridge the right of the people to be heard through their representatives in Congress is incompatible with our institutions, subversive of American liberty, and *revolutionary in its tendency*."

The resolutions were sent to Washington to be presented in the House.

> Some of these [resolutions from the convention in Ashtabula County Convention] attracted attention, and were said to rank among the ablest state papers of the twenty-seventh Congress.[381] —Joshua R. Giddings

On April 22, the House was made fully aware of the public outcry of the 16th Congressional District of Ohio regarding the conduct of the House's censure of their representative:

> Friday, April 22, 1842. Mr. Botts [of *Virginia*] rose to a point of order . . . . Under the order of the house of the 29th ultimo, Mr. Patrick G. Goode laid on the clerk's table resolutions adopted at a meeting of citizens of the county of Ashtabula . . . approving the conduct of Joshua R. Giddings . . . also strongly disapproving the course pursued by the House on the 22nd of the same month toward Mr. Giddings . . . which resolutions were laid on the table.[382]

The Southern contingent wanted the resolutions from Ashtabula tabled. A debate ensued that called into question whether the Ashtabula measures were presented as petitions or resolutions. At one point, the Southern member's growing frustration and concern over Giddings and his Creole Resolutions, as well as the Ashtabula resolutions, sought to deflect the issue by striking out against the easiest target available. In a highly agitated state, Mr. Botts of Virginia, waving a copy of *The Emancipator* about, excitedly accused one Joshua Leavitt of being the culprit behind much of the unrest in the House.

Mr. B was proceeding to show that it was due to the dignity of the body that they should not permit themselves to be thus censored—that they should receive no resolutions, coming from any quarter, which involved a censure of the proceedings of the House [the resolutions from Ashtabula condemning the House for censoring Giddings], or defamatory to the character of the House; and he was not about to show that this was not the only instance of it. If it was not due to the Northern men that they should protect their own dignity and character, he held it due to the members from the South; and he was about to move [pointing to a gentleman who holds a seat at one of the desks allotted to reporters . . .] for expulsion of that man, who had a seat by courtesy in this House, and employed himself in defaming it, and characterizing one portion of the house as dough-faces and slaves: he alluded to the editor of the Emancipator and Free America—a paper he received regularly, he knew not how![383]

Leavitt, for his part, believed that the battle to break the Gag Rule was still in play. He had maintained a steady correspondence with Giddings, offering advice and encouragement. Along with many others, he was confident that Giddings would regain his seat.

And Mr. Raymar (North Carolina) desired to be informed by the gentleman from Ohio, (Mr. Gorde), whether his colleague, (Mr. Giddings), if he went home, and returned, (as the gentleman had stated the fact of a resignation having taken place), intended to charge the government with double mileage?[384]

What concerned the Southern representatives was not only the fact that the constituents of Ohio's 16th District were determined to return Giddings to the House as soon as possible, but that nonpartisan conventions all over the district resolved that Giddings should present the Creole Resolutions as soon as voters sent him back to Washington. Giddings reported with pride and accuracy to Adams, "There is a spirit of independence going forth among the people that shows our population to have been descended from the Pilgrim Fathers."

In a special election held on April 26, 1842, Giddings carried a crushing 7,469 to 393 majority over his Democratic opponent. On May 7, it was reported in the *Niles Weekly Register* that, "J.R. Giddings, re-elected on the 26th ult. representative in Congress from Ohio, to fill the vacancy from his own resignation took his seat in the House on May 5th."

John Quincy Adams wrote the following in his diary:

May 5, 1842. Morning visit from Mr. Lay . . . Next came Mr. Joshua Leavitt, with the gratifying intelligence that Joshua R. Giddings was here, reelected by a majority of upwards of 3,000 of his old constituents of the Sixteenth Congressional District of Ohio.

Giddings's return to Washington greatly bolstered the anti-slavery contingent in Congress. At the same time, the Southern contingent was fully aware of the threat to slavery that was poised by the mandate that Giddings reintroduce the Creole Resolutions.

But the most remarkable effect of this popular feeling manifested in the House of Representatives by the members who voted for the resolutions of censure. They well understood the instructions of the author [Giddings], to again present the resolutions, which had now been published throughout the free States, and to maintain the doctrines which they asserted.[385]
—Joshua R. Giddings

In vain, Southern members tried to stop Giddings from reintroducing the Creole Resolutions. Their ploy was to avoid, altogether, petition day. Each time the appointed day was on the calendar, Southern members called for a suspension of the rules due to "pressing" business. This antic went on for several weeks. Regardless, it was inevitable that Giddings would find the opportunity to reinstate the Creole Resolutions on the House floor.

On Friday, June 3, 1842, Giddings made his first speech since his return to Congress. It was regarding a matter relating to the Committee of the Whole on a question of the reduction in the size of the army to its 1821 standard. Only forty members were present in the House at that moment. Mr. Giddings rose and stated that "he had some observations to make, and he thought he could make them while the absent members were being called in."

Giddings began to inject the topic of the Seminole Wars in Florida and then, on a pretext of a statement made earlier by Mr. Cushing, stated:

He [Giddings] next took issue with the gentleman from Massachusetts [Mr. Cushing] who had said this nation has a question with Great Britain on a point of honor, arising out of the *Creole* case. In the first place, he laid down the position that with the case the free States of the Federal Union had nothing whatever to do; and then he entered largely into that case, and viewed it, as he said, as a jurist. He made some allusion to himself, in connection with the recent action of the House towards him in reference to the case. After proceeding sometime:

Mr. J. G. FLOYD called him to order for irrelevancy.

The CHAIRMAN was understood to be of the opinion that the gentleman from Ohio was in order.

Giddings again held forth on the *Creole* case. He restated his position that, ". . . with the Creole case this government had nothing to do . . ."

Mr. Andrews called Giddings to order.

"The CHAIRMAN said he thought the gentleman was in order.

Mr. ANDREWS, (with a peculiarity of manner which convulsed the House with laughter,) Oh, you do, do you?

Mr. Giddings resumed his argument, to show that with the Creole case this Government had nothing to do.[386]

After several more interruptions, Giddings resumed his remarks. He reestablished his argument that federal jurisprudence held jurisdiction over interstate commerce and emphasized the fact that slavery could only exist legally by state municipal codes. Despite challenges made by several Southern members, the mandate of his quick re-election and return to Congress allowed Giddings the prerogative to proceed.

> The speech was listened to with respectful attention, and although he spoke with severity of language respecting the slave trade and of those who in official stations encouraged that commerce in men and woman, yet he was not called to order.[387]

The iconic moment—when the Gag Rule was finally dismantled and left as a discarded shell of its previous power—ended with a whimper, rather than a bang. Although the Gag Rule would technically remain on the books until 1845, its effectiveness dissipated with the reintroduction of the Creole Resolutions on June 3, 1842, by Representative Joshua Reed Giddings, newly returned member of the House of Representatives, from the 16th Congressional District of Ohio.

"From that date," wrote Giddings twenty years later, "freedom of debate was substantially regained," and the Gag Rule ". . . morally ceased to operate."[388]

Morally ceased to operate.

It was over.

The importance of the actions that occurred in the second session of the 27th Congress were characterized by Giddings when he wrote:

> [R]eflecting men saw clearly that the slaveholding influence had passed its culminating point. The institution no longer exerted undisputed sway. The regaining the right of petition and freedom of debate constituted the first step in the important reformation which may be said to have been fairly inaugurated during the year 1842.[389]

It was the beginning of the end of slavery. In the following week, anti-slavery petitions were received and referred to committee regarding the District of Columbia. Although it persisted on the books, on December 3, 1844, the Gag Rule was officially voted out. In his diary, Adams ends the notation for that day with the following lines: "The question was then put on the resolution; and it was carried—108 to 80. Blessed, forever blessed, be the name of God!"

29
Freedom

Though it cost the blood of MILLIONS OF WHITE MEN, LET IT COME: Let justice be done though the heavens fall. —John Quincy Adams, 1844

A dams's fear that the Union could be dismantled by means other than force is evident in his musings on February 4, 1842:

I specially refuted the pretense that the Union could be dissolved only by force, and cited the example of the peaceable dissolution of the Confederation Union by the present Constitution of the United States.[390]

Now, with the Gag Rule no longer in force, a legislated separation of a state from the union was no longer a viable option.

During the time the Gag Rule was in force, there were two states admitted to the Union, based on resolutions prior to the enactment of the Gag Rule: Arkansas and Michigan, one free, the other slave. Texas would be allowed into the Union as a slave state along with Florida in 1845, followed by the free states of Iowa (1846), Wisconsin (1848), and California (1850).

By breaking the Gag Rule, Adams and his select committee ensured that nullification and secession would now be illegal, and considered an act of rebellion against the federal government and the Constitution. And by the powers vested in the Constitution, the federal government would have the legal authority to put down such a rebellion.

Adams realized that eventually the slavery question would be resolved, but at a cost. In a moment on the House floor in 1844, Adams predicted the inevitable clash between North and South:

It was during this debate that an incidental remark was made by Mr. Adams ... Mr. Dillett, of Alabama ... Like other Representatives from the South, he appeared anxious to assail Mr. Adams. He [Mr. Dillett] held in his hand the report of a speech delivered by the object of his assault to the colored people of Pittsburg, Pennsylvania. From this, he read the following passage: 'We know that the day of your redemption must come. The time and manner of its coming we know not: It may come in peace, or it may come in blood; but, *whether in peace or in blood,* LET IT COME.' Having read this sentence, he [Mr. Dillett] invoked attention to it, and in order that all might appreciate it, he read it a second time; and as his voice died away, Mr. Adams, in his seat, with peculiar emphasis, added, "*I say now, let it come.*" Dillett, apparently indignant at what he regarded the audacity of Mr. Adams, added, 'Yes, the gentleman now says let it come, though it *cost the blood of thousands of white men.*" To which Mr. Adams rejoined: "*Though it cost the blood of* MILLIONS OF WHITE MEN, LET IT COME: *Let justice be done though the heavens fall.*"[391]

The slavery question continued to plague the nation and was finally resolved in the great American Civil War. In the 1860s, several states, led by South Carolina, illegally seceded from the Union and attempted to create the Confederate States of America. The actions taken some twenty years earlier by the select committee guaranteed President Lincoln the constitutional prerogative to direct the federal government to put down the rebellion. If the South had legally legislated the secession, the federal government would not have had recourse in keeping seceding states from leaving the Union. If the federal government attempted to stop such a legal separation, the South could have enlisted the help of foreign nations in its struggle to become independent on the grounds that they would have been a legal nation.

Instead, European nations stayed clear of the conflict until it was decided on the battlefield. When it was finally decided at Appomattox, Virginia, in April of 1865, the South lay in ruins along with its institutions.

The defeat of the rebellious armies of the South finally brought about the end of Southern plans to create an agrarian society based on the machinery of the South. On January 1, 1863, President Lincoln issued the Emancipation Proclamation, which declared that all persons held in slavery in the states of rebellion were free. Two years later, Congress enacted the Thirteenth Amendment to the Constitution of the United States of America, ending slavery.

John Quincy Adams continued to serve in the House of Representatives until February 21, 1848. After answering roll, Adams rose with a paper in his hand when a paralysis returned that had plagued him. He collapsed and was carried from the House floor. His last words were: "This is the last of earth; I am content."

Two days later, his spirit peacefully departed.

On the death of Adams, the torch was passed to a new generation who believed in a strong Union and the end of slavery. It is ironic that in the backbenches of the House, where new members were seated, a representative from a district in Illinois witnessed the final days of Adams. His name was Abraham Lincoln, and Mr. Lincoln served as a pallbearer when Adams was interred at the Congressional Cemetery in Washington, DC.

Adams's nemesis, John C. Calhoun, realized the opportunity to reform the Constitution to reflect Southern ideals and Jeffersonian philosophy was lost with the breaking of the Gag Rule. Calhoun's comments on the Creole Incident, in a speech made in the Senate, 19 August 1842 supporting ratification of the Web-ster-Ashburton Treaty, are telling in the way that he concedes to the inevitable.

> The Treaty is opposed, not only for what it contains, but also for what it does not; and, among other objections of the kind, because it has no pro-vision in reference to the case of the *Creole*, and other similar ones . . . In the meantime, the case of the *Creole* occurred, which, as shocking and out-rageous as it is, was but the legitimate consequence of the principle main-tained by Lord Palmerston, and on which he closed the correspondence in the case of the *Enterprise*.

> Such was the state of the facts when the negotiation commenced in refer-ence to these cases; and it remains now to be shown in what state it has left them. In the first place, the broad principles of the law of nations, on which he placed our right in his resolutions, have been clearly stated and conclu-sively vindicated in the very able letter of the Secretary of State [Calhoun slips by the point that the British Government rejected all arguments pre-sented in said letter], which has strengthened our cause not a little, as well from its intrinsic merit as the quarter from which it comes. In the next place, we have an explicit recognition of the principles for which we contend, in the answer of Lord Ashburton, who expressly says that, 'on the great general principles affecting the case,' [the *Creole*] 'they do not differ;' and that is followed by 'an engagement that instructions shall be given to the Gover-nors of her Majesty's colonies on the Southern borders of the United States, to execute their own laws with careful attention to the wishes of their Gov-ernment to maintain good neighborhood; and that there shall be no offi-cious interference with American vessels driven by accident or violence into their ports. The laws and duties of hospitality shall be executed.'

> Here, again, he would repeat, that such stipulations in the treaty itself would have been preferable, but who can deny, when he compares the state of the facts, as they stood before and since the close of this negotiation, that we have gained—largely gained—in reference to this important subject…I have now stated my opinion fully and impartially on the treaty, with the connected subjects. On reviewing the whole, and weighing the reasons for and against ratification, I cannot doubt that the former greatly preponderate.[392]

In the conclusion of Calhoun's remarks to the Senate over the Webster-Ash-burton Treaty, he acquiesces to the jurisdictional sovereignty of the federal gov-ernment over the individual states:

> Indeed, it would be difficult to imagine a system more so than our Federal Republic—a system of State and General Governments, so blended as to constitute one sublime whole; the latter having charge of the interests common to all, and the former those local and peculiar to each state.[393]

This address by Calhoun is a masterwork in avoiding reality by sidestep-ping the turn of events caused by the Creole Incident. With the Gag Rule all but broken, Calhoun's presidential aspirations and his desire to reform the Constitution were now a thing of the past. The South had reached its legislative high water mark and was now left to stumble down a path to illegal secession.

The last time Calhoun attended a session of the Senate was on March 13, 1850. Senator John Caldwell Calhoun died on March 31, 1850, at Hill's Boarding House, Washington, DC. His last words were, "I am now perfectly comfortable."

Joshua Reed Giddings went on to a long career in government. For his work in breaking the Gag Rule, he was presented with a gold watch and family Bible, fittingly enough, from the congregation of abolitionist Henry Highland Garnet's church in New York City. The gifts were from "The Colored People of New York and Brooklyn" in recognition of Giddings as the "Champion of American Freedom."[394]

Giddings wrote a book in the 1860s that chronicled the events that led to secession, *A History of the Rebellion: Its Authors and Causes*.

Giddings paid tribute to J. Q. Adams and recognized him as a mentor who had no equal. In a letter to then candidate Lincoln in 1860, Giddings made a pointed reference, comparing Senator Clay to Adams, as to whom Lincoln should model himself after.

Mr. Clay defeated himself and friends in 1844 by attempting to make his opinions acceptable to all. Let me advise you to avoid his example [Clay] in that respect, rather and to follow that of Mr. Adams.[395]

In April 1861, President Lincoln appointed Giddings consul general to Canada. While at a friend's house in Montreal on May 26, 1864, Joshua Reed Giddings was analyzing a difficult three-cushion billiard when he suffered a fatal stroke.

Joshua Leavitt remained active in abolitionist politics. In the late 1840s, along with Salmon P. Chase, he helped create a coalition between antislavery Conscience Whigs and Barnburner Democrats called the Free-Soil Party. This group later evolved into the Republican Party that elected its first president in 1860: Abraham Lincoln. Along with Adams, Giddings, and others, Leavitt continued to lead the assault on the issue of slavery in Congress. His daring use of the Creole Incident in breaking the Gag Rule greatly facilitated the planter's loss of power in Congress and led eventually to the enactment of the Thirteenth Amendment, which outlawed slavery in the United States. He lived long enough to see emancipation and the power of the South broken. Joshua Leavitt died on September 8, 1873 in Brooklyn, New York, at the age of seventy-nine.

George Bourne continued to aid those fleeing the horrors of slavery, and his home was a point of refuge along the Underground Railroad. He vigorously continued to urge for the "immediate and total abolition" of slavery and warned his contemporaries of the consequences of continuing such a system, until by its growth, it should endanger the Union.

Bourne never revealed his true involvement in the Creole Incident, although it was widely reported:

[T]he slaves were instructed in how to carry out the revolt by a Baptist

Minister named George Bourne.[396]

Whether he visited and advised slaves "with regard to their course, and [had] given them directions how to proceed" in either Norfolk or in Richmond was information he took to the grave. Bourne died in 1845.

As to the ship, the *Creole* was insured on its fateful voyage for $16,000. The cargo was insured for $50,000. In the National Archives master abstracts for certificates of registration in Record Group 41, Records of the Bureau of Marine Inspection and Navigation, there is an indication that the final document for the brig *Creole* was surrendered on October 26, 1842, because the "vessel wrecked" in the lower Mississippi. No additional information was located.

When it comes to the freed slaves, many of the 135 passengers on the *Creole* were given passage on a ship to Jamaica. Colonial authorities feared an American reprisal to recapture the newly freed slaves, and it was thought best to disperse the passengers to other British colonies throughout the Caribbean.

On April 16, 1842, British authorities in Nassau, Bahamas, discharged from their prison those individuals being held on charges of mutiny and murder:

> The chief justice at Nassau said, "No British court could try a foreigner for an offense committed against another foreigner on the high seas, except for the crime of piracy," and thus took the ground of Judge Thompson with respect to the [*La*] *Amistad* Africans. He then undertook to show that Madison Washington and his associates had not been guilty of piracy. Piracy is larceny committed on the sea. Larceny consists in the taking and conveying away the property of another, with the intention of defrauding the owner of it, and of converting it to the use of the taker-applying it to the profit of the thief. "If," said the judge "a man takes a horse from a stable and rides it a certain distance and then abandons it, this is no larceny," as he took the horse mainly for the purpose of conveyance, and did not subsequently convert it to his own use. The judge stated that it was notorious to everyone at Nassau, that the protests of the officers of the *Creole* made at New Orleans, contained gross miss-statements of facts.[397]

In concluding the decision of the court, the chief justice in Nassau addressed the liberated men, and said: "It has pleased God to set you free from the bonds of slavery—may you hereafter live the lives of good and faithful subjects of Her Majesty's government."

It is believed that many, if not all of the "nineteen," settled in the Bahamas. In a 1999 edition of *The Scene*, a publication for the islands of the Bahamas, an article appeared about the Creole Incident. It concluded by stating:

> Slaves of the *Creole* melted into the new Bahamian society; some of the names listed in the dispatch are similar to the ones in Bahamian society today and include names such as Madison Washington.[398]

It is known that, after his release, Elijah Morris settled in Gambier Village on the island of New Providence, eight miles from Nassau. In August of 1970, Dr. Gail Saunders, former Director of The Bahamas Archives, sat down with and interviewed a Mr. Arthur Fernandez, born in the late 1870s, then in his nineties.

During the interview Dr. Saunders asked Mr. Fernandez, ". . . Elijah Morris? He came off the *Creole?*"

Fernandez answered, "When he come here in the village [Gambier] . . . my father, he was already here. When Morris come, he wasn't sold, he wasn't sold for any . . . because he come from America."

As for Madison Washington, little is known of what became of him after the Creole Incident. At the time, he was well regarded and frequently praised by his contemporaries in the abolitionist movement. Fredrick Douglass wrote a fictional account of the exploits of the revolt on board the *Creole* titled "The Heroic Slave" and mentioned him frequently in several of his speeches.

> Madison Washington, he has made some noise in the world by that act of his, it has been made the ground of some diplomacy: -he fled from Virginia for his freedom. . . he left his wife and little ones in slavery—he made up his mind to leave them, for he felt that in Virginia he was always subject to be removed from them; he ran off to Canada, he was there for two years, but there in misery; for his wife was perpetually before him, he said within himself—I can't be free while my wife's a slave.[399]

At an address delivered by Douglass in New York, New York on April 23, 1849:

> He went to Virginia, [Madison Washington] against the entreaties of friends, against the advice of my friend Gurney . . . He went contrary to the advice of another . . . Robert Purvis was the man: he advised him not to go, and for a time he was inclined to listen to his counsel . . . He told him it would be of no use for him to go, for that as sure as he went he would only be himself enslaved, and could of course do nothing towards freeing his wife.[400]

Another famous abolitionist, John Brown, who had knowledge of Madison Washington, had a brief correspondence with him. Prior to his raid at Harpers Ferry, Brown attempted to recruit Madison. A fugitive from the eastern shore of Maryland named Thomas Thomas was sent by Brown to see Madison in the Bahamas. Thomas returned to report that Madison was not interested in returning to the States.[401]

On a spring day in April of 1842, Madison Washington, Elijah Morris, Ben Blacksmith, Doctor Ruffin, Richard Butler, Phil Jones, Robert Lumpkin or "Limpley," Peter Smallwood, Warner Smith, Walter Brown, Horace Beverly, America, Addison Tyler, William Jenkins, Pompey Garrison, George Basden and George Portlock walked into the morning sun of Nassau, as free men.

One by one, the surviving fugitives who had led the revolt on board the *Creole* filed out into the new day, no longer in chains, answerable only to themselves. The early morning air of the islands filled their lungs as they blinked back the new day's bright sun. They gathered outside the prison gate and stood about, not sure what to do with themselves. The thought of freedom seemed, at first, unreal.

It had always been a dream, something that was talked about on the same level as owning one's own place, traveling, or working one's own fields. The thought was constant, but each time, they had to remind themselves it was only a dream.

Yet, that time had arrived. They were free.

What occurred to Madison Washington after his release can only be, at this point, pure conjecture. The only evidence, uncovered by this investigation, was the brief correspondence with John Brown prior to Brown's raid at Harper's Ferry in 1859, that would seem to suggest that Madison Washington was still in the Nassau area in 1859. It is a known fact that Elijah Morris and some of the other 18 that were held on charges of mutiny and murder in Nassau did settle in Gambire Village, located just outside of Nassau, Bahamas.

As to Madison being reunited with Susan, there has been no reliable, primary source material that would affirm or deny a reunification of the two. However, based on his actions in the Creole Incident, there is little doubt that Madison Washington was a determined man.

With that in mind, I now ask one indulgence: to beg leave from factual research to draw a plausible conclusion. I hold no claim and have no basis on primary source material, but instead, rely on the better angels of the heart.

Consider: On the day of his release, Madison Washington would have looked about, a free man. As he began to walk into Nassau he would have stopped and smiled when he heard a voice call his name. A figure off to one corner of a building that lined the road spoke to him. He slowly walked toward the person who had addressed him in an all-too-familiar voice.

She would have run to him and thrown her arms around his neck with tears of joy running down her cheeks.

They would kiss softly, as he whispered in her ear, "We are free."

As she smiled up at him, they would lock, arm in arm and casually walk down the street, around the corner and into history.

—THE END—

End Notes

PROLOGUE

[1] Henry Clay *The Papers of Henry Clay*. Volume 9: The Whig Leader, January 1, 1837. Edited by Robert Seager III (The University Press of Kentucky. 1988) 625

[2] From the manifest of the brig Creole. Boarded at Richmond, Va., 20th October, 1841.

40	Dick King	black	25	5' 9"	
41	Bill Moore	"	20	5' 11"	
42	Rob Lucy	"	19	5' 8 1/2"	
43	H Gaines	brown	25	5' 8'	
44	Jos Twine	"	23	5' 7 1/2"	
45	J Jones	black	22	5' 6 1/2"	
46	W Clarke	yellow	17	5' 4 1/2"	
47	Doctor Ruffin	brown	25	5' 6"	
48	H Beverly	black	19	5' 9 1/2"	
49	Rob. Pullen	"	22	5' 5"	
50	P Dorsey	brown	23	5' 5"	
51	B. Ross	black	17	5' 5 1/2"	
52	B Gibson	black	17	5' 7"	
53	H Overton	"	33	5' 5 1/2"	
54	Phil Jones	"	17	5' 6 1/2"	
55	R Carter	brown	17	5' 4"	
56	P White	black	18	5' 6"	
57	H Garret	"	30	5' 4"	
58	A Bird	"	35	5' 8 1/2"	
59	G Robinson	"	25	5' 9 1/2"	
60	P Smallwood	brown	23	5' 10 1/2"	
61	H Wood	black	22	5' 7 1/2"	
62	Nelson Walker	"	18	5' 7 1/2"	
63	Addison Tyler	"	23	5' 5 1/2"	
64	C Carter	"	16	5' 3"	
65	Lucy Carter	brown	17	5' 4"	female
66	M Corbin	black	17	5' 6"	"
67	P Page	"	17	5' 4"	"
68	Lydia Gordon	brown	17	5' 5"	

Stayed aboard Creole and returned to New Orleans.

69	L Ellis	black	16	5' 3 1/2"	"
70	C Moore	"	19	5' 2"	"
71	Lucy Grisby	"	26	5' 2"	"
72	Arrene Lester	brown	15	5' 2"	"
73	Nelly Brown	black	18	5' 1"	"

74	Sarah Washington	brown	15	5' 1 1/2"	
75	Mary Loyd	black	10	4' 7"	"
76	H Grigsby	"	8	4' 6 1/2"	"
77	S Clarke	"	10	4' 6"	"
78	Agness Crew	"	15	5' 5"	"
79	Julia Ann Francis	brown	16	5' 2"	"
80	E Hardister	black	28	5' 2"	"

Belonging to Thos McCargo. Boarded at Richmond, Va., 28 October, 1841

81	Henery White	brown	23	5' 11"	male
82	Madison Washington	black	22	5' 9 1/2"	"
83	William Wilks	"	26	5' 8 1/2	"
84	James Bruce	"	18	5' 4"	"
85	William Denly	"	18	5' 5"	"
86	Jacob Hagewood	"	17	5' 4 1/2	"
87	Elijah Morris	"	23	5' 5 1/2"	
88	Marshall Pendleton	brown	22	5' 6 1/2"	
89	John Linsay	black	21	5' 8"	"
90	Edmond Tallenford	"	21	5' 6 1/2"	"
91	Chs Oliver	"	18	5' 6 1/2"	"
92	David Parker	"	18	5' 4 1/4"	"
93	Myer Long	"	17	5' 2 1/4"	
94	Ben Blair	brown	15	4'11 1/2"	"
95	Lewis Carter	yellow	18	5' 6 1/2"	"
96	Andrew Bunkind	black	25	5' 7"	"
97	Willy Glover	"	22	5' 5 1/2"	
98	Geo.		22	5' 4 1/4"	"
110	Rebecca Evans	"	30	5' 4 1/2"	"
111	Ann Wilson	"	15	5' 3/4"	"
112	Elisa Palmer	"	20	5' 6 1/2"	"
113	Elizabeth Celler	"	14	5' 1"	"
114	Mahala Young	brown	14	5' 0"	"
115	Ann Field	black	17	5' 2"	
116	Mitta Gains	"	15	4' 10"	"
117	Milla Jewett	"	26	5' 1 1/4"	"
118	Charlotte Jones	yellow	10	4' 4"	"
119	Alsey Smith	"	13	4' 10"	"
120	Frankey Furgrison	"	40	5' 1"	"
121	Mary C Sergpar				

[3] Niles' National Register, Volume 61

[4] The log of the brig Creole, Remarks. Monday, Oct. 25, 1841

[5] The log of the brig Creole, Remarks. Thursday, 28th Oct. 1841

[6] The log of the brig Creole, Remarks. Remarks on board the brig Creole. Thursday, 28th Oct. 1841

[7] The log of the brig *Creole*, Remarks. Monday, Oct. 29, 1841

[8] The log of the brig *Creole*, Sunday October 30, 1841

[9] The log of the brig *Creole*, Thursday November 4, 1841

[10] Deposition of Zephaniah C Gifford. Taken by Consulate of the United States of America, John F Bacon, at Nassau, Bahamas. November 9, 1841. *Correspondence on The Slave Trade with Foreign Powers. Presented to both Houses of Parliament by Command of Her Majesty,* 1843 LONDON: Printed by William Clowes and Sons, Stamford Street.

[11] ibid

[12] The deposition of Zephaniah C. Gifford, taken at New Orleans, State of Louisiana, by notary public William Young Lewis on December 2, 1841.

CHAPTER 1

[13] Cited in: CO 318/123, 1835 Volume 4. Removal of Liberated Africans from Cuba. Minute on the Condition and Disposal of Captured Africans at the Havana. 24th October, 1835.

[14] History Matters. The U.S. Survey Course on the Web. http://historymatters.gmu.edu/d/6811/ In 1831 a slave named Nat Turner led a rebellion in Southhampton County, Virginia. A religious leader and self-styled Baptist minister, Turner and a group of followers killed some sixty white men, women, and children on the night of August 21 [1831]. Turner and 16 of his conspirators were captured and executed, but the incident continued to haunt Southern whites. Blacks were randomly killed all over Southhampton County; many were beheaded and their heads left along the roads to warn others. In the wake of the uprising planters tightened their grip on slaves and slavery.

[15] Diary of John Quincy Adams. August 14, 1835. *The Diary of John Quincy Adams. 1794-1845 American Diplomacy, and Political, Social, and Intellectual Life, from Washington to Polk.* Edited by Allan Nevins. (Charles Scribner's Sons, New York 1951), 463.

[16] Old Sturbridge Village's collection: Title, *Moore Family Papers, Antislavery Petition,* c. 1835. Library Call No. 1974.1.1.14.3.

[17] Lynn Hudson Parson, *John Quincy Adams.* (Rowman & Littlefield Publishers, Maryland, 1999), 226.

[18] Nat Turner revolt, Southampton County, VA., August 21-22. Some 60 Whites were killed. Nat Turner was not captured until October 30. Nat Turner was hanged, Jerusalem, VA., Nov. 11, 1831.

[19] Cong. Globe, 24 Congress, 1 Session., p. 10

[20] Article I, Section 2, paragraph 3. Deals with the 3/5 representation vote of slaves.

Article IV, Section 2, paragraph 3. Deals with fugitive slaves.

Article I, Section 9, Clause I Deals with importation of slaves.

Representatives and direct Taxes shall be apportioned among the several States which may be included within this Union, according to their respective Numbers, which shall be determined by adding to the whole Number of free Persons, including those bound to Service for a Term of Years, and excluding Indians not taxed, three fifths of all other Persons.

ARTICLE I, SECTION 2, CLAUSE 3

No Person held to Service or Labour in one State, under the Laws thereof, escaping into another, shall, in Consequence of any Law or Regulation therein, be discharged from such Service or Labour, but shall be delivered up on Claim of the Party to whom such Service or Labour may be due.

ARTICLE IV, SECTION 2, CLAUSE 3

The Migration or Importation of such Persons as any of the States now existing shall think proper to admit, shall not be prohibited by the Congress prior to the Year one thousand eight hundred and   eight, but a Tax or duty may be imposed on such Importation, not exceeding ten dollars for each Person.

ARTICLE I, SECTION 9, CLAUSE I

The Migration or Importation of such Persons as any of the States now existing shall think proper to admit, shall not be prohibited by the Congress prior to the Year one thousand eight hundred and eight, but a Tax or duty may be imposed on such Importation, not exceeding ten dollars for each Person.

[21] American Anti-Slavery Society, Constitution, 4 December 1833. Adopted at the founding convention of the American Anti-Slavery Society held at Philadelphia, December 4, 1833. ARTICLE II. -- The objects of this Society are the entire abolition of Slavery in the United States. While it admits that each State, in which Slavery exists, has, by the Constitution of the United States, the exclusive right to legislate in regard to its abolition in said State, it shall aim to convince all our fellow-citizens, by arguments addressed to their understandings and consciences, that Slaveholding is a heinous crime in the sight of God, and that the duty, safety, and best interests of all concerned, require its immediate abandonment, without expatriation. The Society will also endeavor, in a constitutional way, to influence Congress to put an end to the domestic Slave trade, and to abolish Slavery in all those portions of our common country which come under its control, *especially in the District of Columbia,* -- and likewise to prevent the extension of it to any State that may be hereafter admitted to the Union.

[22] Cong Globe, 24th Congress, 1st Session. (1836), 170.

CHAPTER 2

[23] Diary of John Quincy Adams. May 17, 1836. The Diary of John Quincy Adams. 1794-1845 American Diplomacy, and Political, Social, and Intellectual Life, from Washington to Polk. Edited by Allan Nevins. (Charles Scribner's Sons, New York 1951), 57.

[24] Jenkins Hill was later renamed Capitol Hill, although the name persisted as late as 1952.

[25] Harriet Martineau WASHINGTON, D. C. A Guide to the Nation's Capital. ed. Randall Bond Truett. (Hastings House, New York, 1942), 121.

[26] E. S. Abdy, Journal of a Residence and Tour in the United States of North America, from April, 1833, to October 1834. Volume 2, (John Murry, London, 1835), 96-97.

[27] Article I § 2, the 3/5 clause—dealing with the counting of each slave as 3/5 of a person for matters of representation in the House; Article 1 § 9, dealing with the end of the African Slave Trade by Treaty in 1808 and Article IV § 2 Clause 3, dealing with fugitive slaves being returned to their owners. Found in the Constitution of the United States, these sections are referred to as "slave clauses." They were nullified with the passing of the Thirteenth Amendment to the Constitution. Of note, none of the clauses mentioned slavery in fact or used the words "slave," "slavery" or "chattel." It left the jurisdiction and enforcement of the institution to state and municipal codes.

[28] Kentucky and Virginia Resolutions of 1799: Thomas Jefferson and James Madison present these resolutions in defiance to the Alien and Sedition Acts of 1789. These resolutions acted to interpose state authority between the federal government and the people when it was deemed that a federal law was unconstitutional. The Alien and Sedition Act, which stemmed from an undeclared war with France, was thought to be just such a law. Most Northern states rejected the Kentucky and Virginia Resolutions as an attempt to usurp the federal supremacy clause found in the Constitution: Article VI.

[29] An excerpt from the "South Carolina Exposition and Protest."

[30] The Supremacy Clause, The United States Constitution. Article. VI. This Constitution, and the Laws of the United States which shall be made in Pursuance thereof; and all Treaties made, or which shall be made, under the Authority of the United States, shall be the supreme Law of the Land; and the Judges in every State shall be bound thereby, any Thing in the Constitution or Laws of any State to the Contrary notwithstanding.

[31] South Carolina's Reply to Jackson's Proclamation of the Force Bill (1832)

[32] The Force Bill, along with *his Nullification Proclamation*, was issued by President Jackson on December 28, 1832 and passed in Congress on March 1, 1833, in response to South Carolina's ordinance of nullification. It empowered President Jackson to use the army and navy, if necessary, to collect tariffs and put down any attempt at rebellion.

[33] John Niven, *John C. Calhoun and the Price of Union*. (Louisiana State University Press, Baton Rouge, 1998), 239.

[34] Of note, in our present political party system, it would be rare for a vice president to publicly oppose his president to the point of advocating that individual states ignore federal law, although not impossible. In Calhoun's time, the vice-president was elected separately from the president and was often from the opposing party of the president elect.

[35] Diary of John Quincy Adams, 1819-20 [Vol. I, 418, Memoirs, IV, 531. 1819-20] March 3, 1820.

[36] Diary of John Quincy Adams, 1819-20 [Vol. I, 418, Memoirs, IV, 531. 1819-20] 327.

[37] Address of John Quincy Adams to his Constituents of the Twelfth Congressional District at Brainier, Mass., 17th October 1842. (Reported Originally for the Boston Atlas. J. H. Eastburn. Printer, 1842), 20.

[38] Josiah Quincy, *Memoir of John Quincy Adams*. (Boston: Phillips, Sampson and Company 1858), 183.

[39] Mr. Adams at Brainier, Mass., 17 October 1842.

[40] John Niven, *John C. Calhoun and the Price of Union* (Baton Rouge: Louisiana State University Press, 1988), 332.

CHAPTER 3

[41] *The Diary of John Quincy Adams*. May 18, 1836 (Longmans, Green and Co., New York, 1929 Ed. Allan Nevins), 465.

[42] *The Diary of John Quincy Adams*, November 26, 1833 (Longmans, Green and Co., New York, 1929 Ed. Allan Nevins), 465.

[43] William Jay, *A View of Action of the Federal Government, in behalf of slavery*. (Utica: J C Jackson the N.Y. Anti-Slavery Society, 1844), 69.

[44] Monday, May 16, 1836 Gales & Seaton Register, United States Senate. Recognition of Texas, page 1456. Senator William Preston, South Carolina.

[45] Congressional Globe, 24th Congress, 1st Session, Monday, February 1, 1836. Remarks of Representative James Henry Hammond of South Carolina's 4th Congressional district.

[46] Adams, John Quincy, Nile's National Register. (June 18, 1836), 278. Speech of Mr. Adams.

[47] Being that Statuary Hall is elliptic it has a unique acoustic feature wherein it creates a reflection of sound waves. John Quincy Adams, while a member of the House of Representatives, discovered this acoustical phenomenon and placed his desk at a focal point of the elliptical ceiling, easily eavesdropping on the private conversations of other House members located near the other focal point.

[48] This concerns an incident that occurred in 1813. It was resolved by the following Act of Congress. Statute I. July 2 1836

Chap CCXCVIII--An Act for the relief of the owners officers and crews of the private armed vessels Neptune and Fox. Be it enacted, &c., That there be paid to the owners, officers, and crews of the private armed   vessels Neptune and Fox, or their legal Allowance for representatives, by the proper officers of the treasury, out of any money not otherwise appropriated, the sum of twenty-five dollars for each of sixty-nine prisoners captured by said Neptune and Fox on the St. Lawrence river, on the nineteenth day of July, eighteen hundred and thirteen, and delivered to the authorized agent of the United States at Sackett's Harbor. Approved July 2 1836.

[49] On leave seeks permission to deviate from an established rule or procedure.

[50] *Congressional Globe,* 24th Congress, 1st Session. (Friday, March 11, 1836). 247

[51] *Congressional Globe*, 24th Congress, 1st Session (Wednesday March 16, 1836). 258

[52] John C. Calhoun. *The Disquisition on Government and A Discourse of the Constitution and Government of The United States of America.* ed. Richard K. Cralle (Published under the directions of the General Assembly of the State of South Carolina. 1851), 440

[53] *Congressional Globe*, 24th Congress, 1st Session. (May 19, 1836), 474

[54] *Congressional Globe*, 24th Congress, 1st Session. (Wednesday, May 19, 1836).

[55] *Congressional Globe,* 26th Cong., 1st Sess. 150 (1840)

CHAPTER 4

[56] It was at this time that a single ship, the *Sea Venture*, from Sir Thomas Gates expedition of nine ships bound for Jamestown wrecked on a small island in Bermuda. This incident is believed to be the inspiration for Shakespeare's 'The Tempest.'

[57] William Waller Hening, *Virginia Slave Laws Statutes at Large*; Being a Collection of all the Laws of Virginia (Richmond, Va., 1809-23), Vol. 11. (New York: R & W & G. Bartow, 1823) 170, 260, 266, 270.

[58] This refers to the end of the monopoly held by the Royal African Company, a slaving company. In 1660, and again in 1663, after the Restoration, the Royal Adventures in African Company was granted a monopoly by charter over all the English slave trade. It is believed that between 1672 and 1689 it transported around 90,000-100,000 slaves to the new world colonies. Source: *The Emergence Of International Business 1200-1800. Vol 5., The Royal African Company*. By K. G. Davies., Longmans, Green and Co. 1957 London. pg. 41

[59] Slave Clauses United States Constitution:

Article I Section 2.

Representatives and direct taxes shall be apportioned among the several states which may be included within this union, according to their respective numbers, which shall be determined by adding to the whole number of free persons, including those bound to service for a term of years, and excluding Indians not taxed, *three fifths of all other Persons*.

Constitution: Article IV. Section 2. Clause 3:

No person held to service or labor in one state, under the laws thereof, escaping into another, shall, in consequence of any law or regulation therein, be discharged from such service or labor, but shall be delivered up on claim of the party to whom such service or labor may be due.

[60] Samuel Flagg Bemis, *John Quincy Adams and The Union*. (New York: Alfred A. Knopf. 1956) 246-47

CHAPTER 5

[61] William Francis Allen; Charles Pickard Ware, *Slave Songs of the United States*. A. Simpson & Co., New York 1867. Page 2

[62] Based in part on the diary of John Quincy Adams dated Thursday, November 30, 1849. Mr. Adams was in route to Washington from Boston and on that night. He was aboard the steamer Narragran (sp?) in the Long   Island Sound, heading for New York City. He wrote; "The night was blustering, and the wind directly ahead."

[63] William Wells Brown, *Madison Washington, The Black Man, His Antecedents, His Genius, and His Achievements*. (1863; reprint, New York: Arno, 1969) 75-83

64 Charles Ball, *Fifty Years in Chains; or, the Life of an American Slave* (New York, 1858).

65 Pauline E. Hopkins, *The Colored American Magazine*. (Vol III, No. 4, August, 1901) 245

66 Richmond Public Library, City Records Manager, Mr. Alexander G. Monroe 1840 Census of Virginia.

67 Charles Ball, *Fifty Years in Chains*; or, *The Life of an American Slave* (New York, 1858)

68 Michael Tadman, *Speculators and Slaves*. (University of Wisconsin Press. 1989) 286. table A5.3.

69 Frances Anne Kemble, *Journal of a Residence on a Georgia Plantation in 1838-1839*. (Brwn Thrasher Books, The University of Georgia Press, 1984) 351.

70 Theodore D. Weld, *American Slavery as it is: testimony of a thousand witnesses*. (Published by The American Anti-Slavery Society, Office, No. 143 Nassau Street, New York, New York 1839).

71 Joseph Sturge, *A Visit To The United States in 1841* (London: Hamilton, Adams, and Co., Paternoster Row, Birmingham: B Hudson, Bull Street 1842) 97

72 Joseph Sturge, *A Visit To The United States in 1841* (London: Hamilton, Adams, and Co., Paternoster Row, Birmingham: B Hudson, Bull Street 1842) 75

73 Theodore D. Weld, *American Slavery as it is: testimony of a thousand witnesses*. (Published by The American Anti-Slavery Society, Office, No. 143 Nassau Street, New York, New York 1839) 15

74 All three of the quotes can be found in: *Slavery And The Internal Slave Trade In The United States Of North America 1841*: Slavery And The Internal Slave Trade In The United States Of North America Being Replies To Questions Transmitted By The Committee Of The British and Foreign Anti-Slavery For the abolition of slavery and the slave trade throughout the world. Presented To The General Anti-Slavery Convention Held In London June, 1840. By The Executive Committee Of The American Antislavery Society. London, Thomas Ward And 1co. Paternoster Row: and to be had at the office of the British and Foreign Antislavery Society, 27, New Broad Street. 1841 16

75 Charles Elliott, Benjamin Franklin Tefft, *Sinfulness of American Slavery* (L. Swormstedt & J. H. Power. For the Methodist Episcopal Church. 1851) 125. *Effects Of Slavery On The State*. Representative Clayton of Georgia first used this term as a reference to slavery. Adams wrote the following in his diary: "Not three days since, Mr. Clayton, of Georgia, called that species of population—that is, slaves—the machinery of the south. Now, that machinery had twenty odd representatives in that hall—not elected by the machinery, but by those who owned it. . . "

lxx J. J. Toler was a speculator in the counties in and around Richmond, Virginia., 1840-1860.

77 John Brow, *Slave Life In Georgia*. Originally published: 1856. Narrative of ex-slave, John Brown, describing a New Orleans pen.

78 William Wells Brown, "Madison Washington," *The Black Man, His Antecedents, His genius, and His Achievements* (1863; reprint, New York: Arno, 1969) 77

CHAPTER 6

[79] Slave song that was popular in the 1830–1840s. Was one of the slave songs sung by Henry Highland Garnet on his visit to England in 1849.

[80] William Wells Brown, "Madison Washington," *The Black Man, His Antecedents, His genius, and His Achievements* (1863; reprint, New York: Arno, 1969) 81

[81] L. Maria Child, *Madison Washington. The Freedmen's Book* (Boston, Ticknor & Fields 1865) 147

[82] George Bourne, *Slavery Illustrated In Its Effects Upon Woman And Domestic Society.* (Isaac Knapp, 25 Cornhill, Boston. 1837) Introduction 26.

[83] William Wells Brown, *The Black Man, His Antecedents, His Genius, And His Achievements.* (4th ed. Boston: R.F. Wallcut. 1863) 81–82

[84] William Wells Brown, *The Black Man, His Antecedents, His Genius, And His Achievements.* (4th ed. Boston: R.F. Wallcut. 1863) 76

[85] Harriet A. Jacobs, *Incidents in The Life of A Slave Girl; written by herself.* (Boston: 1861) 9

[86] John W. Blassingame *The Slave Community; Plantation Life In The Antebellum South.* (Oxford University Press, New York-Oxford 1979) 224-25

[87] Frances Anne Kemble *Journal of a Residence on a Georgian Plantation in 1838-1839.* (University of University of Georgia Press 1984) 101

[88] Frances Anne Kemble *Journal of a Residence on a Georgian Plantation in 1838-1839.* (University of University of Georgia Press 1984) 360

[89] Theodore Dwight Weld, *AMERICAN SLAVERY AS IT IS: Testimony of a Thousand Witnesses* (The American Anti-Slavery Society, Office, No. 143 Nassau Street. New York 1839) 172.

[90] George Bourne, *Picture of Slavery In The United States of America.* (Published 1834. Republished 1972 Negro History Press. Detroit, Michigan) 97

CHAPTER 7

[91] William Wells Brown, *My Southern Home.* (A. G. Brown & Co Boston 1880) 92-93

[92] John W. Blassingame *The Slave Community; Plantation Life In The Antebellum South.* (Oxford University Press, New York-Oxford 1979)

[93] Edited by Eli Brown, *Rambles in the path of the Steam-horse.* (Wm. Bromwell and Wm. White Smith. No. 195 Chestnut Street, Baltimore, Maryland 1855) 20

[94] John Anderson. *The Story of the Life of John Anderson, a Fugitive Slave.* (W. Tweedie, London 1863) 129

[95] Michael Tadman, Speculators and Slaves. (The University of Wisconsin Press. 1989) 143

CHAPTER 8

[96] *The Narrative of Lunsford Lane* (Boston, 1842).

[97] Josiah Henson *Uncle Tom's Story of His Life: An Autobiography of the Rev. Josiah Henson* (London, 1877). Josiah Henson spent thirty years on a plantation in Montgomery County, Maryland before he escaped slavery and became a Methodist preacher, abolitionist, lecturer, and founder of a cooperative colony of former slaves in Canada. His memoirs, published in 1849, provided Harriet Beecher Stowe with her model of Uncle Tom.

[98] Frances Anne Kemble *Journal of a Residence on a Georgian Plantation in 1838-1839.* (University of University of Georgia Press 1984), 99-100.

[99] Frances Anne Kemble *Journal of a Residence on a Georgian Plantation in 1838-1839.* (University of University of Georgia Press 1984), 11.

[100] Peter Randolph, *Slave Cabin to the Pulpit* (Boston, 1893). Peter Randolph, who grew up in slavery on a plantation in Prince George County, Virginia, received his freedom in 1847 following his owner's death, and then served as an antislavery agent, a newspaper editor, and as a Baptist minister in the North and in Canada. Following the Civil War, he served as minister in the Ryland or Old African Baptist Church in Richmond, Virginia.

[101] National Humanities Center Resource Toolbox. The Making of African American Identity: Vol. I, 1500-1865 RELIGIOUS PRACTIC Selections from the WPA interviews, 1936-1938

[102] Peter Randolph, *Slave Cabin to the Pulpit: The Autobiography of Rev. Peter Randolph* (James H Earle. Boston, 1893), 203.

[103] Josiah Henson Uncle Tom's Story of His Life: An Autobiography of the Rev. Josiah Henson (London, 1877), 18.

[104] This figure was based on research supported by information derived from; *The Slave Community, Plantation Life In The Antebellum South.*, John W. Blassingame. Oxford University Press. 1979 pg 245-46., several slave narratives, Frances Anne Kemble, *Journal of a Residence on a Georgia Plantation*. Although it would be difficult to compile an accurate number of slaves whipped each year, the slave narratives that exist strongly suggest that 50% is a safe estimate.

[105] Charles Ball, *Fifty Years in Chains; or, The Life of an American Slave* (New York, 1858), 96.

[106] Lunsford Lane, *The Narrative of Lunsford Lane* (Boston, 1845), 2-3.

[107] Lewis Clarke. *Interesting Memoirs and Documents Relating to American Slavery, and the Glorious Struggle Now Making for Complete Emancipation* (London, 1846), 80. Lewis Clarke, the son of a Scottish weaver and a slave mother, was born in Kentucky in 1815. Despite an agreement that she was to be freed upon her husband's death, Clarke's mother and her nine children remained in slavery. After he learned that he was going to be sold in New Orleans, Clarke successfully fled through Ohio across Lake Erie to Canada in 1841.

[108] Eber Pettit, *Sketches in the History of the Underground Railroad* (Fredonia, N.Y., 1879), 81. Margaret Ward and her infant son Samuel Ringgold Ward, slaves from Maryland.

[109] Loren Schweninger, "To the Honorable: Divorce, Alimony, Slavery and the Law in Antebellum North Carolina." *North Carolina Historical Review* April 2009, 127-179.

[110] Unruly Women: The Politics of Social and Sexual Control in the Old South (Gender and American Culture) by Victoria E. Bynum, University of North Carolina Press, Chapel Hill and London. 1984

[111] Benjamin Drew, *The Refugee* or *The Narratives Of Fugitive Slaves In Canada. Related by themselves.* (John P Jewett and Company, Cleveland, Ohio and Worthington. New York Sheldon, Lamport and Blakeman, London, Tribune and Co, 1856), 137.

[112] George Bourne, *Pictures Of Slavery in the United States of America.* (Edwin Hunt 1834. Middletown, Con. Republished 1972 Negro History Press, Detroit, Michigan), 88.

CHAPTER 9

[113] William Francis Allen, Charles Pickard Ware, and Lucy McKim Garrison, Slave Songs of the United States. (New York: A. Simpson & Co., 1867), 112-113.

[114] George Bourne, *Picture of Slavery in The United States of America.* (Isaac Knapp 1838), 30.

[115] Frances Anne Kemble, *Journal of a Residence on a Georgia Plantation, Journal of a Residence on a Georgian Plantation in 1838-1839.* (University of University of Georgia Press 1984), 255.

[116] Josiah Henson, *Uncle Tom's Story of His Life: An Autobiography of the Rev. Josiah Henson* (R. B. Russel & Co. London, 1877), 23.

[117] Theodore D. Weld, *American Slavery as it is: testimony of a thousand witnesses.* (Published by The American Anti-Slavery Society, Office, No. 143 Nassau Street, New York, New York 1839), 16.

[118] Frances Anne Kemble, *Journal of a Residence on a Georgia Plantation, Journal of a Residence on a Georgian Plantation in 1838-1839.* (University of University of Georgia Press 1984), 31.

[119] Frederick Douglass, *Life and Times of Frederick Douglass.* (Park Publ. Co. Hartford, Con. 1881), 151.

[120] Lewis Clarke *From The Sufferings of Lewis and Milton Clarke* Dictated by Themselves Boston: Bela Marsh, 1846

[121] Eber Pettit, *Sketches in the History of the Underground Railroad* (Fredonia, N.Y., 1879), 83.

[122] Handsawing: flat handsaws were used as whips. Source: James McKaye. *The Mastership and Its Fruits: The Emancipated Slave Face to Face with His Old Master.* (W.C. Bryant & Co., Printers. 41 Nassau Street, Corner of Liberty 1864), 9.

[123] Michael Tadman, *Speculators and Slaves.* (The University of Wisconsin Press. 1989), 187.

[124] Advertisement, *New Orleans Commercial Bulletin* (30th September, 1845)

[125] William Wells Brown, *The Narrative of William W. Brown, a Fugitive Slave* (Addison Wesley Publishing Company 1969), 144-45.

CHAPTER 10

[126] Milton C. Sernett, *Abolition's Axe: Beriah Green, Oneida Institute, and the Black Freedom Struggle.* (Syracuse University Press, Syracuse, New York. 1986)

[127] Wilbur H. Siebert, *The Underground Railroad; from Slavery to Freedom.* (The Macmillan Company. London. 1899), 56.

[128] Mrs. Amoretta Frasier relating a childhood incident involving her neighbor, a Mrs. Johnson and her involvement in the Underground Railroad. From the "*Westfield Republican*," April 1, 1959. 12, column II.

[129] Milton C. Sernett, *Common Cause: The Antislavery Alliance of Gerrit Smith and Beriah Green.* (Syracuse University, Library Associates Courier., Volume XXI. Number 2 Fall 1986), 58.

[130] Address by Abraham D Shadd, 12 July, 1831 Black Abolitionist Papers 1830-1846

[131] The American Neptune: article. Hugh H. Davis, *The American Seaman's Friend Society.* (Vol. 39. January 1979), 45.

[132] Hugh Davis, *Joshua Leavitt; Evangelical Abolitionist.* (Louisiana State university Press, Baton Rouge and London. 1990), 104.

[133] Samuel Flagg Bemis, *John Quincy Adams and The Union.* (New York, Alfred A. Knopf. 1956), 334.

[134] Samuel Flagg Bemis, *John Quincy Adams and The Union.* (New York, Alfred A. Knopf. 1956), 331.

[135] osiah Quincy LL. D, *Memoir of John Quincy Adams.* (Boston: Phillips, Sampson and Company. 1858), 385-87.

CHAPTER 11

[136] George Bourne, *Picture of Slavery in the United States of America.* (Published by Edwin Hunt, Middletown, Conn. 1834)

[137] Theodore Bourne, *Rev. George Bourne. The Pioneer of American Antislavery.* (Methodist Quarterly Review, January 1882) 71

[138] Theodore Bourne, *Rev. George Bourne. The Pioneer of American Antislavery.* (Methodist Quarterly Review, January 1882) 73

[139] George Bourne, *Picture of Slavery in the United States of America.* (Published by Edwin Hunt, Middletown, Conn. 1834) 143-44

[140] William Lloyd Garrison, *The Letters of William Lloyd Garrison, Volume II: A House Dividing Against Itself: 1836-1840.* (Edited By Louis Ruchames. Harvard Press. 1971) 484

[141] George Bourne, *Picture of Slavery in the United States of America.* (Published by Edwin Hunt, Middletown, Conn. 1834) 143-44

[142] George Bourne. Picture of Slavery in the United States of America. Middletown, Connecticut 1834. page 143-44

[143] (ibid. p. 159)

[144] (ibid. p. 39)

CHAPTER 12

[145] Christian Spectator: *People Of* Color 1825 No.1, Vol VII. 240. Certain contributions to the Christian Spectator by Leavitt appeared anonymously under the pseudonym S.F.D.

[146] William Jay, *Slavery in America*. (Leavitt, Lord & Co. New York, 1835) 149.

[147] Michael Tadman, *Speculators and Slaves; Masters, Traders and Slaves in the Old South*. (University of Wisconsin Press. 1989) 80-81

[148] William Jay, *Slavery in America*. (Leavitt, Lord & Co. New York, 1835) 279n *Register*, 9 Jan. 1830.

[149] Joshua Leavitt. *The Anti-Slavery Reporter*, (June 21, 1843) 98-99

[150] Theodore Weld, *Slavery as It Is*. (The American Anti-Slavery Society, Office, No. 143 Nassau Street. New York 1839) 20

[151] Hugh Davis, *Joshua Leavitt, Evangelical Abolitionist*. (Louisiana State University Press, Baton Rouge and London; 1990)

[152] Samuel Flagg Bemis, *John Quincy Adams and The Union*. (New York, Alfred A. Knopf. 1956. Adams diary, Aug. 11, 1835)

[153] Plug-uglies: An Irish gang of New York City, in the Five Point area, a notorious slum centered on the five-cornered intersection of Anthony (now Worth St.), Cross (now Mosco), and Orange (now Baxter) on Manhattan island.

[154] Henry Mayer, *All on Fire*. (Saint Martin's Press: New York, 1998) 263-4.

[155] James M. McPherson, *The Fight Against the Gag Rule: Joshua Leavitt and Anti-slavery Insurgency in the Whig Party, 1839-1842*. (The Journal of African American History. Volume 48, Number 3 July 1963) 177

[156] Wilbur H. Siebert, *The Underground Railroad, from Slavery to Freedom*. (The MacMillan Company, London. 1899) 303-306

[157] Alex Tyrrell, *Joseph Sturge and the Moral Radical Party in Early Victorian England*. (Christopher Helm, London. 1987) 110

[158] 1833 Emancipation Act: Ends slavery in the British Empire, 1 August, 1834

[159] Act of 1820, STATUTE I. Section 4. May 15, 1820. CHAP. CXIII. --An Act to continue in force "An act to protect the commerce of the United States, and punish the crime of piracy," and also to make further provisions for punishing the crime or piracy.

[160] Positive Law: is also described as the law that applies at certain time (present or past) and at certain place, consisting of statutory law, and case law, as far as it is binding. n. statutory man-made law, as compared to "natural law," which is purportedly based on universally accepted moral principles, "God's law," and/or derived from nature and reason. The term "positive law" was first used by Thomas Hobbes in Leviathan (1651).

CHAPTER 13

[161] Wilbur H. Siebert, *The Underground Railroad; from Slavery to Freedom*. (The Macmillan Company. London. 1899) 125-26

[162] Benjamin Drew, *The Refugee Of The Narratives Of Fugitive Slaves In Canada, related by themselves with an account of the history and condition of the colored population of upper Canada*. (John P. Jewett and Company. Cleveland, Ohio: Jewett, Proctor and Worthington. New York: Sheldon, Lamport and Blakeman London: Trubner and Co. 1856) 18

[163] *Memoirs of Joseph John Gurney: with selections from his journal*. In two Volumes. Volume 2. Ed. Joseph Bevan Braithwaite, (Norwich: Fletcher and Alexander. London MDCCCLIV 1854) 179

[164] William Lloyd Garrison, *The Letters of William Lloyd Garrison*, Volume II: A House Dividing Against Itself: 1836-1840, Edited by Louis Ruchames. (Harvard Press) 484

[165] L Maria Child, *The Freedmen's Book*. (Ticknor And Fields. Boston 1866) 148

[166] William Still, *The Underground Railroad*. (Aron Press, New York 1968 [original 1872]) 65. This is a letter written by a fugitive from Canada. I use the majority of the letter with few changes as I found it relates well to the same situation Madison was in. The original letter was written by a I. Forman, in Toronto, May 7, 1854.

CHAPTER 14

[167] *The Frederick Douglass Papers, Series One, Volume 2., 1847-54.*, ed. John W. Blassingame. Yale University Press 1982. p. 154-55; An address delivered in New York, New York, on 23 April. 1849)

[168] This description of Madison Washington was found in William Wells Brown, "Madison Washington, "*The Black Man, His Antecedents, His Genius, and His Achievements*. (1863; reprint, New York: Arno, 1969)

[169] George Hendrick, Willene Hendrick, *Black Refugees in Canada: Accounts of Escape During the Era of Slavery*. (McFarland & Co., Inc. Publishers 2010) 35

[170] *The Frederick Douglass Papers; Series One, Volume 1, 1841-46.*, ed. John W. Blassingame. New Haven & London. Yale University Press. 1979

[171] A quote from a speech given by Henry Highland Garnet at the National Convention of Colored People, Buffalo, New York, August 15th-19th, 1843.

[172] *The Frederick Douglass Papers, Series One, Volume 2., 1847-54.*, ed. John W. Blassingame. Yale   University Press 1982., pp. 154-55

[173] Richard J. Powell, *Cutting a Figure: Fashioning Black Portraiture* (Uni of Chicago, 2008. Chicago) 30–32.

[174] Richard J. Powell, *Cutting a Figure: Fashioning Black Portraiture* (University Of Chicago Press 2008) 228 #19. First City: Philadelphia and the Forging of Historical Memory., Gary B. Nash (University of   Pennsylvania Press. 2002) 193

[175] Winthrop D. Jordan, *The White Man's Burden, Historical Origins of Racism In The United States*. (Oxford University Press 1974) 79

[176] Winthrop D. Jordon, *The White Man's Burden, Historical Origins of Racism In The United States.* (Oxford University Press ©1974) 79

[177] L Maria Child, *The Freedmen's Book.* (Boston. Ticknor And Fields. 1866) 150

[178] William Wells Brown, "Madison Washington," Source: *The Black Man, His Antecedents, His Genius, and His Achievements.*, (1863; reprint, New York: Arno, 1969), pp. 75-83

[179] *The Freedmen's Book.* By L Maria Child., Boston. Tickmor and Fields. 1866

CHAPTER 15

[180] Coffle: Droves of slaves, chained or roped together. In this manner, forced to walk from one market to another. Usually accompanied by musicians, the slaves being forced to 'sing' or 'strike up lively', this to "reinforce among white observers the myth that blacks were carefree people. . . and to separate the coffle gang from making contact with fellow slaves." *A Visit To The United States in 1841.*, by Joseph Sturge. Boston, Dexter S. King. 1842

[181] Richard J. Follett, *The Sugar Masters: Planters and Slaves in Louisiana's Cane World, 1820-1860.* (Louisiana State University Press, Baton Rouge. 2005) 77

[182] Richard J. Follett, *The Sugar Masters: Planters and Slaves in Louisiana's Cane World, 1820-1860.* (Louisiana State University Press, Baton Rouge. 2005) 175

[183] Frederic Bancroft, *Slave Trading In The South* (Fredrick Ungar Publishing Co., New York. 1959) 106

[184] Advertisement for Lewis B. Levy, 4 Wall Street, The Richmond Directory and Business Advertiser, for 1852. 27

[185] John Brown, *Slave Life in Georgia: A Narrative of the Life, Sufferings, and Escape of John Brown, a Fugitive Slave, Now in England*, ed. Louis Alexis Chamerovzow (W. M. Watts. London 1855) 112

[186] Michael Tadman, *Speculators and Slaves, Masters, Traders and Slaves in the Old South.* (The University of Wisconsin Press. Madison 1989) 98

[187] Solomon Northup, *Twelve years a slave: Narrative of Solomon Northup, a citizen of New-York, kidnapped in Washington City in 1841, and rescued in 1853, from a cotton plantation near the Red River in Louisiana* (Auburn, N.Y.: 1856), 78-82.

[188] Michael Tadman, *Speculators and Slaves, Masters, Traders and Slaves in the Old South.* (The University of Wisconsin Press. Madison 1989) 99

CHAPTER 16

[189] International Treaties Concerning Slave Trade;

1807

Great Britain passes the Abolition of the Slave Trade Act abolishing the Transatlantic slave trade and levying fines on British captains importing slaves of up to £100 per slave. United States entirely abolishes Slave Trade. British minister in Lisbon instructed to lobby for Treaty to abolish Portuguese slave trade

1808

British West Africa Squadron is established at Sierra Leone to suppress the British slave trade. British Minister in Madrid instructed to lobby for Treaty to abolish Spanish slave trade.

1810

Portugal signs Treaty with Great Britain to abolish slave trade gradually, and in the mean time to prohibit it in places where it was discontinued by other powers.

1818

'Felony Act' makes Slave Trade a felony. British subjects engaged in it will be punished with transportation or five years imprisonment.

1814

Denmark signs treaty with Great Britain, to prohibit slave trade. Holland decrees to forbid Dutch slave trade on Coast of Africa. Austria, Russia, Prussia and France engage at Congress to assist Great Britain in abolishing the slave trade. Spain signs treaty with Great Britain to permit slave trade solely for the supply of her own possessions.

1815

Great Britain, Austria, France, Portugal, Prussia, Spain and Sweden sign a Declaration denouncing the slave trade at the Congress of Vienna. Portugal signs treaty with Great Britain declaring Portugal slave trade north of the equator illegal, fixing a period for its entire abolition, and permitting the Trade only for its Transatlantic possessions. Napoleon issues a decree abolishing all French slave trade

1817

Louis XVIII issues a decree abolishing French slave trade. Portugal signs treaty with Great Britain conceding the Right of Search (allowing the Royal Navy to search vessels suspected of trading slaves), establishing Mixed Commissions, and regulating Portuguese slave trade south of the equator. Spain signs treaty with Great Britain abolishing the slave trade north of the equator, conceding Right of Search, establishing Mixed Commissions and commit to abolish the slave trade entirely after 30 May 1820.

1818

Netherlands sign treaty with Great Britain to suppress their slave trade, conceding Right of Search and establishing Mixed Commissions

1820

United States passes a law declaring the American slave trade an act of piracy punishable by death.

1822

Spain adds an article to the 1817 Treaty, authorizing the condemnation of vessels proved to have had slaves on board on the voyage in which they were taken. Netherlands adds an article to the 1818 Treaty for the same purpose.

1823

Netherlands add an article to the 1818 Treaty authorizing vessels engaged in the slave trade be condemned for slave trade equipment and broken up. Portugal add an article to the 1817 Treaty authorizing the condemnation of vessels proved to have had slaves on board on the voyage in which they were taken. Anti-Slavery Committee is formed to campaign for the total abolition of slavery. Members include Thomas

Clarkson, Henry Brougham, William Wilberforce and Thomas Foxwell Buxton.

1824

Act of Parliament declares the slave trade an act of piracy, punishable by death. Sweden signs treaty with Great Britain to suppress their slave trade, conceding Right of Search, establishing Mixed Commissions and authorizing the condemnation of vessels equipped for the slave trade. Buenos Aires pass law declaring the American slave trade an act of piracy

1825

Buenos Aires and Columbia sign Treaty with Great Britain committing to the total abolition of the slave trade and forbidding it in its own dominions.

1826

Brazil signs treaty with Great Britain to abolish its slave trade in three years, and in the interim, to adopt the 1817 Treaty between Portugal and Great Britain. Mexico signs Treaty with Great Britain committing to the total abolition of the slave trade and forbidding it in its own dominions.

1827

France passes law to punish those engaged in the slave trade by fine, imprisonment and banishment.

1831

France signs treaty with Great Britain conceding a limited right of search. Brazil passes decree to punish those engaged in the slave trade by fines and corporal punishment, and declaring that slave vessels arriving in Brazil will be confiscated. Freed slave Mary Prince publishes *The History of Mary Prince*, an account of her experiences as a slave. The book becomes a powerful instrument in the campaign against slavery.

1832

Brazil orders for ships to be searched on their arrival at Rio to enforce the 1831 Decree.

1833

France signs treaty with Great Britain authorizing the condemnation of slave vessels equipped for the slave trade. The Abolition of Slave Act abolishes slavery in all of Great Britain's colonies. Twenty million pounds is granted in compensation to slave holders. The Act declares free all slaves under the age of 6 years. Former slaves must serve as apprentices for 4 years before being freed. William Wilberforce dies three days after the Bill is passed by Parliament

1834

Denmark and Sardinia sign treaty with Great Britain and France, agreeing to the terms of the previous treaties between the two nations in 1831 and 1833.

Spain signs treaty with Great Britain entirely abolishing the slave trade, granting the Right of Search, establishing Mixed Commissions, authorizing that vessels equipped for the slave trade be condemned and broken up, and declaring that slaves liberated by the Mixed Commission should be delivered to the government whose cruiser made the capture Sweden and Norway add an article to 1824 Treaty, stipulating that vessels condemned for the slave trade should be broken up before sale.

Russia issues a circular withdrawing her protection from slave vessels making use of her flag.

1836

Portugal issues a decree abolishing the slave trade, limiting the number of slaves to be transported by colonists, committing to punish Portuguese slave traders and authorizing the condemnation of vessels equipped for the slave trade.

1837

Netherlands add an article declaring that vessels condemned for the slave trade should be broken up before sale. Bolivia signs treaty with Great Britain to co-operate in the total abolition of the slave trade and prohibiting its subjects engaging in the trade. Tuscany signs treaty with Great Britain and France agreeing to the terms of the previous treaties between the two nations in 1831 and 1833.

1838

Naples signs treaty with Great Britain and France agreeing to the terms of the previous treaties between the two nations in 1831 and 1833. Britain pass an Act of Parliament reducing the punishment for the slave trade from that of death to transportation, or imprisonment for three years.

Enslaved people are emancipated in British colonies when the apprenticeship scheme fails.

1839

Chile and Venezuela sign treaty with Great Britain, conceding the Right of Search, the establishment of Mixed Commissions, authorizing the condemnation of vessels equipped for the slave trade, and declaring that liberated slaves are to be given over to the government whose cruisers made the capture. Argentine Confederation and Uruguay sign treaty with Great Britain on the same terms as the 1835 Treaty with Spain. Act of Parliament passed authorizing British cruisers to detain Portuguese slave vessels and British Vice-Admiralty courts to condemn them.Haiti signs treaty with Great Britain and France agreeing to the terms of the previous treaties between the two nations in 1831 and 1833.Slaves revolt on board the slave ship Amistad off the coast of Cuba, resulting in the arrest of the Africans on arrival in the United States. American abolitionists rally to their cause. Pope Gregory XVI issues a Bull against the slave trade.

1840

Greece issues a decree against the slave trade. Bolivia signs treaty with Great Britain on the same terms as the 1835 Treaty with Spain.

1841

Mexico signs treaty with Great Britain declaring slave trade an act of piracy, conceding a Right of Search, authorizing that vessels equipped for the slave trade should be condemned and broken up before sale, and declaring that liberated slaves are to be given over to the government whose cruisers made the capture. Tunis forbids the export of slaves from her possessions and commits to suppress the slave trade. Austria, France, Prussia and Russia sign treaty with Great Britain for the more effectual suppression of the slave trade, extending the Right of Search, authorizing the condemnation of vessels equipped for slave trade. Austria, Prussia and Russia declare the slave trade to be an act of piracy.

1842

Portugal signs a treaty with Great Britain giving British cruisers Right of Search, authorizing the condemnation of vessels equipped for slave trade, establishing Mixed Commissions, declaring the slave trade to be an act of piracy, regulating the number of slaves to be carried by Portuguese subjects, declaring that liberated slaves are to be given over to the government whose cruisers made the capture. United States signs Treaty with Great Britain agreeing to keep a fleet of guns on the Coast of Africa for the suppression of the slave trade. Chile passes a law declaring the slave trade to be an act of piracy. Tunisia abolishes the slave trade and any children born to slaves are declared free.

[190] The United States, Appellants, Vs. Cinque, And Others., Africans, Captured In The Schooner *Amistad*, By Lieut. Gedney, Delivered On The 24th Of February And 1st Of March, 1841. With A Review Of The Case Of The Antelope, Reported In The 10th, 11th And 12th Volumes Of Wheaton's Reports. New York, Sept. 6, 1839

[191] Lewis Tappan, *The Life Of Arthur Tappan*. (Published by Hurd and Houghton. Cambrodge: Riverside Press 1870) 317

[192] John Quincy Adams' diary entry from March 29th, 1841

[193] Hugh Davis, *Joshua Leavitt; Evangelical Abolitionist*. (Louisiana State University Press, Baton Rouge and London. 1990) 177-78

[194] Richard Peters, *Reports of Cases Argued and Adjudged in the Supreme Court of the United States. January Term 1841*. Vol 15. Mr. Baldwin for the defendant. United Statres *v* Amistad. January, 1841. 553-554

[195] The English Reports, King's Bench Division. Volume CVII; King's Bench Division XXXVI Barnwall and Cresswell, Volumes 1 to 4. (Wiliam Green & Sons, Limited, Edinburgh, Stevens & Son's Limited, London) 456

[196] *The British and Foreign Anti-Slavery Reporter*, June 21, 1843. (Lancelot Wild, 13 Catherine Street, Stand) 99

[197] Constitution of the United States of America: Article IV. Section 2. Clause 3.

[198] Excerpt from Chief Justice Marshall's decision; Gibbons v Ogden, 1824. Source: *The Supreme Court and the Constitution*; 3d Edition., ed. Stanley I. Kutler. W.W. Norton & Company, New York. 1984. pp. 90-96

[199] This relates to a law enacted by South Carolina that was struck down by the Federal Courts; The Negro Seaman's Act. This law was in response to an attempted revolt by slaves led by Denmark Vesey in 1822.

[200] Gibbons v. Ogden, 22 U.S. 1, 9 Wheat. 1, 6 L. Ed. 23 (1824)

[201] Source: L http://teachingamericanhistory.org/library/index.asp?document=179

The U.S. Congress passed this piece of landmark legislation to end the profitable international slave trade on March 2, 1807, and President Thomas Jefferson promptly signed the act, making it law. The act went into effect on January 1, 1808, prohibiting from that time on the importation of African slaves to the United States.

[202] Gibbons v. Ogden, 22 U.S. 1, 9 Wheat. 1, 6 L. Ed. 23 (1824)

[203] Gibbons v. Ogden, 22 U.S. 1, 9 Wheat. 1, 6 L. Ed. 23 (1824)

[204] Bank Of Augusta V. Earle, 38 U.S. 519 (1839) 38 U.S. 519 (Pet.)

[205] Excerpt from Chief Justice Taney's decision, *Proprietors of the Charles River Bridge v. Proprietors of the Warren Bridge* (1837).

[206] Josiah Quincy, LL. D, *Memoir of John Quincy Adams*, (Phillips, Sampson and Company, Boston. 1858) [Remarks of Mr. Adams after a conversation with Oliver

Wilcott, successor to Alexander Hamilton as Sec. of State under Washington. No specific date was given in the book, aprox. June 1830] 199.

[207] Ford, Worthington, Chauncey. *John Quincy Adams: His connection with the Monroe Doctrine (1823)* (Cambridge J. Wilson and Son. 1902) 80

[208] Samuel Flagg Bemis, *John Quincy Adams and The Union.* (Alfred A. Knopf. 1956. New York) 327

[209] Based on the name *Whiggamore*, member of a Scottish group that marched to Edinburgh in 1648 to oppose the court party.

[210] Webster remained as Secretary of State, later replaced by Able Parker Upshur in June of 1843, who served until his death, when Tyler appointed Calhoun.

CHAPTER 17

[211] Diary of John Quincy Adams, April 4, 1841.

[212] The British and Foreign Anti-Slavery Reporter, May 4, 1842. (Lancelot Wild, 13 Catherine Street, Stand) 288

[213] Robert J. Morgan, *A Whig Embattled.* (Archon Books, 1974) 12

[214] Clyde Wilson, *The Papers Of John C Calhoun, XV 1839-1841.* (Uni. of South Carolina Press, 1983) 804

[215] Cong Globe, Twenty-sixth Congress; House of Representatives. Vol 8 No. 9 Saturday, January 18, 1841

[216] Cong Globe, Twenty-sixth Congress; House of Representatives. Vol 8 No. 9 Tuesday, January 28, 1841

[217] ibid

[218] William Lee Miller, *Arguing About Slavery: John Quincy Adams and the Great Battle in the United States Congress.* (Vintage Books, A Division of Random House, Inc. 1995) 371

[219] James M. McPherson, *The Fight Against The Gag Rule: Joshua Leavitt And Anti-slavery Insurgency In The Whig Party*, 1839-1842. (The Journal of Negro History. July, 1963) 187

[220] **United States v. The Amistad 40 U.S. (15 Pet.) 540 Opinion of Justice Story.**

[221] ibid

CHAPTER 18

[222] Payne v. Tennessee, 501 U.S. 808, 827 (1991).

[223] Joshua Leavitt to Myron Holley, July 12, 1839, in Miscellaneous Manuscripts, New York Historical Society.

[224] Angelina Grimke and her sister, Sarah, were the daughters of a slaveholding judge from Charleston, South Carolina. Regardless, the sisters became anti-slavery early on. They moved to Philadelphia in 1819 and joined the Society of Friends. By 1835 Angelina was writing anti-slavery pamphlets for the *Liberator,* William Lloyds Gar-

rison's Anti-Slavery publication. Both became active in woman's rights and in 1838 Angelina married Theodore Weld.

[225] *Abolitionism and American Religion: History of the American Abolitionist Movement A Bibliography of Scholarly Articles.* ed. John R. McKivigan. (Indiana University-Prude University. Indianapolis Garland Publishing A member of Taylor & Francis Group, New York & London. 1999) 79

[226] *Abolitionism and American Religion: History of the American Abolitionist Movement A Bibliography of Scholarly Articles.* ed. John R. McKivigan. (Indiana University-Prude University. Indianapolis Garland Publishing A member of Taylor & Francis Group, New York & London. 1999) 83

[227] Hugh Davis, *Joshua Leavitt, Evangelical Abolitionist.* (Louisiana State University Press, London 1990)

[228] February 4, 1833, speech in House of Representatives by John Q Adams. Congressional Globe.

[229] Congressional Globe. February 4, 1833, speech in House of Representatives by John Q Adams.

[230] Josiah Quincy, LL. D., *Memoir of John Quincy Adams.* (Phillips, Sampson and Company. Boston 1858) 385-87 Mr. Adams at Brainier, Mass., 17th October, 1842.

[231] Josiah Quincy, LL. D., *Memoir of John Quincy Adams.* (Phillips, Sampson and Company. Boston 1858) 385-87 Mr. Adams at Brainier, Mass., 17th October, 1842.

[232] Josiah Quincy, LL. D., *Memoir of John Quincy Adams.* (Phillips, Sampson and Company. Boston 1858) 210-211 February 4, 1833, speech in House of Representatives by John Q Adams.

[233] *The Papers of John C Calhoun, XV 1839-1841.* ed. Wilson, Clyde. (Uni. of South Carolina Press. 1983). Ironically, one year before the date (Nov. 7, 1841) Calhoun wrote in a letter to Henry Deas, et. al. Fort Hill, Nov. 7, 1840.

[234] Mr. Adams at Brainier, Mass., 17th October, 1842.

[235] Joshua R. Giddings, *History of the Rebellion: Its Authors and Causes.* (Follett, Foster & Co. New York 1861) 125-26

[236] Joshua R. Giddings, *History of the Rebellion: Its Authors and Causes.* (Follett, Foster & Co. New York 1861) 107

[237] Sprigg's Boarding house was located at the present day site of the Library of Congress, Washington, D.C.

[238] Hugh Davis, *Joshua Leavitt; Evangelical Abolitionist.* (Louisiana State university Press, Baton Rouge and London. 1990) 199

[239] Weld, *Letters of Theodore Dwight Weld, Angelina Grimke Weld and Sarah Grimke, 1822 - 1844.* ed. Gilbert H. Barnes and Dwight L. Dumond. Weld to Angeline G. Weld, Jan. 1, 1842 (The American Historical Association, The Albert J. Beveridge Memorial Fund. D. Appleton-Century Company. New York.1934) 882-883:

[240] James M. McPherson, "Fight Against the Gag Rule: Joshua Leavitt and Antislavery Insurgency in the Whig Party, 1839-1842" *The Journal of Negro History*, Vol. 48, No. 3 (July, 1963) 177-195

[241] *Emancipator*, Jan. 16, 1840; Giddings Papers, Ohio Historical Society

[242] James M. McPherson, "Fight Against the Gag Rule: Joshua Leavitt and Antislavery Insurgency in the Whig Party, 1839-1842" *The Journal of Negro History*, Vol. 48, No. 3 (July, 1963) 177-195

[243] James M. McPherson, "Fight Against the Gag Rule: Joshua Leavitt and Antislavery Insurgency in the Whig Party, 1839-1842" *The Journal of Negro History*, Vol. 48, No. 3 (July, 1963) 177-195

[244] Giddings Papers, Ohio Historical Society.

[245] James Brewer Stewart, *Joshua R. Giddings and the Tactics of Radical Politics*. (The Press of Case Western Reserve University. Cleveland 1970) 65

[246] Mr. Justice Story opinion of the Court. THE UNITED STATES, APPELLANTS, v. THE LIBELLANTS AND CLAIMANTS OF THE SCHOONER AMISTAD, HER TACKLE, APPAREL, AND FURNITURE, TOGETHER WITH HER CARGO, AND THE AFRICANS MENTIONED AND DESCRIBED IN THE SEVERAL LIBELS AND CLAIMS, APPELLEES.—Supreme Court Of The United States 40 U.S. 518 January, 1841 Term

[247] Richard Peters, *Reports of Cases Argued and Adjudged in the Supreme Court of the United States. January Term 1841.* Vol 15. Mr. Baldwin for the defendant. United States *v* Amistad. January, 1841. 553-554

[248] THE UNITED STATES, APPELLANTS, v. THE LIBELLANTS AND CLAIMANTS OF THE SCHOONER AMISTAD, HER TACKLE, APPAREL, AND FURNITURE, TOGETHER WITH HER CARGO, AND THE AFRICANS MENTIONED AND DESCRIBED IN THE SEVERAL LIBELS AND CLAIMS, APPELLEES. SUPREME COURT OF THE UNITED STATES40 U.S. 518 JANUARY, 1841 Term

CHAPTER 19

[249] Frederic Bancroft, *Slave Trading in the Old South*. (J. H. Furst Company. Baltimore 1931)102-103.

[250] George Bourne, *The Picture of Slavery in the United States of America*. (Edwin Hunt, Middletown, Conn. 1834) 111

[251] *NILES NATIONAL REGISTER* Fifth Series N0. 21 Vol. XI Baltimore January 23 1842 Vol LXI The case Of The Brig Creole: Page 323 -24

[252] Edward P. Crapol, *John Tyler, the Accidental President*. (University of North Carolina Press, 2006) 98

[253] *Mutiny and Murder on board the Brig Creole*. Slaves Set Free by British Authorities. New Orleans Bulletin. December 3, 1841

[254] *The Domestic Slave Trade,* Case of the brig Creole. Boston Liberator: December 24, 1841, From the N. Y. Journal of Commerce; Page 2

[255] *The Case Of The Creole*, Times, Friday, January 14, 1842

[256] *The Case Of The Creole*, Times. London. January 14, 1842

CHAPTER 20

[257] From the slave spiritual 'Better Days Are Coming.' Circa early 1830s

[258] Source: National Archives; master abstracts for certificates of registration in Record Group 41, Records of the Bureau of Marine Inspection and Navigation.

[259] Source: National Archives; master abstracts for certificates of registration in Record Group 41, Records of the Bureau of Marine Inspection and Navigation.

[260] Judah Philip Benjamin was a lawyer for the Louisiana Insurance Company when the slave owners sought indemnification against the company over the loss of property (slaves) in the Creole Case. Born a British citizen in Christiansted, British Virgin Islands, he immigrated to the United States, went to Yale law school, became a United States Senator from Louisiana, served in the Confederate government as; Attorney General, Secretary of War and Secretary of State and was considered to be second in command and "the brains of the Confederacy." As the Confederacy fell, Benjamin escaped the United States and made his way to England where he was made counsel to Queen Victoria. His book *Treatise on the Law of Sale of Personal Property* became a standard in civil law and was a principal textbook in law schools in both the United States and England.

[261] Theodore Dwight Weld, *American Slavery As It Is: Testimony of a Thousand Witnesses.* (American Anti-Slavery Society. New York 1839) 75.

[262] *NILES NATIONAL REGISTER*, Fifth Series N0. 21 Vol. XI., Baltimore, January 22, 1842 [Vol. LXI Whole No. 1,582] The Case Of The Brig Creole: Page 323 -24 & London Times, Friday, January 28, 1842

[263] NILES NATIONAL REGISTER Fifth Series N0. 21 Vol. XI Baltimore January 23 1842 Vol LXI The case Of The Brig Creole: Page 323 -24

[264] The log of the brig *Creole*.

[265] *Correspondence on The Slave Trade: From January 1 to December 31, 1842, inclusive. Accounts and Papers: SLAVE TRADE.* Vol LIX. LONDON: Printed by William Cloves and Sons, Stamford Street. For Her Majesty's Stationary Office. 1843 Class D, Correspondence with Foreign Powers. 152

CHAPTER 21

[266] John Niven, *John C. Calhoun and the Price of Union.* Louisiana State University Press. Baton Rouge. 1988. Page 182. Letter to M. McCalla, Thomas M. Hickey, Benjamin Taylor, and G.W. Johnson. Washington, June 27, 1840

[267] John Niven, *John C. Calhoun and the Price of Union.* (Louisiana State University Press. Baton Rouge. 1988) 6

[268] Josiah Quincy, LL. D, *Memoir of John Quincy Adams.* (Phillips, Sampson and Company. Boston 1858.) 177

[269] John Quincy Adams letter to Henry Clay, 7 September 1831

[270] John Niven, *John C. Calhoun and the Price of Union.* (Louisiana State University Press. Baton Rouge. 1988). 239. Calhoun to Virgil Maxcy, Fort Hill, September 11, 1830.

[271] Charles Grove Hanes, *The Role of the Supreme Court in American Government and Politics, 1789-1835*. (Russell & Russell. New York 1960) 109

[272] *The Papers of John C Calhoun, XV 1839-1841*. ed. Clyde Wilson. (Uni. of South Carolina Press, 1983) Letter to A.T. Moore and others, Madison County, Miss. Fort Hill, Sept. 17, 1840

[273] *The Papers of John C Calhoun, XV 1839-1841*. ed. Clyde Wilson. (Uni. of South Carolina Press, 1983) Fort Hill, 31st October 1841

[274] *The Papers of John C Calhoun, XV 1839-1841*. ed. Clyde Wilson. (Uni. of South Carolina Press, 1983) Fort Hill, October 1841. Letter from J.C. Calhoun to Dixon H. Lewis.

[275] *The Papers of John C Calhoun, XV 1839-1841*. ed. Clyde Wilson. (Uni. of South Carolina Press, 1983) To Col. James Edward Calhoun, Fort Hill, 1st November, 1841.

[276] *The Papers of John C Calhoun, XV 1839-1841*. ed. Clyde Wilson. (Uni. of South Carolina Press, 1983) Letter to Dixon H. Lewis [Fort Hill, October, 1841.

[277] Melville, Herman, "The Bell Tower," *Putman's Monthly* Magazine. Vol. II No. 32 [Benito Cereno and the Piazza Tales: *The Bell Tower*] Dix & Edwards, New York: July – December 1855. 459 - 471

CHAPTER 22

[278] Merriam-Webster dictionary.

[279] Source: The Anti-Slavery Reporter. London The Creole Memorial to Lord Aberdeen; February 23, 1842., p. 27-28.

[280] Personally appeared before me, John F Bacon, consul of the United States of America at Nassau, Bahamas, William H Merritt, who being sworn, deposeth and saith:

[281] November 9, 1841: Deposition of William H. Merritt. Sworn before Robert Duncome, Police Magistrate of Nassau, Bahamas. The files of J. J. Burnside, Justice of the Peace, Nassau Bahamas. 1841

[282] Ibid

[283] Ibid

[284] November 9, 1841: From the disposition of Zephaniah C. Gifford, the 1st mate of the brig *Creole*, Sworn before Robert Duncome, Police Magistrate of Nassau, Bahamas. The files of J. J. Burnside, Justice of the Peace, Nassau Bahamas. 1841

[285] From the disposition of Lucius Stevens, the second mate of the brig *Creole*, given to Consulate of the   United States of America, John F Bacon, on November 13, 1841; Nassau, Bahamas.

[286] Deposition of Lucius Stevens, by John F. Bacon, Consulate of the United States of America, Nassau, Bahamas, November 10, 1841.

[287] November 10, 1841: From the disposition of Lucius Stevens, the second mate of the brig *Creole*, Sworn   before Robert Duncome, Police Magistrate of Nassau, Bahamas. The files of J. J. Burnside, Justice of the Peace, Nassau Bahamas. 1841

[288] Protest of Zephaniah C. Gifford, acting master of the brig *Creole*, given on

December 2, 1841 at New Orleans, Louisiana, to William Young Lewis, Notary Public. *Accounts and Papers, Thirty-Two Volumes. Slave Trade. Session 2 February-- August 1843.* United States. Page 154.

[289] Source: 27th Congress, 2d Session: Message From The President Of The United States, January 20, 1842., State of Louisiana, City of New Orleans., Depositions of William Devereux, the cook on brig *Creole,* Henry Speck, John Silvy, Jaques Lacombe, Francis Foxwell and Blinn Curtis, all seamen on brig *Creole,* taken before W Y Lewis, a Notary Public at New Orleans, on December 2, 1841, Page 40

[290] Ibid

[291] London Times, Friday, January 14, 1842

CHAPTER 23

[292] Source: National Archives; Affidavits from the crew and passengers of the Brig Creole. November 1841.

[293] Definition of coast pilot. 1: one who pilots coasting vessels. :an official publication giving a description of a particular section of coast and usually sailing directions for coastal navigation. https://www.merriam-webster.com/dictionary/coast%20pilot

[294] NILES NATIONAL REGISTER, Fifth Series N0. 21 Vol. XI; Jan. 22, 1842, Pg. 324. The Protest of the officers and Crew of the American brig *Creole* bound from Richmond to New Orleans, whose cargo of slaves mutinied on the 7th of November, 1841 off the Hole in the Wall.

[295] Deposition of Zephaniah C. Gifford, taken by William Young Lewis, notary public, State of Louisiana, City of New Orleans. December 2, 1841. Pg 41.

[296] William Wells Brown, "Madison Washington," in *The Black Man, His Antecedents, His genius, and His Achievements.* Page 82

[297] NILES NATIONAL REGISTER, Fifth Series N0. 21 Vol. XI., Baltimore, January 22, 1842 [Vol. LXI   Whole No. 1,582]   The Case Of The Brig Creole: Page 323 -24 & London Times, Friday, January 28, 1842

[298] William Wells Brown, "Madison Washington," in *The Black Man, His Antecedents, His genius, and His Achievements.* Page 81 – 82

[299] R. Edward Lee, *Madison Washington, Slave Mutineer,* (Blacfax, Winter/ Spring1998, Vol. 8 Issue 36) 8.

[300] L. Maria Child, *The Freedman's Book.* (Ticknor & Fields. Boston 1865) 153

[301] Pauline E. Hopkins, *Short Fiction By Black Woman, 1900 – 1920; A Dash For Kiberty;* (founded on an article written by Col. T. W. Higginson, for the Atlantic Monthly, June 1861) 98

[302] For a further in depth reading, regarding Susan's role in 19th century literature, I recommend: *Dusky Powder Magazines: the Creole Revolt (1841) in nineteenth century American literature.,* by Celeste-Marie Bernier (2002). PhD thesis, University of Nottingham. Access from the University of Nottingham repository: http://eprints.nottingham.ac.uk/11502/1/246387.pdf

[303] Niles' Register; Vol. LX or X Jan. 22, 1842 ed. Jeremiah Huges. (Printed by the

Editor. Baltimore) 325.

[304] Department of Archives; Nassau, Bahamas. Governors Dispatches And The Executive Council Minutes. November 9, 1841

[305] Accounts and Papers *Thirty-Two Volumes*. Slave Trade. Session 2 February – 24 august 1843. Vol. LIX. *Presented to both Houses of Parliament by Command of Her Majesty*, 1843. Printed by William Cloves and Sons, Stamford Street, for Her Majesty's Stationary Office. London: Class D––1842. Protest of the crew of the brig *Creole*. New Orleans, November 18, 1842, by W.Y. Lewis, Notary Public. Page 158

[306] *Accounts and Papers. Thirty-Two Volume. Slave Trade VOL. LIX. Presented to both Houses of Parliament by Command of her Majesty's Government. Class D-1842* (Printed by William Clowes and Sons. London 1843)131. Deposition of William Woodside. Consulate of the United States of America. Nassau, Bahamas, November 13, 1841.

[307] Patrice M. Williams, Assistant Director of Archives, Nassau Bahamas. Apr 22, 2010. Department Archives: archives@batelnet.bs

[308] Department of Archives; Nassau, Bahamas. Governors Dispatches and The Executive Council Minutes.

[309] *Accounts and Papers. Thirty-Two Volume. Slave Trade VOL. LIX. Presented to both Houses of Parliament by Command of her Majesty's Government. Class D-1842* (Printed by William Clowes and Sons. London 1843) 156. Deposition of Zephaniah C. Gifford, at New Orleans, December 2, 1841.

[310] *Accounts and Papers. Thirty-Two Volume. Slave Trade VOL. LIX. Presented to both Houses of Parliament by Command of her Majesty's Government. Class D-1842* (Printed by William Clowes and Sons. London 1843)156. Deposition of Zephaniah C. Gifford, at New Orleans, December 2, 1841.

[311] Department of Archives; Nassau, Bahamas. Governors Dispatches and The Executive Council Minutes.

CHAPTER 24

[312] *No. 146 The Earl of Aberdeen to Mr. Everett. Foreign Office, April 18, 1842. House of Common papers. Accounts and Papers: Thirty-Two Volumes. Slave Trade. 2 February– 24 August 1843. VOL. LIX. Class D—1842. 1842* (Printed by William Clowes and Sons. London 1843) 193

[313] London Times, Friday, January 14, 1842.

[314] Times of London, Friday, January 14, 1842

[315] *Accounts and Papers. Thirty-Two Volume. Slave Trade VOL. LIX. Presented to both Houses of Parliament by Command of her Majesty's Government. Class D-1842* (Printed by William Clowes and Sons. London 1843) 112 No. 136. Mr. Fox to the Earl of Aberdeen. Washington, December 28, 1841.

[316] *Accounts and Papers. Thirty-Two Volume. Slave Trade VOL. LIX. Presented to both Houses of Parliament by Command of her Majesty's Government. Class D-1842* (Printed by William Clowes and Sons. London 1843)

[317] Minutes of 7 February 1842, paragraph 430: Dr Lushington gave his opinion that

the British authorities have no power to give up the negroes found aboard the Creole, and now in custody in Nassau on the alleged charge of mutiny and murder, either as slaves or felons and Lord Broughton and Mr. Macaulay agreed with this opinion.

318 *The Frederick Douglass Papers, Series One, Volume 2., 1847-54.*, ed. John W. Blassingame. (Yale University Press, 1982) 154-55. An address delivered in New York, New York, on 23 April. 1849

319 *Memoirs of Joseph John Gurney: with selections from his journal.* ed. Joseph Bevan Braithwaite. (In two Volumes. Volume 2. Pg 179. Norwich: Fletcher and Alexander. London MDCCCLIV 1854)

320 Memorial from the British and foreign Anti-Slavery society, presented to the Right Honorable the Earl of Aberdeen, Her Majesty's principal Secretary of State for Foreign Affairs., February 2, 1842. No. XIX. CASE OF THE CREOLE

321 *Accounts and Papers. Thirty-Two Volume. Slave Trade VOL. LIX. Presented to both Houses of Parliament by Command of her Majesty's Government. Class D-1842* (Printed by William Clowes and Sons. London 1843) 131 Disposition of William Woodside, shipmaster of the bark Louisa, given to Consulate of the United States of America, John F Bacon, on November 13, 1841; Nassau, Bahamas.

322 Pax Britannica: a Latin term, *The British peace.* A time period extending from the end of the Napoleonic Wars [1815] to the start of WW I [1914]. The growth and domination of the Royal Navy over worldwide commerce and the establishment of the British Empire.

323 Regarding: How England could have stopped US expansion to the Pacific (as constituted in 1840). We often fall into the habit of viewing history from a present-day perception. A map of 1840 North America will show how the Oregon Territory touches the Texas Territory, establishing a veritable wall against the westward expansion by the United States. England was in control of the Oregon Territory in 1840. The settlement at the 49th parallel would not occur until 1846, establishing present day boundaries between US and Canada. If England, in the early 1840s, had gained control, possessed or annexed Texas, it would have effectively stopped US expansion to the Pacific.

324 Source: The Anti-Slavery Reporter. London

325 Source: The Anti-Slavery Reporter. London. A letter from Simeon S. Joceklyn; Corresponding Secretary of the American and Foreign Anti-Slavery Society to the Secretary of the British and Foreign Anti-Slavery Society; April 1, 1842.

326 This is the same Edward Everett who would give a speech at Gettysburg, Pennsylvania, prior to President Lincoln's Gettysburg Address, November 19, 1863.

327 Webster dispatch to Everett, Department of State [Jan. 29th, 1842] *Accounts and Papers: Thirty-Two Volumes.* Slave Trade. Session 2 February––24 August 1843. Vol. LIX. pp 161-64. LONDON: printed by William Clowes and Sons, Stamford Street, for Her Majesty's Stationary Office. 1843

328 ibid: Webster dispatch to Everett, Department of State [Jan. 29th, 1842]

329 ibid: Webster dispatch to Everett, Department of State [Jan. 29th, 1842]

330 *Accounts and Papers. Thirty-Two Volume. Slave Trade VOL. LIX. Presented to both Houses of Parliament by Command of her Majesty's Government. Class D-1842* (Printed by William Clowes and Sons. London 1843) From the letter of Her Majes-

ty's Secretary of State for Foreign Affairs; Lord Aberdeen. April 18, 1842. Written to Mr. Everett, United States Minister in England.

[331] *Accounts and Papers. Thirty-Two Volume. Slave Trade VOL. LIX. Presented to both Houses of Parliament by Command of her Majesty's Government. Class D-1842* (Printed by William Clowes and Sons. London 1843) From the letter of Her Majesty's Secretary of State for Foreign Affairs; Lord Aberdeen. April 18, 1842. Written to Mr. Everett, United States Minister in England.

[332] *Accounts and Papers. Thirty-Two Volume. Slave Trade VOL. LIX. Presented to both Houses of Parliament by Command of her Majesty's Government. Class D-1842* (Printed by William Clowes and Sons. London 1843) From the letter of Her Majesty's Secretary of State for Foreign Affairs; Lord Aberdeen. April 18, 1842. Written to Mr. Everett, United States Minister in England.

CHAPTER 25

[333] Letter to M. McCalla, Thomas M. Hickey, Benjamin Taylor, and G.W. Johnson. Washington, June 27, 1840

[334] New Orleans Picayune, December 3, 1841.

[335] Henry Clay, *The Papers of Henry Clay. Volume 9*: The Whig Leader, January 1, 1837. Washington, December 24, 1841. From a letter to James B. Clay

[336] *The Papers Of John C Calhoun, XV 1839-1841.* ed. Wilson, Clyde. (Uni. of South Carolina Press, 1983) 808. Letter to Col. James Edward Calhoun, Fort Hill, 1st November, 1841

[337] Samuel Flagg Bemis, *John Quincy Adams and The Union.* (New York, Alfred A. Knopf. 1956) 42 "On January 28, 1840. . . The House adopted the tightest Gag yet voted a standing rule (the Twenty-first, later numbered the Twenty-fifth Rule) to govern all future sessions: 'No petition, memorial, resolution or other paper, praying for the abolition of slavery in the District of Columbia, or any state or territory or the slave trade between states and territories of the United States in which it now exists, shall be received by the House, or entertained what so ever.'"

[338] Stanley I Kutler, *The Supreme Court and the Constitution, Third Edition* (University Of Wisconsin, W.W. Norton and Sons1984) 96

[339] Josiah Quincy, LL. D., *Memoir of John Quincy Adams.* (Phillips, Sampson and Company Boston. 1858) March 21, 1841

CHAPTER 26

[340] Weld. *Letters of Theodore Dwight Weld, Angelina Grimke Weld and Sarah Grimke, 1822-1844.* Edited by Gilbert H. Barnes and Dwight L. Dumond. P. 88-883 *Weld to Angeline G. Weld, Jan.1, 1842*

[341] James Brewer Stewart, *Joshua R. Giddings and the Tactics of Radical politics.* (The Press of Case Western Reserve University. Cleveland 1970) May 18, 1842; Leavitt Papers

[342] James Brewer Stewart, *Joshua R. Giddings and the Tactics of Radical Politics.* (The Press of Case Western Reserve University. Cleveland. 1970) 69

[343] Theodore D. Weld, *American Slavery As It Is: Testimony Of A Thousand Witnesses.* (Published by The American Anti-Slavery Society, Office, No. 143 Nassau Street, New York, New York 1839). "First Hand Views of Slavery." 1839

[344] Mr. Adams at Brainier, Mass., 17th October, 1842.

[345] Theodore Weld's description of Adams's remarks concerning the Georgia petition; (Weld to Angelina G. Weld and Sarah Grimkè, Washington, Jan. 23, 1842, *Weld-Grimkè Letters*, II, 899-1000.)

[346] Joshua R. Giddings, *History of the Rebellion: Its Authors and Causes.* (Follett, Foster & Co. New York 1861) 118

[347] Joshua R. Giddings, *History of the Rebellion: Its Authors and Causes.* (Follett, Foster & Co. New York 1861) 70

[348] Hugh Davis, *Joshua Leavitt, Evangelical Abolitionist.* (Louisiana State University Press, Baton Rouge and London. 1990) 190

[349] Josiah Quincy, LL. D., Memoir *of John Quincy Adams.* (Phillips, Sampson and Company. Boston 1858) 252-54. Presented in Congress February, 1837

[350] Josiah Quincy, LL. D., Memoir *of John Quincy Adams.* (Phillips, Sampson and Company. Boston 1858) 252-54. Presented in Congress February, 1837

[351] *Cong Globe* 27th Congress 24th of January, 1842. Adams presents a petition of forty-five citizens of Haverhill, Massachusetts, praying that Congress would take measures to peaceably dissolve the Union.

[352] *Cong Globe* 27th Congress 2d Session, January 25, 1842. House of Representatives. 173

[353] Joshua R. Giddings, *History of the Rebellion: Its Authors and Causes.* (Follett, Foster & Co. New York 1861) 167 fn.

[353] *Cong. Globe* 27th Congress House of Representatives; January 25, 1842 "Whereas, The federal constitution is a permanent form of government, and of perpetual obligation, until altered or modified in the mode pointed out in that instrument; and the members of this House, deriving their political character and powers from the same, are sworn to support it; and the dissolution of the Union necessarily implies the destruction of that instrument, the overthrow of the American republic, and the extinction of our national existence: a proposition, therefore, to the representatives of the people, to dissolve the organic laws framed by their constituents, and to support which they are commanded by those constituents to be sworn before they can enter into the execution of the political powers created by it and entrusted to them, is a high breach of privilege, a contempt offered to this House, a direct proposition to the legislature and each member of it to commit perjury, and involving necessarily in its execution and its consequences the destruction of our country, and the crime of high treason."

CHAPTER 27

[355] Joshua R. Giddings, *History of the Rebellion: Its Authors and Causes.* (Follett, Foster & Co. New York 1861) 158

[356] Calhoun protesting the abolitionist petitions on slavery in the Senate. *Register of*

Debates, XIII, Pt. II, 2184-5. February 6, 1837.

[357] Calhoun's *La Amistad* Resolutions; Adopted by the Senate, April 15, 1840. *Congressional Globe*, VIII, pp. 267, 328)

[358] *The Anti-Slavery Reporter*. London February 23, 1842; Pg. 28

[359] Joshua R. Giddings, *History of the Rebellion: Its Authors and Causes*. (Follett, Foster & Co. New York 1861) 181

[360] Ibid. page 181

[361] William Lee Miller, *Arguing About Slavery, John Quincy Adams and the Great battle in the United States Congress*. (Vintage Books, a division of Random House, Inc. New York 1995) 27

[362] *Cong. Globe* 27th Congress United States House of Representatives, Tuesday, March 21, 1842. pg. 342

[363] *Cong. Globe* 27th Congress United States House of Representatives, Tuesday, March 22, 1842. pg. 342

[364] Creole Resolutions: Presented in the United States House of Representatives by the Honorable Joshua R. Giddings from Ohio's 16th Congressional District, The 27th Congress; March 21, 1842 and again on June 3, 1842: *Congressional Globe*; United States House of Representatives, Monday, March 21, 1842.

- Resolved, That, prior to the adoption of our Federal Constitution, each of the several States comprising this Union exercised full and exclusive jurisdiction over the subject of slavery within its own Territory, and possessed full power to continue or abolish it at pleasure.

- Resolved, That by adopting the Constitution, no part of the aforesaid powers were delegated to the Federal Government, but were reserved by, and still pertain to, each of the several States.

- Resolved, That by the 8th section of the 1st article of the Constitution, each of the several States surrendered to the Federal Government all jurisdiction over the subjects of commerce and navigation upon the high seas.

- Resolved, That slavery being an abridgment of the natural rights of man, can exist only by force of positive municipal law, and is necessarily confined to the territorial jurisdiction of the power creating it.

- Resolved, That when a ship belonging to the citizens of any State of this Union leaves the waters and territory of such State and enters upon the high seas, the persons on board cease to be subject to the slave laws of such State, and thenceforth are governed in their relations to each other by, and are amenable to the laws of the United States.

- Resolved, That when the brig Creole, on her late passage to New Orleans, left the territorial jurisdiction of Virginia, the slave laws of that State ceased to have jurisdiction over the persons on board said brig, and such persons became amenable only to the laws of the United States.

- Resolved, That the persons on board the said ship, in resuming their natural rights of personal liberty, violated no law of the United States, incurred no legal penalty, and are justly liable to no punishment.

- Resolved, That all attempts to regain possession of, or to re-enslave, said persons, are unauthorized by the Constitution or laws of the United States, and are incompatible with our national honor.

- Resolved, That all attempts to exert our national influence in favor of the coastwise slave trade, or to place this nation in the attitude of maintaining a "commerce in human beings," are subversive of the rights and injurious to the feelings and the interests of the free States; are unauthorized by the Constitution and prejudicial to our national character.

[365] Joshua R. Giddings, *History of the Rebellion: Its Authors and Causes*. (Follett, Foster & Co. New York 1861) 183

[366] ibid., p. 182

[367] ibid., p. 183

[368] ibid.

[369] ibid., p. 184

[370] ibid.

[371] *Cong. Globe* 27th Congress United States House of Representatives, Tuesday, March 22, 1842, pg. 342

[372] ibid.

[373] ibid.

[374] Giddings, pp. 185–86

[375] ibid. pp. 188–89

CHAPTER 28

[376] ibid., p. 191

[377] *Cong. Globe* 27th Congress House of Representatives, Friday, April 22, 1842. pg. 439

[378] Giddings, p. 190

[379] ibid., p. 192

[380] ibid footnote pg. 191.

[381] ibid.

[382] *Niles Weekly Register* Vol 62., April 22, 1842. pg. 142

[383] *Cong. Globe* 27th Congress House of Representatives, Friday, April 22, 1842. pg. 439

[384] *Niles Weekly Register* Vol. 63 March 23, 1842, pg. 62. (Actual date cited was March 22, 1842).

[385] Giddings, *History of the Rebellion: Its Authors and Causes*. (Follett, Foster & Co. New York 1861) 192

[386] *Cong. Globe* 27th Congress the House of Representatives, June 3, 1842, pp. 575–76

[387] Giddings, p. 193

388 ibid.

389 ibid., p. 195

CHAPTER 29

390 John Quincy Adams diary 43, 1 January 1842 - 8 July 1843, page 39 [electronic edition]. *The Diaries of John Quincy Adams: A Digital Collection.* Boston, Mass. Massachusetts Historical Society, 2004. http://www.masshist.org/jqadiaries Diary of John Quincy Adams. Washington. February 4, 1832.

391 Joshua R. Giddings, *History of the Rebellion: Its Authors and Causes.* (Follett, Foster & Co. New York 1861) 217-18

392 *The Papers of John C Calhoun,* XV 1839–1841. ed. Wilson, Clyde. (University of South Carolina Press, 1983) Calhoun's comments on the *Creole* Incident in a speech made in the Senate, 19 August, 1842, supporting ratification of the Webster-Ashburton Treaty.

393 (ibid. p. 409) From the conclusion of Calhoun's speech. Source: *The Papers of John C Calhoun,* XV 1839–1841, ed., Wilson, Clyde., University of South Carolina Press, 1983. Calhoun's comments on the *Creole* incident in a speech made in the Senate, 19 August, 1842, supporting ratification of the Webster-Ashburton Treaty.

394 James Brewer Stewart, *Joshua R. Giddings and the Tactics of Radical Politics.* (The Press of Case Western Reserve University. Cleveland 1970) 262 [Julian, Giddings, 363; John A. Bingham to JRG, March 4, 1859, Giddings MSS]

395 Series 1. General Correspondence. 1833-1916: Joshua R. Giddings to Abraham Lincoln, Tuesday, June 19, 1860 (Advises Lincoln to emulate John Quincy Adams) Library Of Congress.Bottom of Form

396 *London Times,* Friday, January 14, 1842.

397 Source: Department of Archives; Nassau, Bahamas. "Governors Dispatches and The Executive Council" Minutes. April 16, 1842

398 Source: *Island Scene* Vol. 3 No. 1, 1999, pg. 36

399 *The Frederick Douglass Papers;* Series One, Volume 1, 1841–46., ed. John W. Blassingame. (New Haven & London. Yale University Press. 1979) 67 From a speech given in Cork, Ireland, Cork's Imperial Hotel, 23 October, 1845.

400 *The Frederick Douglass Papers,* Series One, Volume 2., 1847–54., ed. John W. Blassingame. (Yale University Press, 1982) 154–55. An address delivered in New York, New York, on 23 April. 1849

401 *Atlantic Monthly;* April 1872, "John Brown in Massachusetts," 413–420

About the Author

John Hyde Barnard is originally from a small, idyllic town in western New York State where he was born on one of the coldest days ever recorded in February. Since then he has pursued life's pleasures, curiosities, and joys, is suspicious of authority - yet is an adherent to tradition, and holds a strong affinity for winter. John is an author and a musician. He presently resides in California and New York.

www.ingramcontent.com/pod-product-compliance
Lightning Source LLC
Chambersburg PA
CBHW060907120626
46553CB00001B/232